ANTI-SOCIAL PATTERNS OF BEGGING AND BEGGARS

ANTI-SOCIAL PATTERNS OF BEGGING AND BEGGARS

Editor
O. P. Goyal

ISHA BOOKS

Anti-social Patterns of Begging and Beggars

Rs. 880

ISBN: 81-8205-150-9

Published in 2005 in India by
Isha Books, D-43, Prithviraj Road,
Adarsh Nagar, Delhi-110 033

Laser Typesetting at : Shree Vaishnavi Creations, Delhi
Printed at : Chawla Offset Press, Delhi

Contents

Preface

Begging is one of the oldest profession on earth. Although varying by geography and the times, begging is universal. Even richest countries like America and Britain have beggars in one form or another. The beggar community feels that due to the increase in mankind's selfishness and small-mindedness, they are not able to make a living.

People who beg are amongst the most damaged and vulnerable people in our society. The vast majority are homeless; they suffer from a combination of poor skills, low income, poor housing, bad health, substance misuse and family breakdown. Few, if any, are in their situation by choice. Personal crises and the traumatising nature of homelessness combined with the difficulties accessing essential services such as healthcare and drug detox services prevent them from escaping their predicament.

Begging is a cross-cutting issue that has implications across many different government strategies, including homelessness, anti-social behaviour, crime and disorder, health and drugs. Begging impacts on crime, increases the fear of crime, concerns the public and effects businesses, the retail trade and tourists. This presents a problem for local authority, police and city and town centre managers.

There is no doubt that begging is a problem that must be tackled head on, not because people who beg are criminals, but because they are caught up in an activity that is dangerous, damaging and humiliating and are trapped in a cycle of poverty and deprivation. Theirs is a plight that cannot be ignored. Using methods of enforcement to deal with begging is wrong because it criminalises an already vulnerable section of our population increasing their contact with the police and criminal justice system. The solutions to begging must be based upon principles of compassion and methods of positive engagement. Methods that empower people by providing them with real and positive choices and by giving them the support necessary to help them overcome the difficulties that they face.

The book finds out the nature of erosion of social norms and cultural patterns among different groups of beggars who lived precariously at the margin of an urban society. It also describes the specific social, cultural and behavioural strategies by which the beggars managed to survive in their miserable socio-economic situation. It brings out the sub-culture of the beggars, in a situation of extreme poverty and social marginality.

Editor

1

Panhandling: A Social Trauma

"Panhandling," is more often referred to as "begging" elsewhere, or occasionally, as "cadging." "Panhandlers" are variously referred to as "beggars," "vagrants," "vagabonds," "mendicants," or "cadgers." The term "panhandling" derives either from the impression created by someone holding out his or her hand (as a pan's handle sticks out from the pan) or from the image of someone using a pan to collect money.

Generally, there are two types of panhandling: passive and aggressive. Passive panhandling is soliciting without threat or menace, often without any words exchanged at all–just a cup or a hand held out. Aggressive panhandling is soliciting coercively, with actual or implied threats, or menacing actions. If a panhandler uses physical force or extremely aggressive actions, the panhandling may constitute robbery.

Isolated incidents of passive panhandling are usually a low police priority. In many jurisdictions, panhandling is not even illegal. Even where it is illegal, police usually tolerate passive panhandling, for both legal and practical reasons. Courts in some jurisdictions have ruled that passive panhandling is constitutionally protected activity. Police can reasonably conclude that, absent citizen complaints, their time is better spent addressing more serious problems. Whether panhandling and other forms of street disorder cause or contribute to more serious crime–the broken windows thesis–is hotly debated, but the debate is as yet unsettled.

Panhandling becomes a higher police priority when it becomes aggressive or so pervasive that its cumulative effect, even when done passively, is to make passersby apprehensive. Panhandling is of greater concern to merchants who worry that their customers will be discouraged from patronizing their business.

Merchants are most likely to call police when panhandling disrupts their commerce. Police must also be concerned with the welfare of panhandlers who are vulnerable to physical and verbal assault by other panhandlers, street robbersor passersby who react violently to being panhandled. Panhandlers often claim certain spots as their own territory, and disputes and fights over territory are not uncommon.

Broadly speaking, public policy perspectives on panhandling are of two types–the sympathetic view and the unsympathetic view. The sympathetic view, commonly but not unanimously held by civil libertarians and homeless advocates, is that panhandling is essential to destitute people's survival, and should not be regulated by police. Some even view panhandling as a poignant expression of the plight of the needy, and an opportunity for the more fortunate to help.

The unsympathetic view is that panhandling is a blight that contributes to further community disorder and crime, as well as to panhandlers' degradation and deterioration as their underlying problems go unaddressed. Those holding this view believe panhandling should be heavily regulated by police.

People's opinions about panhandling are rooted in deeply held beliefs about individual liberty, public order and social responsibility. Their opinions are also shaped by their actual exposure to panhandling–the more people are panhandled, the less sympathetic they are toward panhandlers. While begging is discouraged on most philosophical grounds and by most major religions, many people feel torn about whether to give money to panhandlers. Some people tolerate all sorts of street disorder, while others are genuinely frightened by it. This tension between opposing viewpoints will undoubtedly always exist.

Panhandling and its variants are only one form of disorderly street conduct and street crime about which police are concerned. Other forms are:

— disorderly conduct of day laborers;
— disorderly conduct of public inebriates (e. g., public intoxication, public drinking, public urination and defecation, harassment, intimidation, and passing out in public places);
— disorderly conduct of transients/homeless (e. g., public camping, public urination and defecation, and sleeping on sidewalks and benches, and in public libraries);
— disorderly youth in public places;
— harassment (usually sexual) of female pedestrians;
— pickpocketing;
— purse snatching;
— robbery at automated teller machines (ATMs);
— trash picking (for food or to salvage aluminum cans and bottles);
— unlicensed street entertainment;and
— unlicensed street vending (also referred to as illegal peddling).

Some of these other forms of disorderly street conduct may also be attributable to panhandlers, but this is not necessarily so. These problems overlap in various ways, and a local analysis of them will be necessary to understand how they do.

Factors Contributing to Panhandling

Understanding the factors that contribute to your panhandling problem will help you frame your own local analysis questions, determine good effectiveness measures, recognize key intervention points, and select appropriate responses.

Whether Panhandling Intimidates Passersby

Panhandling intimidates some people, even causing some to avoid areas where they believe they will be panhandled. Onethird of San Franciscans surveyed said they gave money to panhandlers because they felt pressured, and avoided certain areas because of panhandling; nearly 40 percent expressed concern for their safety around panhandlers. But most studies conclude that intentional aggressive panhandling is rare, largely because panhandlers realize that using aggression reduces their income, and is more likely to get them arrested or otherwise draw police attention to them.

Whether panhandling intimidates passersby depends, of course, on how aggressive or menacing the panhandler is, but it also depends on the context in which panhandling occurs. In other words, an act of panhandling in one context might not be intimidating, but the same behavior in a different context might. Among the contextual factors that influence how intimidating panhandling is are:

— the time of day (nighttime panhandling is usually more intimidating than daytime panhandling);

— the ease with which people can avoid panhandlers

(panhandling is more likely to intimidate motorists stuck in traffic than it is those who can drive away);

— the degree to which people feel especially vulnerable (for example, being panhandled near an ATM makes some people feel more vulnerable to being robbed);

— the presence of other passersby (most people feel safer when there are other people around);

— the physical appearance of the panhandler (panhandlers who appear to be mentally ill, intoxicated or otherwise disoriented are most likely to frighten passersby because their conduct seems particularly unpredictable);

— the reputation of the panhandler (panhandlers known to be aggressive or erratic are more intimidating than those not known to be so);

— the characteristics of the person being solicited (the elderly tend to be more intimidated by panhandlers because they are less sure of their ability to defend themselves from attack);

— the number of panhandlers (multiple panhandlers working together are more intimidating than a lone panhandler); and

— the volume of panhandling (the more panhandlers present in an area, the more intimidating and bothersome panhandling will seem).

Typical Profile of a Panhandler

Typically, relatively few panhandlers account for most complaints to police about panhandling. The typical profile of a panhandler that emerges from a number of studies is that of an unemployed, unmarried male in his 30s or 40s, with substance abuse problems, few family ties, a high school education, and laborer's skills.

Some observers have noted that younger people–many of whom are runaways or otherwise transient–are turning to panhandling. A high percentage of panhandlers in U. S. urban areas are African- American. Some panhandlers suffer from mental illness, but most do not. Many panhandlers have criminal records, but panhandlers are nearly as likely to have been crime victims as offenders. Some are transient, but most have been in their community for a long time.

Contrary to common belief, panhandlers and homeless people are not necessarily one and the same. Many studies have found that only a small percentage of homeless people panhandle, and only a small percentage of panhandlers are homeless. Most studies conclude that panhandlers make rational economic choices–that is, they look to make money in the most efficient way possible. Panhandlers develop their "sales pitches," and sometimes compete with one another for the rights to a particular sales pitch. Their sales pitches are usually, though not always, fraudulent in some respect. Some panhandlers will admit to passersby that they want money to buy alcohol (hoping candor will win them favor), though few will admit they intend to buy illegal drugs.

Many panhandlers make it a habit to always be polite and appreciative, even when they are refused. Given the frequent hostility they experience, maintaining their composure can be a remarkable psychological feat. Panhandlers usually give some consideration to their physical appearance: they must balance looking needy against looking too offensive or threatening.

Most panhandlers are not interested in regular employment, particularly not minimum-wage labor, which many believe would scarcely be more profitable than panhandling. Some panhandlers' refusal to look for regular employment is better explained by their unwillingness or inability to commit to regular work hours, often because of substance abuse problems. Some panhandlers buy food with the money they receive, because they dislike the food served in shelters and soup kitchens.

The Donors

In some communities, nearly everyone who routinely uses public places has been panhandled. Many who get panhandled are themselves people of modest means. Wealthy citizens can more readily avoid public places where panhandling occurs, whether consciously, to avoid the nuisances of the street, or as well as on food merely because their lifestyles do not expose them to public places. Estimates of the percentage of people who report that they give money to panhandlers range from 10 to 60 percent. The percentage of college students who do so (between 50 and 60 percent) tends to be higher than that of the general population. There is some evidence that women and minorities tend to give more freely to panhandlers.

Male-female couples are attractive targets for panhandlers because the male is likely to want to appear compassionate in front of the female. Panhandlers more commonly target women than men,but some find that lone women are not suitable targets because they are more likely to fear having their purses snatched should they open them to get change.

Conventioneers and tourists are good targets for panhandlers because they are already psychologically prepared to spend money. Diners and grocery shoppers are good targets because dining and grocery shopping remind them of the contrast between their relative wealth and panhandlers' apparent poverty. Regular panhandlers try to cultivate regular donors; some even become acquaintances, if not friends.

Locations of Panhandlers

Panhandlers need to go where the money is. In other

words, they need to panhandle in communities and specific locations where the opportunities to collect money are best–where there are a lot of pedestrians or motorists, especially those who are most likely to have money and to give it.

Panhandling is more common in communities that provide a high level of social services to the needy, because the same citizens who support social services are also likely to give money directly to panhandlers; panhandlers are drawn to communities where both free social services and generous passersby are plentiful. With respect to specific locations, panhandlers prefer to panhandle where passersby cannot readily avoid them, although doing so can make passersby feel more intimidated. Among the more common, specific panhandling locations are the following:

- near ATMs, parking meters and telephone booths (because ATM users, motorists and callers are less likely to say they do not have any money to give);
- near building entrances/exits and public restrooms with a lot of pedestrian traffic;
- on or near college campuses (because students tend to be more sympathetic toward panhandlers);
- near subway, train and bus station entrances/exits (because of high pedestrian traffic, and because public transportation users are likely to be carrying cash to buy tickets or tokens);
- on buses and subway trains (because riders are a "captive audience");
- near places that provide panhandlers with shade and shelter from bad weather (such as doorways, alcoves and alleys in commercial districts);
- in front of convenience stores, restaurants and grocery stores (because panhandlers' claims to be

buying food or necessities for them or their children seem more plausible, and because shoppers and diners often feel especially fortunate and generous);

— at gas stations (because panhandlers' claims that they need money for gas or to repair their vehicle seem more plausible);

— at freeway exits/entrances (because motorists will be stopped or traveling slowly enough to be able to give money);

— on crowded sidewalks (because it is easier for panhandlers to blend in with the crowd should the police appear);

— at intersections with traffic signals (because motorists will be stopped); and

— near liquor stores and drug markets (so the panhandlers do not have to travel far to buy alcohol or drugs).

There are typically daily, weekly, monthly, and seasonal patterns to panhandling; that is, panhandling levels often follow fairly predictable cycles, which vary from community to community. For example, panhandling may increase during winter months in warm-climate communities as transients migrate there from cold-weather regions.

Panhandling levels often drop around the dates government benefits are distributed, because those panhandlers who receive benefits have the money they need. Once that money runs out, they resume panhandling. Panhandling on or near college campuses often follows the cycles of students' going to and coming from classes. There are usually daily lulls in panhandling when those panhandlers who are chronic inebriates or drug addicts go off to drink or take drugs. Regular panhandlers keep fairly routine schedules, typically panhandling for four to six hours a day.

Income Spending Patterns among Panhandlers

Most evidence confirms that panhandling is not lucrative, although some panhandlers clearly are able to subsist on a combination of panhandling money, government benefits, private charity, and money from odd jobs such as selling scavenged materials or plasma.

How much money a panhandler can make varies depending on his or her skill and personal appeal, as well as on the area in which he or she solicits. Estimates vary from a couple of dollars (U. S.) a day on the low end, to $20 to $50 a day in the mid-range, to about $300 a day on the high end. Women–especially those who have children with them–and panhandlers who appear to be disabled tend to receive more money. For this reason, some panhandlers pretend to be disabled and/or war veterans. Others use pets as a means of evoking sympathy from passersby. Panhandlers' regular donors can account for up to half their receipts.

Panhandlers spend much of their money on alcohol, drugs and tobacco, although some money does go toward food, transportation and toiletries. Panhandlers rarely save any money, partly because they risk having it stolen, and partly because their primary purpose is to immediately buy alcohol or drugs.

Income from panhandling could clearly have significant health effects: higher income is strongly associated with better health, and panhandling could have a positive effect if earnings were used to obtain food or housing. On the other hand, use of panhandling income to buy alcohol or illicit drugs could be harmful to health.

Although panhandlers have been studied from a sociologic perspective, little quantitative information is available on income and spending among panhandlers. The characteristics of homeless people have been described, but the relevance of this information is uncertain because not all homeless people panhandle, and those who do so may be atypical.

Recenlty survey was conducted among of panhandlers in Toronto to determine their demographic characteristics, income from panhandling and other sources, spending patterns and attitudes toward panhandling. Between February and April 2001, the survey team located panhandlers by systematically searching major streets and subway stations during the late afternoon in a 6-km^2 region of downtown Toronto. To avoid double-counting, a single investigator visually screened all panhandlers.

The survey team decided in advance that panhandlers would be offered a nonnegotiable amount of money in exchange for their participation. Participants were not allowed to solicit donations during the 20-minute interview and could not bargain for greater amounts of reimbursement. The survey team sought to determine the lowest payment that would elicit a high response rate by offering $10, $1, $4, $5, $7 and $8 to sequential groups of panhandlers. The number of participants offered each level of reimbursement was recorded, and all individuals who refused to participate were asked to explain the reason for refusal. The survey team hypothesized that acceptance of a particular level of reimbursement would be a crude validation of a participant's estimated panhandling earnings during the same 20-minute period.

The survey consisted of 90 questions. Demographic characteristics and substance use were assessed using mostly closed-ended questions. Respondents were asked to state their monthly income from each of 9 possible sources and their spending in each of 15 categories. Subjects were asked "Do you enjoy panhandling?" (yes or no) and "Why?" (open ended) and "Which would you prefer: a minimum-wage job ($6.85 per hour) or panhandling?" and "Why?" (open ended). The St. Michael's Hospital Research Ethics Board in Toronto approved this study.

Of 67 panhandlers approached, 54 (81%) agreed to participate. Thirteen individuals declined to be interviewed, of whom 8 stated they could earn more by panhandling and 5 cited noneconomic reasons. Excluding the 5 individuals who declined for noneconomic reasons, acceptance rates at each payment level were 43% at $1, 100% at $4, 67% at $5, 100% at $7, 91% at $8 and 90% at $10. Three participants refused to provide information about their income or spending.

When asked if they enjoyed panhandling, 23 participants (43%) replied "yes," commonly because of the opportunity to "meet people," 26 (48%) answered "no," often describing panhandling as "degrading," and 5 (9%) were undecided. Overall, 38 (70%) stated that they would prefer a minimum-wage job, typically citing a desire for a "steady income" or "getting off the street." However, many felt they could not handle conventional jobs because of mental illness, physical disability or lack of skills.

Panhandlers in Toronto reported a median monthly income of $300 from panhandling and $638 from all sources. The amount of payment that panhandlers were willing to accept for participating in a 20-minute survey was generally consistent with their self-estimated earnings from panhandling for the same length of time. This suggests that few panhandlers earn extremely large amounts of money. Their single largest reported expense was food, followed by tobacco, then alcohol and/or illicit drugs.

These findings differ significantly from those of John Stackhouse, a journalist who briefly lived on the street in Toronto working as a panhandler and who reported that panhandlers can earn more than $200 per day and typically spend "almost all their begging money on their addictions" and very little on food. These differences may be partly explained by the fact that high-earning panhandlers were presumably less likely to participate in our survey, and these individuals may have formed the basis for Stackhouse's observations.

The survey team found that the majority of panhandlers in Toronto are homeless and living in extreme poverty. They found that the amount of money panhandlers spend on alcohol and illicit drugs is significant, but much lower than some have suggested. The health effects of a loss of panhandling income are uncertain, because panhandlers might reduce their food intake, reduce their substance use or find other sources of income.

For the one-fourth of panhandlers who rent a room or apartment, however, any loss of income could easily lead to homelessness. Future studies of panhandlers should attempt to verify income and spending patterns objectively and examine differences in these variables by sex, housing status and health status.

Factors Influencing Panhandling

Broad economic, social and legal factors influence the overall level of panhandling, as well as community tolerance of it. Tolerance levels appear to have declined significantly during the 1990s, at least in the United States, leading to increased pressure on police to control panhandling.

The state of the economy, at the local, regional and even national level, affects how much panhandling occurs. As the economy declines, panhandling increases. As government benefit programs become more restrictive, panhandling increases.

At least as important as economic factors, if not more so, are social factors. The stronger the social bonds and social network on which indigent people can rely for emotional and financial support, the less likely they are to panhandle. Thus, the weakening of social bonds throughout society affects the indigent most negatively.

As substance abuse levels rise in society, as, for example, during the crack epidemic, so too do panhandling levels. As the skid rows in urban centers are redeveloped, the indigent people who live there move to areas where their panhandling is less tolerated. As people with mental illnesses are increasingly released into the community, often without adequate follow-up care, panhandling also increases. Where there are inadequate detoxification and substance-abuse treatment facilities, panhandling is high.

As courts strike down laws that authorize police to regulate public disorder, and as police are less inclined to enforce such laws, panhandling flourishes. Arrest and incarceration rates may also affect panhandling levels: convicted offenders often have difficulty getting jobs after release, and some inevitably turn to panhandling.

Responses to Panhanling

The following are potentially useful measures of the effectiveness of responses to panhandling:

— number of complaints filed with police about panhandling;

— number of complaints filed with other organizations or people (e. g., neighborhood/business associations, elected officials) about panhandling;

— levels of concern expressed about panhandling (from surveys);

— number of known chronic panhandlers (based on complaints, contacts and arrests);

— costs of police response to panhandling complaints;

— evidence that panhandling has been displaced to

other areas, or is resulting in an increase in other forms of nuisance behavior or crime (e. g., trash scavenging, shoplifting, theft from autos, purse snatching, prostitution, drug dealing);and

— indicators of the economic health of the area beset withpanhandling (e. g., property vacancy rates, shoppers' presence, commerce levels, tax receipts, private-security expenditures).

The following response strategies provide a foundation of ideas for addressing the particular problem. These strategies are drawn from a variety of research studies and police reports. Several of these strategies may apply to your community's problem. It is critical that you tailor responses to local circumstances, and that you can justify each response based on reliable analysis.

In most cases, an effective strategy will involve implementing several different responses. Law enforcement responses alone are seldom effective in reducing or solving the problem. Do not limit yourself to considering what police can do: give careful consideration to who else in your community shares responsibility for the problem and can help police better respond to it.

Most researchers and practitioners seem to agree that the enforcement of laws prohibiting panhandling plays only a part in controlling the problem. Public education to discourage people from giving money to panhandlers, informal social control and adequate social services (especially alcohol and drug treatment) for panhandlers are the other essential components of an effective and comprehensive response.

Panhandling, like many other forms of street disorder, is controlled more through informal means than through formal enforcement. Panhandlers, merchants, passersby, social workers, and police beat officers form an intricate social network of mutual support and regulation. They all have something to gain by cooperating with one another (and, consequently, to lose by not cooperating with one another). Panhandlers obviously gain money, food and some social interaction from their activity; they risk losing them if they act too disorderly. Merchants will usually tolerate some panhandling, though seldom directly in front of their businesses.

Some merchants even give panhandlers food or hire them to do odd jobs such as wash store windows. Passersby gain freedom from the harassment and intimidation of persistent and menacing panhandlers, along with the positive feelings they experience from truly voluntary charity.

Social workers are more likely to be able to help those street people who are not frequently arrested for panhandling. Police beat officers can cultivate panhandlers as informants, helping the officers stay current with what is happening on the street.

Enforcement Responses

Whether or not you emphasize enforcement of laws that regulate panhandling, it is important that the laws be able to survive legal challenge. Police should have valid enforcement authority to bolster other responses they use, including issuing warnings to panhandlers. Laws that prohibit aggressive panhandling or panhandling in specified areas are more likely to survive legal challenge than those that prohibit all panhandling.

If enforcement of panhandling laws will be a key component of your strategy, and if you think the panhandling laws you rely on are vulnerable to legal challenge, you should consult legal counsel to help you draft and propose new legislation.

Warning panhandlers and ordering them to "move along" are perhaps the most common police responses to panhandling. Many police beat officers develop working relationships with regular panhandlers; they use a mix of formal and informal approaches to keeping panhandling under control.

Most officers do not view panhandling as a serious matter, and are reluctant to devote the time necessary to arrest and book offenders. Moreover, even when they have the authority to issue citations and release the offenders, most officers realize that panhandlers are unlikely to either appear in court or pay a fine. Prosecutors are equally unlikely to prosecute panhandling cases, typically viewing them as an unwise use of scarce prosecutorial resources.

Panhandler arrests are rare,but when they occur, this is the typical scenario: An officer issues a panhandler a summons or citation that sets a court date or specifies a fine. The panhandler fails to appear in court or fails to pay the fine. A warrant is issued for the panhandler's arrest. The police later arrest the panhandler after running a warrant check during a subsequent encounter. The panhandler is incarcerated for no more than a couple of days, sentenced to time already served by the court, and released. Because prosecutors and judges are unlikely to view isolated panhandling cases as serious matters, it is advisable to prepare and present to the court some background information on panhandling's overall impact on the community. A problemimpact statement can help prosecutors and judges understand the overall negative effect the seemingly minor offense of panhandling is having on the community.

In the United Kingdom, police can apply to the courts for an "antisocial behavior order" against individuals or groups as one means of controlling their persistent low-level offending. Violations of the orders can result in relatively severe jail sentences. It is unknown how effective the orders have been in controlling panhandling.

1. Prohibiting aggressive panhandling

Laws that prohibit *aggressive* panhandling are more likely to survive legal challenge than laws that prohibit *all* panhandling, and are therefore to be encouraged. A growing number of jurisdictions have enacted aggressive-panhandling laws, most within the past 10 years.

Enforcing aggressive-panhandling laws can be difficult, partly because few panhandlers behave aggressively, and partly because many victims of aggressive panhandling do not report the offense to police or are unwilling to file a complaint. Police can use proactive enforcement methods such as having officers serve as decoys, giving panhandlers the opportunity to panhandle them aggressively.

Some agencies have provided officers with special legal training before enforcing aggressive-panhandling laws. Enforcing other laws panhandlers commonly violate–those regarding drinking in public, trespassing, disorderly conduct, etc. –can help control some aspects of the panhandling problem.

Police need not heavily enforce aggressive-panhandling laws in order to control panhandling; the informal norms among most panhandlers discourage aggressive panhandling anyway. Panhandlers exercise some influence over one another's behavior, to minimize complaints and keep police from intervening. Enforcing aggressive-panhandling laws can serve to reinforce the informal norms because aggressive panhandling by the few makes panhandling less profitable for others. Aggressive-panhandling laws typically include the following specific prohibitions:

- confronting someone in a way that would cause a reasonable person to fear bodily harm;
- touching someone without his or her consent;
- continuing to panhandle or follow someone after he or she has refused to give money;

— intentionally blocking or interfering with the safe passage of a person or vehicle;
— using obscene or abusive language toward someone while attempting to panhandle him or her; and
— acting with intent to intimidate someone into giving money.

2. Prohibiting panhandling in specified areas

Many courts have held that laws can restrict where panhandling occurs. Panhandlers are increasingly being prohibited from panhandling:

— near ATMs;
— on public transportation vehicles and near stations and stops;
— near business entrances/exits;
— on private property, if posted by the owner; and
— on public beaches and boardwalks.

One legal commentator has proposed a novel approach to regulating panhandling: zoning laws that would strictly prohibit panhandling in some areas, allow limited panhandling in other areas, and allow almost all panhandling in yet other areas. The literature does not report any jurisdiction that has adopted this approach as a matter of law, though clearly, police officers informally vary their enforcement depending on community tolerance levels in different parts of their jurisdiction.

3. Prohibiting interference with pedestrians or vehicles.

Some jurisdictions have enacted laws that specifically prohibit impeding pedestrians' ability to walk either by standing or by lying down in the way. Enforcement can be difficult where such laws require police to establish the panhandler's intent to obstruct others. The city of Seattle drafted a law that eliminated the need to establish intent, and that law survived a legal challenge. Where panhandling occurs on roads, as car window-washing usually does, enforcing laws that prohibit interfering with motor vehicle traffic can help control the problem.

4. Banning panhandlers from certain areas as a condition of probation.

Because panhandling's viability depends so heavily on good locations, banning troublesome panhandlers from those locations as a condition of probation, at least temporarily, might serve to discourage them from panhandling and, perhaps, compel them to consider legitimate employment or substance abuse treatment. Convicted panhandlers might also be temporarily banned from publicly funded shelters. Alternatively, courts could use civil injunctions and restraining orders to control chronic panhandlers' conduct, although actual use of this approach does not appear in the literature. Obviously, police will require prosecutors' endorsements and judicial approval to advance these sorts of responses.

5. Sentencing convicted panhandlers to appropriate community service.

Some jurisdictions have made wide use of community service sentences tailored to the particular offender and offense. For example, officers in St. Louis asked courts to sentence chronic panhandlers to community service cleaning the streets, sidewalks and alleys in the area where they panhandled.

6. Requiring panhandlers to obtain solicitation permits.

Some cities, including Wilmington, Del., and New Orleans, have at some time required panhandlers and window washers to obtain solicitation permits, just as permits are required from street vendors and others who solicit money in public. Little is known about the effectiveness of such permit schemes.

Public Education Responses

7. Discouraging people from giving money to panhandlers, and encouraging them to give to charities that serve the needy.

In all likelihood, if people stopped giving money to panhandlers, panhandling would cease. Public education campaigns are intended to discourage people from giving money to panhandlers. They typically offer three main arguments:

1) panhandlers usually use the money to buy alcohol and drugs, rather than goods and services that will improve their condition;
2) giving panhandlers small amounts of money is insufficient to address the underlying circumstances that cause them to panhandle; and
3) social services are available to meet panhandlers' food, clothing, shelter, health care, and employment needs.

Some people do not understand the relationship between panhandling and substance abuse, or are unaware of available social services, however obvious these factors may seem to police. Public education messages have been conveyed via posters, pamphlets, movie trailers, and charity collection points. A poster campaign was an important element of the New York City Transit Authority's effort to control subway panhandling. In Nashville and Memphis, Tenn., special parking meters were used as collection points for charities that serve the needy. Some police officers have invested a lot of their own time making personal appeals to discourage people from giving money to panhandlers. Some cities, such as Evanston, Ill., have hired trained civilians to make such appeals. Not everyone will be persuaded by the appeals; some will undoubtedly perceive them as uncaring.

8. Using civilian patrols to discourage panhandling.

In Baltimore, a business improvement district group hired police-trained, uniformed, unarmed civilian public-safety guides to intervene in low-level disorder incidents, and to radio police if their warnings were not heeded. Portland, Ore., developed a similar program,as did Evanston.

9. Encouraging people to buy and give panhandlers vouchers, instead of money.

Some communities have instituted programs whereby people can buy and give panhandlers vouchers redeemable for food, shelter, transportation, or other necessities, but not for alcohol or tobacco. Typically, a private nonprofit organization prints and sells the vouchers and serves as the broker between buyers and merchants. Some vouchers are printed in a way that makes them difficult to counterfeit. Vouchers are often accompanied with printed information about where they can be redeemed and what social services are available to the needy. Window signs and flyers are commonly used to advertise voucher programs. There is some risk, however, that panhandlers will exchange the vouchers for money through a black market,or that few people will buy the vouchers, as has been reported in some jurisdictions.

Situational Responses

10. Modifying the physical environment to discourage panhandlers from congregating in the area.

Among the environmental features conducive to or facilitating panhandling are the following: access to water; restrooms; unsecured garbage dumpsters; and places to sit or lie down, protected from the elements. These physical features can be modified to discourage panhandling. Police in Santa Ana, Calif., as part of a larger effort to control aggressive panhandling, persuaded business owners to modify many physical features of their property, to make it less attractive to panhandlers, without inconveniencing customers. A number of police efforts to address broader problems related to transient encampments–problems that included panhandling–entailed removing the transients from the encampments and referring them to social service agencies.

11. Regulating alcohol sales to chronic inebriates who panhandle in the area.

Because many panhandlers are chronic inebriates, and because they spend so much of their panhandling money on alcohol, enforcing laws that prohibit alcohol sales to intoxicated people or chronic inebriates is one means of discouraging panhandling in the area. Several police agencies have reported using this approach in their efforts to control panhandling and other problems related to chronic inebriates. Alternatively, merchants might be persuaded to change their sales practices to discourage panhandlers from shopping at their stores.

12. Controlling window-washing materials

Several police agencies have reported on ways to control how squeegee men/panhandlers acquire, store and use window-washing materials. Santa Ana police asked nearby businesses to remove an outdoor water fountain that squeegee men were using to fill their buckets. Vancouver, British Columbia, police discovered where squeegee men stored their buckets and squeegees, and had property owners secure the storage places. They also had gas station owners engrave their squeegee equipment with identifying marks to deter theft by panhandlers.

13. Promoting legitimate uses of public places to displace panhandlers.

Police in Staffordshire, England, encouraged the

municipal authority to promote street musicians in public places where panhandlers abounded, as one means to discourage panhandlers from begging in the area. The underlying logic was that passersby would likely notice the distinction between those who solicit money in exchange for something pleasant, and those who panhandle but offer nothing in return. Passersby would theoretically be less inclined to give money to panhandlers, thereby discouraging panhandling. Similarly, the New York/New Jersey Port Authority promoted new and attractive businesses in the Manhattan bus terminal as part of a larger strategy to reduce crime and disorder, including panhandling. Complaints about panhandling in the terminal declined by one-third over a four-year period.

Social Services/Treatment Response

14. Providing adequate social services and substance abuse treatment to reduce panhandlers' need to panhandle.

To address some of the underlying problems of many panhandlers, police may need to advocate new social services, or help coordinate existing services. Police can be and have long been instrumental in advocating and coordinating social services for panhandlers, and in referring people to those services. Fontana, Calif., police coordinated a highly successful program that provided panhandlers and other transients with a wide range of health care, food, job training, and housing placement services. They offered treatment as an alternative to enforcement; they enforced laws regulating street disorder, including panhandling, and transported those willing to accept treatment to the social service center.

Short-term substance-abuse treatment programs, however, are not likely to be effective for most panhandlers–their addictions are too strong–and most who participate in short- term programs quickly revert to their old habits. Unfortunately, long-term programs cost more than most communities are willing to spend. Police could advocate the most chronic offenders' being given priority for long-term treatment programs, or the courts could mandate such programs. Some social service outreach efforts target those people identified as causing the most problems for the community. In Madison, Wis., detoxification workers even took to the streets to proactively monitor the conduct of their most difficult clients. Some panhandlers will, of course, refuse social service and treatment offers because they are unwilling to make the lifestyle changes usually required to stay in the programs.

15. Enforcing laws that prohibit all panhandling.

Many laws that prohibit all panhandling were written long ago and are vaguely and broadly worded: consequently, they are unlikely to survive a legal challenge.

2

Hunger and Food Security: Current Trends

Hunger is the most extreme form of poverty, where individuals or families cannot afford to meet their most basic need for food. Hunger manifests itself in many ways other than starvation and famine. Most poor people who battle hunger deal with chronic undernourishment and vitamin or mineral deficiencies, which result in stunted growth, weakness and heightened susceptibility to illness. Countries in which a large portion of the population battles hunger daily are usually poor and often lack the social safety nets we enjoy, such as soup kitchens, food stamps, and job training programs. When a family that lives in a poor country cannot grow enough food or earn enough money to buy food, there is nowhere to turn for help.

Today our world houses 6.3 billion people. The United States is a part of the developed or industrialized world, which consists of about 50 countries with a combined population of only 0.9 billion, less than one sixth of the world's population. In contrast, approximately 5 billion people live in the developing world. This world is made up of about 125 low and middle-income countries in which people generally have a lower standard of living with access to fewer goods and services than people in high-income countries. The remaining 0.4 billion live in countries in transition, which include the Baltic states, eastern Europe and the Commonwealth of Independent States.

World hunger is increasing, with an estimated 842 million people going to bed hungry every night. Most people suffering from hunger live in Africa and Latin America, but 34 million are in the former Soviet Union and 10 million live in the rich industrialised countries. This startling evidence of the growing division between rich and poor on a world scale appears in a recent report published by the United Nations Food and Agriculture Organisation (FAO).

In the developing world, more than 1.2 billion people currently live below the international poverty line, earning less than $1 per day. Among this group of poor people, many have problems obtaining adequate, nutritious food for themselves and their families. As a result, 798 million people in the developing world are undernourished. They consume less than the minimum amount of calories essential for sound health and growth. Undernourishment negatively affects people's health, productivity, sense of hope and overall well-being. A lack of food can stunt growth, slow thinking, sap energy, hinder fetal development and contribute to mental retardation.

Economically, the constant securing of food consumes valuable time and energy of poor people, allowing less time for work and earning income. Socially, the lack of food erodes relationships and feeds shame so that those most in need of support are often least able to call on it.

Poor nutrition and calorie deficiencies cause nearly one in three people to die prematurely or have disabilities, according to the World Health Organization. Pregnant women, new mothers who breastfeed infants, and children are among the most at risk of undernourishment. 153 million children under 5 in the developing world are underweight. Worse yet, 11 million children younger than 5 die every year, more than half from hunger-related causes. Most of these deaths are attributed, not to outright starvation, but to diseases that move in on vulnerable children whose bodies have been weakened by hunger.

The four most common childhood illnesses are diarrhea, acute respiratory illness, malaria and measles. Each of these illnesses is both preventable and treatable. Yet, again, poverty interferes in parents' ability to access immunizations and medicines. Chronic undernourishment on top of insufficient treatment greatly increases a child's risk of death. In the developing world, 27 percent of children under 5 are moderately to severely underweight. 10 percent are severely underweight. 8 percent of children under 5 are moderately to severely wasted, or seriously below weight for one's height, and an overwhelming 32 percent are moderately to severely stunted, or seriously below normal height for one's age.

There are 830 million undernourished people in the world today and 791 million live in developing countries. The undernourished have an average deficit of more than 300 kilocalories per person per day. The largest number of people who suffer nutritional deficiencies live in Asia and the Pacific region, where poverty, unsafe water and poor sanitation contribute to poor health

In the Asia and Pacific region 525 million or 17% of the total population of 3 billion suffer from undernourishment and the worst hit countries are North Korea, Mongolia, Cambodia and Bangladesh. In addition, there are millions of drought-affected people in Tajikistan, Pakistan, Iran, Armenia and Georgia.

But the worst conditions continue to be, largely, in Africa. One out of every three people in Sub-Sahara Africa is undernourished. High government debt burdens, inadequate funding for health and education, pervasive poverty, poor agricultural productivity, weak public institutionsand the AIDS pandemic all are major causes.

In Sub-Sahara Africa 180 million or 33% of the total population of 539 million suffer from under-nourishment and the worst hit countries include Angola, Burundi, Sierra Leone, Guinea, Somalia, Sudan, Ethiopia and Eritrea.

In the Near East and North Africa, 33 million or 9% of the total population of 360 million suffer from under-nourishment and the worst hit country is Afghanistan.

In the Latin America and Caribbean region, 53 million or 11% of the total population of 481 million suffer from under-nourishment and the worst hit countries are Haiti, Nicaragua, Bolivia and Honduras.

Many countries of the former Soviet Union and Eastern Europe undergoing the transition from centrally-planned to market-based economies have experienced economic hardship and rising levels of under-nutrition during the last decade.

Hunger in Industrial Countries

Hunger is much less widespread and severe in the industrial countries than in Somalia or Bangladesh. But even in industrial countries, millions of people do not have an adequate diet. Children in low-income and single-parent households, homeless people and members of ethnic minorities are especially vulnerable. Widespread hunger among children in the United States is clearly unnecessary and especially shocking.

In 1985, 20 million people were hungry in the United States. By 1995 that number had increased to 30 million. The Food Stamp Program, the main federal government food assistance channel, currently serves 26 million people (about 10 percent of the U.S. population) per month A similar number of people relies on private charitable food assistance, provided by a national network of 150,000 agencies. A 1995 survey of 29 major U.S. cities by the U.S. Conference of Mayors found that requests for emergency food increased by an average of 9 percent over the previous year. Emergency programs were, on average, unable to meet 18 percent of those requests.

In 1994, 38 million people (14.5 percent of the population) lived in poverty. The U.S. government's measure of poverty is based on the income needed to purchase a minimally adequate diet. The poverty rate was 9 percent for non-Hispanic whites and 31 percent for both African Americans and persons of Hispanic origin. People who are poor are those who are likely to be hungry, so it is no surprise that a recent government survey found that food insecurity is also higher among African Americans and Hispanics than whites.

Canadian hunger is paradoxical.4 Canada ranks first in the world among 174 countries in the United Nations Development Programme's (UNDP) 1996 Human Development Index, based on education, wealth and health. Yet as of 1994, 2.5 million people (9 percent of the populace) relied on private charitable food assistance from a network of 456 food banks. In 1992 there were 2 million people using food banks. The largest province, Ontario, had the largest number of food bank users, while Quebec, the second largest province, had the fastest rate of increase. Emergency food demand also exploded in Regina, the heart of the wheat belt, and Edmonton, capital of the oil-rich province of Alberta.

Those particularly vulnerable to hunger include people on public assistance, working poor people, families with children (especially female-headed, single-parent families with young children), single men, disabled people, Black Canadians, those of First Nations (i.e., indigenous) and Latin American ancestry, and refugees.

Countries in Western Europe are experiencing economic hardship. In France, 200,000 to 600,000 people are homeless, including 30,000 in Paris. Four million French people live in substandard housing and more than 3 million (12 percent of the work force) are looking for jobs. Unemployment in Germany, once Europe's "economic engine," has reached 11 percent, about the same level as for the European Union as a whole.

In the United Kingdom, 1.5 million families receiving government welfare payments were too poor to provide their children with an adequate diet in 1994. Poor children are susceptible to illness and even death as a result. Emergency food assistance agencies are spreading rapidly in Western Europe. But despite indicators of vulnerability to hunger, there are no systematic studies of the extent of food insecurity in the region.

In Australia, one of eight people—about 2 million—lived below the poverty line between 1990 and 1992. Many poor Australians depend on charitable food assistance, and some periodically go without food in order to obtain shelter or clothing. In the Northern Territory, up to 20 percent of Aboriginal children under age 2 are malnourished. Nationally, Aborigine infants are three times more likely to die in infancy than non-Aboriginal children.

Childhood hunger is widespread in the United States despite enormous affluence. Even short periods of undernutrition can affect children's behavior, cognitive development and future productivity. Children who are hungry are more than three times as likely to experience unwanted weight loss, more likely to have frequent headaches, and are four times more likely to suffer from fatigue and have difficulty concentrating. Children who are hungry have a hard time learning, are more often sick and absent from school and have a much harder time paying attention in class.

The Urban Institute estimates that the 1996 welfare act will push another 1.1 million children below the poverty line. Congress refused to include funds to monitor the effects of the act on hunger and poverty.

The United States already has the highest child poverty rate of any industrial country.U.S. child poverty was substantially higher than in any other country. There are a number of reasons for the disparity. The gap between rich and poor people tends to be greater in the United States. A study of income inequality in 1995 in 25 industrial countries found inequality ratios (the ratio between incomes of people at the 90th percentile and 10th percentile of the income distribution) range from 2.25 in the Slovak Republic to 6.84 in Russia. The United States has the second highest inequality ratio, 5.67. Although the United States enjoys one of the world's highest standards of living, its sharp income inequality means that rich people are, on average, far better off than rich people elsewhere, while poor people tend to be worse off than in other wealthy countries.

Most other industrial-country governments' policies have a stronger effect on hunger and poverty, especially among children. Virtually every other industrial-country government assures access to health care for all citizens. The United States tends to rely on means-tested welfare programs, basing assistance on strict income and asset limits. Instead, other developed-country governments provide "universal" benefits regardless of income or wealth. Typical benefits include child allowances (monthly payments to families with children); guarantees of child support payments for single parents, either from the absent parent or the government; and child care. In addition, tax policies of most industrial nations help reduce poverty more significantly than do U.S. policies.

In France, every mother receives $2,400 upon the birth of a child, a monthly allowance of $120 following the birth of a second child, and free hospital and medical care before and after each birth. Working mothers are entitled to a six-month paid maternity leave and up to three years of unpaid leave without losing their jobs. The United Kingdom continues to provide generous universal child allowances and national health care after 17 years of political rule by anti-welfare state forces.

The combination of relatively low benefit levels and over-reliance on means-tested programs contribute to poverty among single-mother families in the United States; they are poorest among nine Western countries. In the mid-1980's, the United States had the lowest levels of support for both single- and two-parent poor families among 36 wealthy countries. Tax and government benefit programs in the United States have a weaker impact on single-parent family poverty than those of other countries. In the 1990s, these programs lifted at least 75 percent of all single-parent families out of poverty in the Netherlands, Sweden and the United Kingdom, compared to 50 percent in France, a third in Germany, 20 percent in Canada and just 4.6 percent in the United States.

The contrast between the long-run trends in the United States and Canada, which have experienced similar economic and demographic changes, suggests the important role of government. The Canadian child poverty rate was 2 percentage points above the United States rate in 1970, but 8 points below it by 1991 due in large part to activist social policy.

All industrial countries face a growing number of economically vulnerable single-parent families, changes in the labor market resulting from economic globalization and an aging population. The costs of the welfare state, especially for old-age assistance and for education to meet demand for technologically skilled workers, have escalated dramatically.

In many countries, there is considerable pressure to reduce spending. Most wealthy nations place a higher priority on programs for elderly people than on those for children. Child care in Italy and the United Kingdom, once free, now requires user fees. Germany, France and Belgium have expanded their reliance on means-testing. The governments of France, Sweden and Germany have all sought to scale back the extensive array of social programs their citizens have long enjoyed. This has led to political protests in France and Germany. Italy is considering raising the retirement age. The Netherlands may tighten eligibility for disability benefits, while many countries are debating more modest unemployment benefits. Japan, which has not provided an extensive safety net, now faces slower economic growth, increased joblessness and substantial budget deficits.

In Canada and the United Kingdom, as in the United States, there are demands that single parents work instead of relying on welfare programs. In Scandinavia and France where single parents regularly combine work and public assistance, benefit programs enjoy much stronger political support.

But while all the industrial countries are curtailing social programs somewhat, the United States has higher rates of childhood hunger and has cut back more drastically than any other industrial nation on programs that help children.

Hunger in Countries in Transition

The transition from planned to market economies in

Central and Eastern Europe and the newly independent states (NIS) of the former Soviet Union has dislocated and created hardships for many people. Poverty and inequality have increased. Food prices have generally increased more rapidly than incomes, which has especially affected unemployed persons, pensioners and others on fixed incomes. The sudden dismantling of government social programs, coupled with slow development of markets and private sector jobs, have contributed to food insecurity In parts of the former Yugoslavia and some NIS countries, violent conflict has uprooted hundreds of thousands of people, leaving them at serious risk of hunger and disease.

Between 1979-1981 and 1990-1992, daily per capita calorie supplies fell from 3,400 to 3,230 in the NIS and Eastern Europe. Problems are especially severe in the Central Asian areas of the NIS, where absolute poverty has increased and nutritional deficiencies are widespread. Poverty rates are 70 percent in Russian Central Asia, compared to 10 percent in Moscow and St. Petersburg. In Russia, 4 percent of children under age 2 were underweight in 1993 and 21 percent stunted (only 10 percent were stunted in 1992).

Hunger in Developing Countries

In the developing world, millions of families face severe and persistent hunger. But there is good news in the developing countries. The number of hungry people (those who have inadequate access to food, and so consume fewer calories than required for an active and healthy life) fell from 918 million during the 1969-1971 period to 906 million in 1979-1981 and further to 841 million in 1990-1992. The proportion of the population of the developing world that goes hungry also dropped, from 35 percent in 1969-1971 to 28 percent in 1979-1981, to 20 percent in 1990-1992. Progress against hunger varied widely among countries and regions. The Food and Agriculture Organization of the United Nations (FAO) reports that among 98 developing countries surveyed, the prevalence of hunger increased in 39 counties, 23 of them in Africa.

Africa

In sub-Saharan Africa, the proportion and absolute number of hungry people has increased between 1969-1971 and 1990-1992. The proportion rose from 38 percent to 43 percent, while the hungry population doubled, from 103 million to 215 million. In Ethiopia and Somalia, the proportion of hungry people increased to more than 55 percent.14 Per capita food consumption among hungry people in Africa declined from 1,490 to 1,470 calories per day, far below minimum requirements of 2,350 calories. Eleven of the 14 countries where relative food inadequacy (the gap between actual food supplies and needs for people with inadequate access to food) is higher than 15 percent are located in sub-Saharan Africa. On the other hand, in Burkina Faso and Tanzania, the proportion of hungry people decreased substantially over the two decade period. The Iringa District in Tanzania has established a model child health program, with a strong emphasis on community participation, that has achieved remarkable reductions in child under-nutrition.

These dismal overall regional trends resulted, in part, from high population growth (2.9 percent for Africa as a whole) and harsh external realities (low export prices, unpayable debts and declining aid). Internal problems have plagued Africa as well, notably governments in many countries that have failed to put a high priority on meeting people's needs. Numerous governments on the continent have been both incompetent and corrupt. In recent years, foreign aid donors and the international financial institutions have pushed for sudden and dramatic shifts toward a reduced government role in African economies. But the international financial institutions themselves now admit that their policy prescriptions have not worked well in Africa....Civil conflict and drought have further undermined food security and good governance on the continent.

The food outlook remains grim. FAO projects that the number of undernourished Africans could rise to 265 million (30 percent of the region's population) by 2010. The International Food Policy Research Institute similarly predicts that growth in food production by the year 2020 is unlikely to outpace population growth in sub-Saharan Africa. Increased exports are unlikely to generate enough foreign exchange to import adequate food, and African countries cannot count on sufficient aid from abroad.15

Asia-Pacific

Most of the world's hungry people live in Asia (62 percent). Nevertheless, between 1969-1971 and 1990-1992, the number of hungry people in Southeast Asia fell from 476 million to 269 million, and the proportion declined from 41 percent to 16 percent. In South Asia, the proportion declined from 33 percent to 22 percent. Because of rapid population growth, the absolute number increased from 238 million people in 1969-1971 to 303 million in 1979-1981, but then dropped back to 255 million in 1990-1992. The proportion of hungry people increased in Afghanistan, Bangladesh, Mongolia, Sri Lanka and Vietnam between 1969-1971 and 1990-1992. In some countries of the region, the undernutrition rate among adults and adolescents is substantial: 49 percent in India and 13 percent in China, for example.

Government policies such as investment in agricultural research, rural development and public health have spurred progress against hunger in Asia and the Pacific. During the 1970s, national public policies, supported by aid donors, along with the hard work of the region's farmers and agricultural scientists, achieved a 33 percent increase in cereal output. India, Indonesia and Thailand have extended basic health and nutrition services to hundreds of thousands of villages, with the active participation of local communities playing an essential role. In each country, this has led to substantial gains in the well-being of children, in particular.

Even very poor countries in the region have carried out effective anti-hunger policies. India has not experienced famine since independence in 1947. According to Indian hunger scholar Amartya Sen, this is due to an administrative system which compensates the loss of entitlement as a result of such calamities as droughts and floods by providing employment—often at cash wages—giving the affected population renewed ability to command food in the market. More recently, Sri Lanka has managed to maintain food security for most citizens despite a debilitating 13-year civil war.

Latin America and the Caribbean

In Latin America and the Caribbean, the proportion of hungry people was constant between 1979-1981 and 1990-1992. But the absolute number increased from 48 million to 64 million due to population growth. Poverty is still widespread. Most governments have attempted to make their economies more market- and export-oriented, but their efforts have not generated enough job opportunities, and disparity in wages between low- and high-skilled jobs has widened.

Middle East and North Africa

In this region, the proportion of hungry people has remained fairly stable, but the absolute number increased—from 27 million in 1979-1981 to 37 million in 1990-1992. Algeria, Saudi Arabia, Tunisia, Lebanon and

Syria experienced high growth in per capita food availability. Kuwait experienced about a 15 percent increase in the number of people with inadequate access to food. Economic sanctions are reported to have caused substantial food and nutrition problems in Iraq, including a dramatic increase in child undernutrition.

Faces of Hunger

The word "hunger" conjures up images of famine and starvation, but most hunger does not result from such emergencies. Instead, hungry people typically live lives of grinding poverty that make it impossible for them to meet their food needs. Hunger statistics represent quiet human suffering and injustice on a scale inconceivable to most of us. The numbers represent flesh-and-blood people who are struggling to survive against extraordinary odds: a Filipino woman, forced to temporarily abandon her two young children so she can find work in the city to pay for food; a Peruvian boy who is forced to leave school to help supplement the meager family income; a new mother in Senegal who walks for six hours, house to house, begging for the equivalent of 10 cents so her sick baby may be seen by a nurse.

Poverty

Poverty is a main cause of hunger. Poor people often lack access to land to grow food or adequate income to buy it. According to the World Bank, the number of poor people in developing countries and countries in transition who live on the equivalent of less than a dollar a day (in 1985 prices) increased from 1.2 billion to 1.3 billion between 1987 and 1993. However, the proportion of such people declined 0.7 percent. Seventy percent of these absolutely poor people are women. Inequality in labor markets, ill treatment in social welfare systems, and lower status and power in the family are some of the reasons for women's poverty.

According to UNDP, 3 billion people—a majority of humanity—live on less than $2 per day, while the world's 358 billionaires have assets exceeding the combined annual incomes of countries with 45 percent of the world's people. As the world's population grows at least 40 percent, from nearly 6 billion people today to 8.5 billion or more by the year 2025, the global labor force will grow even faster, by 60 percent, increasing from 2.5 billion to 4 billion workers. Add today's several hundred million unemployed or underemployed workers, and the pressing need is to create 2 billion new economic opportunities over the next 30 years.

Child Undernutrition

Hunger hits young children especially hard. Poor nutrition during the first few years of life can result in permanent physical and mental damage, and often death. In 1990, 179 million of the developing world's children under the age of 5—one out of three—were undernourished, as measured by being underweight. Seventy-five percent of the underweight children lived in the Asia-Pacific region. South Asia's child undernutrition rate was much higher than that of any other region (58 percent, compared to 30 percent in sub-Saharan Africa).

The possible reasons for high levels of child undernutrition in South Asia include the large population size, high population density and the rainy climate, which spreads diseases such as intestinal disorders that cause malnutrition.

Two hundred fifteen million children under age 5 in the developing world (40 percent), are stunted (i.e., have low heights for their age, indicating chronic undernutrition). The rates, again, are highest in South Asia. An estimated 95 million children under age 15 in developing countries work to help their poverty-plagued families. An equal number are homeless, destitute "street children," vulnerable to hunger.

Micronutrient Malnutrition

Even when people are able to obtain the calories and protein they need, they may still suffer from life-threatening malnutrition. Micronutrient malnutrition, especially iodine deficiency disorders, vitamin A deficiency and iron deficiency anemia, seriously undermines the health and productivity of poor people. Over 2 billion people worldwide are vulnerable to this "hidden hunger"..., which has deep consequences. Lack of vitamin A can cause blindness and death from infectious disease. Iron deficiency is a cause of anemia, which lowers productivity by reducing work and school performance and increasing susceptibility to disease. In 1990, anemia afflicted more than half the pregnant women in the developing world, putting them at heightened risk of death in childbirth or bearing low birth-weight babies, who in turn are vulnerable to disease and impaired development.

Iodine deficiency can lead to goiter (an enlargement of the thyroid gland) and mental retardation. There are significant iodine deficiency problems in some European countries as well as in the developing world. The Chinese Ministry of Pubic Health recently reported that iodine shortages during infant brain development have left 10 million people mentally retarded, including hundreds of thousands of cretins (people with severe mental and physical impairment).

Ironically, although the costs of micronutrient malnutrition can be enormous—up to 5 percent of a country's gross domestic product in disability and lost lives and productivity—relatively inexpensive public health interventions can prevent micronutrient deficiency disorders. Iodizing salt supplies cost about 5 cents per person per year. Consumption of small amounts of green, leafy vegetables provides adequate vitamin A. For 6 cents per child per year, children over 6 months of age can also receive three doses of vitamin A capsules. It is likewise inexpensive to fortify sugar and cooking oil with vitamin A. Pregnant women can increase their iron intake with a daily tablet of iron sulfate that costs one-fifth of a cent.

It would not be difficult to overcome this widespread "hidden hunger." But it requires a sustained government commitment. Active community involvement—education, advocacy and carrying out of programs—is critical, too. The good news is that many governments are committed to tackling the problem. In 1995, the United Nations Children's Fund (UNICEF) reported that 58 of 94 countries with iodine deficiency problems were on track to iodize 95 percent of their salt supplies by the end of the year. China is making a major effort to fully iodize its salt supply by the year 2000. Bangladesh, Brazil, India, Malawi and the Philippines provide children with vitamin A capsules in conjunction with immunization efforts.[26]

Urbanization of Hunger

By the year 2025, about 61 percent of the world's population will live in urban areas, compared to 45 percent in 1995. The urban population will increase by 1 million people per week, from 2.5 billion to 5.1 billion.[28] This urbanization is taking place mostly in developing countries, where urban poverty and hunger are also increasing.

Although the proportion of hungry people living in rural areas remains high in the developing world as a whole, in some developing counties, urban malnutrition rates exceed those of rural areas.[29] Slum dwellers are especially susceptible to malnutrition; in Bangladesh, the infant mortality rate in urban areas is 70 per thousand live births, while the rate is 138 in slums, where government services are virtually nonexistent. In Manila, the slum rate is three times greater than that in non-slum areas.30 In Washington, D.C., the infant mortality rate is 18, but it is eight for the United States as a whole.

Urban poor people in the developing world live in "life-"and "health-threatening" conditions in overcrowded huts that lack basic services. Miserable sanitation and other aspects of urban slums sometimes make urban health and nutrition qualitatively different from the rural situation. Strategic policies are needed to grapple with these problems.

Hunger in Complex Emergencies

Complex emergencies, caused mainly by civil wars, are the main cause of today's famines. These situations often lead to starvation and life-threatening disease by displacing people on a large scale and causing economic, political and social institutions to fail. These situations also intensify population pressure on available resources and contribute to environmental degradation. In some cases, natural disasters such as drought aggravate the problems. Bread for the World Institute's Countries in Crisis: Hunger 1996 showed that undernutrition, illness and micronutrient deficiencies are widespread among uprooted people.32 According to the U.S. Mission to the United Nations, 41.5 million people are at risk of starvation and death due to complex emergencies in 1996.

The story of Maria Ingabire Uwamahoro is all too typical. A refugee from Rwanda, she is walking with thousands of others to Zaire. Only three of her five children accompany her. She fears for the two oldest, who were away gathering firewood when she was forced to flee her home suddenly to protect herself and the younger children. The older ones may have made it to a refugee camp or may be dead. Her husband, Minani, was killed while working at the tea factory.

On the day Maria left home, she had been weeding her fields of sorghum and beans. Her farm was one of hundreds crowded together in a patchwork quilt of small squares that covered the sloping hills and mountainsides. Most of the trees that once protected the topsoil had been cut down. The family had been given that rocky piece of land because Minani was the youngest brother of eight; after the family land was subdivided, this small plot was all that was left. Even before the war everyone in the area was desperate. There was simply too little land and too many people.

The number of people currently affected by complex emergencies declined from 45 million in 1993-1994, but it is still 60 percent higher than 10 years ago. In light of "donor fatigue," emergency aid is under threat. The prospects of meeting emergency food needs are not bright. By 2005, emergency needs could grow to between 5.7 million and 6.2 million metric tons of food, according to U.S. Department of Agriculture estimates. When this is added to chronic food aid needs for food deficit countries, total food aid requirements could reach 26 million metric tons by 2005. But only 10.6 million metric tons of grain may be available for both purposes at that time.

Hunger Deaths

Malnutrition is a significant factor in approximately 16 million deaths a year, or about one-third of all deaths. Particularly in Africa, total malnutrition-related deaths are increasing, and moderate malnutrition results in more deaths than does severe malnutrition. Many deaths related to hunger and poor nutrition occur beyond those resulting from the emergencies that receive the most attention. The urgent need for primary health care and nutrition—a need which governments must help address—for many of the world's most vulnerable groups exists not only during, but also before and after humanitarian emergencies. UNICEF and the World Health Organization (WHO) estimate that 12.4 million children under 5 die annually from malnutrition and preventable diseases. But starvation accounts for just 150,000 to 200,000 deaths a year, or less than 0.4 percent of approximately 46 million global deaths in a routine year. During the second half of the 20th century, annual average starvation deaths have declined, although the number of disasters has apparently increased. This results largely from improvements in health science, a shrinking world, due in part to improved communications and trade, and the timely availability of aid. Since 1960, the largest famines have claimed several hundred thousand lives, but not millions, a fact not well known. The lowering of starvation deaths over time may be viewed as a success of public policies, human development and international cooperation. Given current trends, starvation deaths could continue to decrease over the next decade. However, other potential trends could cause increased starvation: possible technological and industrial disasters, genocidal activities, complex emergencies, nuclear terrorism or the breakdown of nation-states. Public health emergencies that disrupt societies and cut vulnerable groups off from support could also accelerate starvation.

Identifying the Food Insecure

The World Food Summit Plan of Action in its para 20 (a) requested governments, in partnership with all actors of civil society, as appropriate, to develop and periodically update, where necessary, a national food insecurity and vulnerability information and mapping system (FIVIMS), indicating areas and populations, including at local level, affected by or at-risk of hunger and malnutrition, and elements contributing to food insecurity, making maximum use of existing data and other information systems in order to avoid duplication of efforts.

The challenge of meeting the World Food Summit goals of halving the number of undernourished by 2015 and promoting food security for all demands that countries design interventions to improve the status of those suffering from hunger. At the time of the Summit these people numbered nearly 830 million in developing countries. Today their number has dropped by only 5 percent, to 790 million in 1996-98.

Identifying and characterising the food insecure is necessary for designing and conducting action to improve their situation and reduce their number. But the factors that make people food insecure are the same ones that make people vulnerable to food insecurity. If direct feeding programmes are contemplated, it may suffice to know precisely who the hungry are. But for long-term action to eradicate hunger, it will be important to tackle the factors that create vulnerability and thus to know more precisely who the vulnerable are. Thus, in order to develop effective policies and interventions to reduce food insecurity, planners must take into account both those who are food insecure at present and those who are vulnerable to food insecurity.

Vulnerability refers to the presence of factors that place people at risk of becoming food insecure. These factors can be external or internal. External factors have the nature of :

— Trends, e.g. depletion of natural resources from which the population makes its living, food price inflation;

— Shocks, e.g. natural disasters, conflict;

— Seasonality, e.g. seasonal employment opportunities, seasonal incidence of disease.

Internal factors are the characteristics of people, the general conditions in which they live and the dynamics of the household that restrict their ability to avoid becoming food insecure in the future.

The difference between food insecure and vulnerable people is one of degree. Vulnerable people have a high probability of becoming food insecure and may fall into food insecurity at any time, as a result of the external or internal factors mentioned above, e.g. as a result of deteriorating soil quality, a flood, a seasonal change in the price of food, an increasing spiral of indebtedness and impoverishment, the loss of an income-earner in the family, the presence of a chronically-ill person in the household. On the other hand, others may see their situations improve as a result of, e.g., new employment opportunities, obtaining a scholarship for a young family member, reduction in fees required for basic health services, opening of a new farm-to market road, building of flood dikes in the area.

For planning purposes, vulnerable individuals can be grouped into categories of people who share common characteristics. Vulnerability can be perceived in a variety of ways, e.g. primarily economic, geographical, cultural or demographic, etc. Examples of different methods of classifying vulnerable groups that have been used by national FIVIMS, include:

— Occupationally, e.g. artisanal fishers in Vietnam;

— Spatially, e.g. marginal urban dwellers living in shanty towns in Guatemala;

— In relation to their environment, e.g. forest dwellers in Turkey;

— Culturally, e.g. San bushmen in Namibia;

— Demographically, e.g. children under five years in Benin;

— According to social condition, e.g. refugees from Sierra Leone in Liberia;

— Physical condition, e.g. handicapped in Chad.

— In relation to a complex combination of characteristics, e.g. sedentary indigenous urban and semi-urban people living in certain zones of Mauritania. The variety of possible classifications reflects the broad range of factors that affect the food security situation of people, and thus the complex multi-dimensional aspects of vulnerability.

Each of these types of classification emphasizes a specific characteristic of individuals that make them food insecure or vulnerable to food insecurity. However, the use of livelihood systems as the entry point for classifying vulnerable groups has proven to be effective in a variety of contexts because various dimensions of vulnerability can be integrated into the categories of livelihood systems.

Livelihood systems encompass the capabilities, material and social resources, and activities required for a particular means of living. Livelihood systems can be described by a main source of livelihood that is quite broad. Landless peasants, communal land herders, agro-pastoral farmers on rainfed land, small-scale livestock producers with no land are some examples of broad livelihood systems that have been used for classifying people into vulnerable groups.

A livelihood system is classified as vulnerable when the system is exposed to various factors that create risk for most people belonging to that system. Within any livelihood-based vulnerable group some people will be more vulnerable than others. Those most likely to be food insecure are those who are economically dependent or otherwise socially marginalised. These include:

At the individual level:

— the elderly

— orphans

— invalids

— pregnant and lactating women and young children

At the household level:

— female-or elderly-headed households

— households belonging to minority groups.

Methods for Profiling Vulnerable Groups

FAO has been developing instruments, procedures and techniques that planners can use to identify food insecure and vulnerable people and to classify them into groups. A major result of this effort has been the development of a method for profiling vulnerable groups. Through the development of vulnerable group profiles, it is possible to identify the food insecure and vulnerable people in a country, where they are located, how many they are and the reasons that they are in this precarious state. This information can then become the basis for policies, programmes and projects to reduce the numbers of food insecure and vulnerable people.

National Brainstorming Sessions

Vulnerable group profiling builds on the work that has already been done by FAO under the FIVIMS initiative. To begin the work of finding out who is food insecure and vulnerable to food insecurity, the secretariat in early 1999 began to encourage countries to hold interdisciplinary brainstorming sessions to establish an initial identification and characterisation of vulnerable groups.

While a review of secondary literature may also be useful for this purpose, the interdisciplinary brainstorming sessions have been found to be especially fruitful. People who know their country well often bring perceptions and insights to an oral discussion that are missed when carrying out a more formal study. The process is often enlightening to the participants and creates a solid base of support for continuing the investigative work about the groups that have been identified. Through this process, vulnerable groups have thus far been identified in 14 countries.

In the draft *FIVIMS Guide for Finding Out Who the Food Insecure Are,* suggestions are made for the conduct of such sessions in all countries that have decided to establish a national FIVIMS. Depending on the size of the country and the degree of decentralization, it may be more useful to have the brainstorming sessions take place on the sub-national (e.g. provincial) level. The brainstorming sessions should result in a first identification, classification and characterisation of the food insecure and vulnerable people, including their location in the country, their main sources of livelihood, demographic characteristics, and dietary patterns, as well as an initial analysis of the factors that make these people food insecure and vulnerable to food insecurity.

Classification of Vulnerable Groups

After the brainstorming session, it is important to construct a classification system for the identified vulnerable groups that uses a consistent set of criteria for characterising all vulnerable groups in the country. The classification of vulnerable groups has to ensure that they are distinct and mutually exclusive. This is essential to avoid double counting in the enumeration of vulnerable people and to prevent un-intended overlap of targeted programmes on certain parts of the food insecure population.

For example, some countries have identified specially vulnerable demographic groups, such as pregnant and lactating women and under-five children. Such demo-graphically characterized individuals most likely belong to other groups that have already been classified according to a livelihood system. Usually not all pregnant and lactating women in a country are vulnerable, but only those belonging to households that are in a precarious situation. In such countries, their special vulnerability would be highlighted in the profile of the livelihood-based vulnerable groups to which they belong.

Some countries have created a category for destitutes that covers dependence on family gifts, on charity, on begging, on petty crime, etc. as sources of livelihood. In this case, destitutes that belong to communities practising other occupations would not be classified as belonging to the livelihood system of their community, but rather to the livelihood system "destitutes".

Estimating the Number of People in each Group

Estimating the approximate number of people in each vulnerable group can be done through a number of means. Often experts and people working with the identified groups can give a rough estimate of how many people belong to that group. Data from the latest national surveys, such as the population census or an agriculture census, can be used to estimate the number of vulnerable people in each group. If these methods are not feasible or satisfactory, it may be necessary to conduct a sample survey of each group.

The Need for Sub-groups

After the initial classification of vulnerable groups into broad categories, it is usually necessary to further refine this classification by dividing the broad categories into sub-groups. In the initial categories, there may be significant differences among the households as regards various factors affecting the food security status and therefore the degree of food insecurity and vulnerability of these households. For example, in Vietnam, a brainstorming session identified "marine fishers" as a broad category of vulnerable people. Subsequently, this broad category was divided into four separate sub-groups, each with its own vulnerability and food insecurity characteristics: beach scavengers and diggers, on-shore fishers, near-shore fishers with a boat, and far-shore fishers.

In the final classification system, each sub-group should represent a separate, clearly distinguishable group of people. Each sub-group should also be characterised by a large degree of homogeneity among the households as to their livelihood system, livelihood strategies and food security status (i.e. at-risk, transitory food insecure, seasonally food insecure or chronically food insecure).

Because of the relatively high level of homogeneity within each sub-group, it should be possible to develop a profile of typical characteristics of households belonging to the sub-group, (where a household is defined as a group of people living on the same incomes and sharing the food). Not all households will possess each of these characteristics, but the general characterisation should permit identification of the main vulnerability factors affecting most households in the group.

Food Securty Status of People within each Subgroup

Once sub-groups have been established, it may be possible to make an initial broad estimation of those that are food secure and those that suffer from or are at risk of food insecurity. One method for determining this is by finding out how many within the vulnerable group have an estimated income well above the poverty line. These are probably the food secure. Among the vulnerable a simple self-assessed hunger-scoring method, for instance, can be used in the absence of more detailed survey data to determine those who are actually hungry and those who are only at risk.

Developing Vulnerable Group Profiles

Understanding the factors that explain the vulnerability of a particular group requires a detailed characterisation of the group. This can be done through profiling each vulnerable group identified at the national or sub-national level.

A vulnerable group profile contains:

— description of the broad livelihood system to which the profiled group belongs and if desired, an estimate of the number of people belonging to that group

— location of the areas where the households of the group live (with a map if possible)

— a minimum information set for the vulnerable group showing typical characteristics of households belonging to the group and information about the various factors that affect the household's food security situation and the household members' access to the food as well as their health status and uptake of food. These factors usually derive from the household's assets and livelihood strategies, the broader contextual factors that impinge upon it and the trends and shocks to which it is subject.

— a brief analysis of possible action areas. Identifying possible action areas that could contribute to the improvement of the food security status of the people of a vulnerable group is a three step process, including:

— A vulnerability analysis. This analysis consists in extracting, from the set of information, the factors and constraints that negatively affect households' food security situation, and individual household members' access to food as well as their health status and uptake of food. The analysis should show how assets, external factors and livelihood strategies combine to create a situation in which households are food insecure or at risk of becoming food insecure.

— An evaluation of opportunities. Opportunities are the positive factors that exist for a food insecure or an at-risk household in their own asset structure or in the external environment, which could potentially contribute to an improvement of the food security status of the household if properly developed. An evaluation of opportunities takes into account the positive characteristics or strengths of a livelihood system.

— An identification of broad areas of interventions and recommendations for action. Recommendations might include, for example, safety net programmes, development programmes and projects, and analysis of current assistance programmes and their relevance to the proposed actions.

FAO is in the process of developing guidelines and methods for carrying out the specific tasks involved in vulnerability profiling for use by countries.

Efforts to Eradicate Exteme Poverty

Halving hunger was one of the UN Millennium Development Goals announced in 1992. The number of people experiencing hunger was supposed to be halved by 2015. Rather than decreasing as the FAO anticipated, the number of hungry people has increased by 4.5 million a year between 1995 and 1997 and from 1999 to 2001. Improved nutrition in some countries is being more than offset by a decline in others.

Amongst the group of countries that suffered a reversal of falling numbers of malnourished were some with large populations such as Sudan, Pakistan, Nigeria, Indonesia and India. The report states, "With reversals in many large countries and progress slowing in others, the pattern of change in the developing countries as a whole shifted from a declining to a rising trend. Between 1995-1997 and 1999-2001, the number of hungry people in the developing countries increased by 18 million wiping out almost half the decrease of 37 million achieved during the previous five years. Unless significant gains are made in large countries where progress has stalled, it will be difficult to reverse this negative trend."

The FAO report highlights the increase in the number of undernourished in those countries it classifies as in transition. It is mainly referring to the countries of the former Soviet Union and Yugoslavia. Figures for 1993-1995 of 25 million undernourished increased to 34 million for 1999-2001—the bulk of the increase being in the Commonwealth of Independent States (the former USSR), which now has nearly 29 million or 10 percent of the population classified as chronically hungry. In these countries the report notes, "Economic transition has been accompanied by far-reaching political and administrative changes that have disrupted trade and exchange relations and led to severe foreign exchange shortages. In addition, agricultural production and marketing systems have broken down."

HIV/AIDS plays a crucial role in the growth of hunger. The report states, "The food crisis that threatened more than 14 million people in Southern Africa in 2002-2003 brought into sharp focus the interactions between HIV/AIDS and food security. It demonstrated that hunger cannot be combated effectively in regions ravaged by AIDS, unless interventions address the particular needs of AIDS-affected households and incorporate measures to prevent and to mitigate the spread of HIV/AIDS."

Those countries where hunger has declined generally do not have a high incidence of AIDS and have not been hit by natural disasters such as drought. Their improvement is extremely precarious and AIDS is spreading rapidly in many of them. Improved nutrition in China and India could soon be reversed.

Reports from Southern Africa have warned of a new kind of emergency in which short-term food shortages overlap with "an unprecedented collapse of health, agricultural production and food security that will endure for decades."

The FAO predict that the AIDS epidemic will stretch well into the century. In mainly claiming the lives of young adults, HIV is severely reducing the number of agricultural workers. The population left is dominated by the very young and the very old.

The report states that by 2020 HIV will have killed 20 percent of the agricultural workforce in Southern African and that currently 60-70 percent of farms are affected by loss of agricultural workers. With the death of young adults the transmission of agricultural knowledge and skills to the next generation is being prevented.

Famine worsens the AIDS epidemic because those affected by famine are more liable to move off the land to urban centres, where the risk of HIV infection is higher and women and children may end up selling sex for money and food—thus becoming more vulnerable to HIV infection. Hunger also makes those already infected with HIV more susceptible to opportunistic infections. Once they have developed full-blown AIDS their capacity to absorb nutrition from food is reduced. Even with drug therapy HIV/AIDS sufferers need to have access to a better diet to help fight the effects of the disease.

In a November 28 press release the World Food Programme Executive Director explained, "Without food aid, the poorest people with HIV will always have to choose between access to medical treatment and their next meal—even where drugs may be free. We are talking about whether to spend money on a bus fare to the nearest clinic or buy basic foodstuffs. No one should have to make that choice."

Some experts are beginning to talk about the interaction between HIV and hunger as "new variant famine"—some have referred to the conjunction as the "perfect storm." In Zambia the deadly combination is known as the "ugly sisters." Following a tour of Zambia last year the UN secretary general's AIDS envoy, Stephen Lewis, said, "It is an absolutely unanswerable measure of AIDS on the one hand and hunger on another hand ... and it leads to a kind of downward spiral on a country, which becomes irreversible if a country does not fight back."

This sentiment was echoed recently by Save the Children's Southern Africa regional director, Greg Ramm, who warned, "We are in a downward spiral. The region as a whole is much more vulnerable to minor shocks than it ever has been before."

Drought has a major impact on food production. The report explains that it accounts for 60 percent of food emergencies. Africa is the driest continent after Australasia, but other countries are affected by erratic rainfall. India receives 70 percent of its rainfall within the short three-month monsoon period. The report stresses the importance of the provision of irrigation, explaining that whilst globally only 17 percent of cropland is irrigated this irrigated cropland provides 40 percent of the world's food supply.

The Consultative Group on International Agricultural Research (CGIAR) held a conference in November in Nairobi under the title Challenge Programme on Water and Food. The conference included scientists, policy-makers and NGOs who met to discuss the issue of food and water.

Global warming and associated climate change is also having an effect. At the recent climate talks in Milan on the Kyoto protocol, UN organisations reported that effects of climate change were leading to an extra 150,000 extra deaths a year. Globally growing seasons are being shortened, adding to malnutrition.

Faced with this mounting crisis the FAO has little to offer. It can only document an unfolding human catastrophe. FAO Director-General Jacques Diouf writes in the foreword to the report, "If the latest data tend to confirm our understanding of factors that contribute to food security, they also confront us with another difficult question: if we already know the basic parameters of what needs to be done, why have we allowed hundreds of millions of people to go hungry in a world that produces more than enough food for every woman, man and child? Bluntly stated, the problem is not so much a lack of food as a lack of political will."

The expertise to address the problem of world hunger exists, but the political will does not exist on the part of the ruling class in the most powerful industrialised countries. Dr. Tewolde Egziabher of the Ethiopian Environmental Protection Authority recently pointed to one of the ways in which the West has prevented Ethiopia becoming self-sufficient in food. Western governments and international financial institutions have insisted that the private sector must control the Ethiopian food supply. They have prevented the government building granaries and food depots that could store grain from one year to the next. As a result, over the last three years Ethiopia has experienced record harvests but now faces famine again.

Ethiopia's experience reveals the extent to which the growth in world hunger is a manmade phenomenon. Prior to the reintroduction of capitalism hunger was unknown in the Soviet Union during peace time, despite a monumentally bureaucratic system of production and distribution. Now 34 million people are chronically hungry in countries where the agricultural land is as potentially productive as any to be found in the United States or Canada.

The FAO offer no analysis of why 10 million go hungry in the most industrialised countries. But their existence is an indictment of the growing gap between the rich and the poor in the advanced capitalist states. The figure shows that hunger is not limited to particular continents, but is even affecting growing numbers of workers in the Western countries.

The United Nations Development Programme (UNDP) issued its annual Human Development Report for 2003 on July 8. The report documents the progress of 175 of the world's poorest countries in the implementation of eight Millennium Development Goals (MDGs) agreed to at the UN General Assembly summit in 2000.

The MDGs were ostensibly designed by the UN as a means of halving poverty, hunger and illness in poorer countries by 2015 and encouraging the so-called "mutual responsibilities of developing and rich countries." But seven of the eight Millennium Goals are directives aimed towards the economies of poorer countries, emphasising the fact that UN's thrust is in line with the International Monetary Fund (IMF) and World Bank. The MDGs place the main responsibility for poverty reduction on the governments of poorer nations and not on Western governments and institutions and the impact of structural adjustment programmes they have imposed.

The MDGs call on developing countries to "focus on improving governance, especially in mobilising resources, allocating them equitably and ensuring their effective use." The UN report also makes the point that the MDGs can only be achieved "if poor countries pursue wide ranging reforms."Only Goal 8, which calls for a strengthening of the partnership between rich and poor countries, places any responsibility on the activities of the more economically advanced countries. An arrogant and shortsighted attitude runs right through the Human Development Report and sets the agenda. But despite this the report is forced to highlight a number of issues that reveal the devastating impact of global capitalism on the vast majority of the world's population.

The UNDP report notes that 54 nations are poorer now than they were in 1990. Twenty of these countries are in Sub-Saharan Africa, while 17 are in Eastern Europe and the Commonwealth of Independent States.

Life expectancy has fallen in 34 countries due primarily to HIV/AIDS. Of 59 priority nations 24 suffer from a high incidence of HIV/AIDS and 31 have "unusually high foreign debts."

The populations of 21 countries are hungrier today than in 1990. In 14 countries more children are dying before the age of five and primary school enrolment is declining in 12 nations.

According to the BBC the UNDP says of its own report that it documents "an unprecedented backslide... in some of the world's poorest nations" and, "More than one billion people still live in extreme poverty, and for many living standards are getting steadily worse."

A statement by Deputy Director for the UN Development Program Jean Fabre sheds some light on the massive redistribution of wealth from poorer nations to richer ones over the past decade. He told reporters, "Economic and political developments in past years have enabled considerable increases in the worlds wealth," but "at the same time, many countries have completely regressed in the past 10 years."

The report notes that in 31 of the poorest countries listed progress towards the MDGs has stalled or begun to reverse. On an assessment of current financial trends some countries would not overcome poverty until the year 2165 and it would take 20 Sub-Saharan African nations until 2147 to halve extreme poverty and until 2165 to cut child mortality rates by two-thirds.

According to the UN Human Development Index—which measures levels of life expectancy, education, adult literacy and income in the poorest nations—twenty-one states have experienced a decline. These included 14 African countries as well as Russia and six former Soviet Republics.

Commenting on the situation in the former Soviet Union after capitalist restoration, Fabre stated, "We have catastrophic falls in several countries, which often are republics of the former Soviet Union, where poverty is actually increasing. In fact poverty has tripled in the whole region."

Per capita income in each of the 42 highly indebted countries in the report is less than $1,500 and between 1990 and 2001 these economies grew on average by only half a percent per year. Despite calls in the report for rich countries to provide debt relief to poorer nations the UN's own statements unwittingly highlight the intransigent and ruthless position of these wealthy countries in enforcing free market policies—and demonstrates that the demands made by the UN on donor countries are just empty phrases that fly in the face of global capitalist reality.

Fabre admits that "the richest countries have established various barriers to the entry of goods on their own territories. There are also important subsidies given to agriculture, artificially maintaining these rich countries agriculture (sectors) above world prices." He went on, "there is, even worse, a dumping of agricultural products from rich countries on countries having weaker economies."

The UN report states that current foreign aid is up from $52.3 billion in 2001 to $57 billion, but still falls well short of the $100 billion minimum needed annually to meet its declared goals. But the UNDP's administrator, Mark Malloch Brown, told BBC News Online that he felt the situation concerning foreign aid was in fact getting worse and quite critical: "Italy, France, Germany, Japan—even the Netherlands, one of the most generous donors—are all making cuts in spending. You've got a real difficulty keeping people on track. Development assistance is the first to go when public spending faces cuts," he said.

The devastating impact of the "Washington consensus" of the World Bank and IMF—the insistence on budget discipline, deregulation and the liberalisation of trade and finance—means that the UNDP report was forced to distance itself from these policies and call for a broader view of development that looked at each country individually. But the report still insists, "Success—or failure—in economic growth is closely linked to how an economy is integrated with global markets."

In one section the UNDP looks at Mali and asks how can this small country become a "successful manufacturing exporter" like China. The report states, "investors consider the country's education and skills level too low to justify the costs imposed by landlockedness, poor health, low nutrition, a tiny domestic market and related barriers." In other words foreign investors will not see a return on their investment and so will not invest. The UNDP goes on to state, "in short Mali does not meet the thresholds required to attract many foreign and domestic investors."

This bizarre section continues by claiming, "Mali could become a successful garment exporter (like Bangladesh) tourist destination and processor of tropical agricultural products." But the country can only do this after, "Key thresholds in health, education, water, sanitation, roads, ports and power are reached."

The glaring contradiction of how an impoverished country is to achieve such a level of development on its own without huge international aid is not raised, or even thought about by the writers of the report.

The approach of rich nations to poorer countries should be to base their support more on "performance" rather than "entitlement", the report states. The countries with wealth should increase assistance to poor countries that "demonstrate good faith efforts to mobilise domestic resources, undertake policy reforms, strengthen institutions and tackle corruption and other aspects of weak governance." This statement reads just like any other issued by the World Bank and IMF.

What the Human Development report of the UNDP will not say—but is revealed by an honest and objective reading of its findings—is that the social and economic disaster destroying the lives of masses of people is the product of the very policies it espouses.

Efforts to address world hunger are not faring well. Progress since the World Food Conference in 1974 has been disappointing. Although the percentage of malnourished (underweight) children has declined, modestly, in most countries in the intervening 25 years, their numbers continue to rise. The data suggest an ongoing race between socioeconomic development and population growth, compounded by an increasingly vulnerable resource base and the fact that, more often than not, the fruits of development have yet to reach millions of people in a manner sufficient to overcome their caloric deficits. Policies and programs explicitly designed to reduce hunger have done so only marginally in most instances, implying that they have not adequately removed the underlying constraints causing hunger in the first place.

Moreover, despite two major international meetings this decade, one on nutrition and the other on hunger itself, there are few grounds for confidence as we look ahead. The hunger dilemma is both conceptual and organizational, and it is not easily circumvented. The dilemma leaves hunger ill-targeted and hunger professionals often frustrated by the constraints they face in trying to erode the constraints to nutritional adequacy experienced by the hungry themselves.

Four children (with their mother), Sudan, 1998. Conflict in Sudan has resulted in many malnourished children (with their education set aside). A hunger agenda must take account of this major cause of hunger.

One might think that hunger would be an easy issue for governments, international agencies, and even universities to embrace. Nobody actually favors the existence of hunger, except occasionally as a weapon of war. Most would agree that hunger is undesirable and that its prevalence in the world connotes something wrong that should be addressed. And, indeed, leaders as diverse as Lenin, Franklin Roosevelt, and Ferdinand Marcos have exploited the rhetorical appeal of hunger as an issue, confident that it symbolizes what they oppose and that their people's ethical, humanitarian, and political beliefs will reward them for pledging to rectify the situation.

Moreover, hunger's political appeal has been strengthened by evidence that protein-energy malnutrition (PEM), the essence of hunger, constrains human competence, productivity, and potential, making it a legitimate issue in development, as well. Hunger, it would seem, has all the advantages of being "big," non-contentious, politically appealing, and— for the development community— professionally respectable, even compelling. Unfortunately, the hunger issue contains several liabilities that have proven to be problematic. Endemic hunger is mostly invisible; its victims are typically peripheral and voiceless; and, rhetoric notwithstanding, political salience is usually low. Moreover, hunger advocates labor in a cluttered policy environment. Most of them have few links to the people for whom they advocate, and their lofty appeals are seldom matched by political mobilization and demands by the hungry on their own behalf.

The hard fact of the matter is that hunger policies are seldom seen as a collective good. They tend to be divisible, even redistributive in their benefits, and hence contentious in nature, especially when it comes to actual resource allocation. Consensus that hunger is unfortunate does not mean commitment to eradicate it, while commitment does not imply agreement on how best to do so. Easy to embrace, hunger is also easy to abandon or distort. Hunger specialists and their allies concerned with social development function in uncertain and unstable terrain laden with obstacles. And that is before they have even started to act.

Role of Governments

Governments have long had difficulty organizing to alleviate hunger. Some have tried interministerial units charged with overseeing and, at times, coordinating the agendas of different ministries. These have typically foundered on the operational autonomy of line ministries and their resistance to being subordinated and coordinated. Other governments have given responsibility for "nutrition" to specific ministries, especially health, in effect squeezing a multisectoral problem into a single sector while trusting, perhaps, that "hunger" will eventually be ameliorated by the country's overall development policies.

The designated ministries often do not know what to do with malnutrition, leaving it to nutritionists who rarely are central players in the ministry's arena. Not infrequently nutrition agendas collide with broader ministry priorities and are similarly marginalized. Meanwhile, the overall development policies being pursued may have little immediate relevance to reducing hunger and in some instances— such as promoting bimodal agricultural systems with a favored commercial sector and a largely neglected subsistence sector— may actually, if unintentionally, intensify hunger.

Role of International Agencies

International agencies have encountered difficulties of their own in determining how best to organize their hunger agendas. USAID has eliminated its Office of Nutrition, absorbing it into a new office of population, health and nutrition. The name of this office clearly expresses the lessened priority given nutrition, with funding allocations being even more skewed. Moreover, attention to protein-energy malnutrition has receded in favor of the micronutrient deficiencies, ostensibly because the latter are more health related. The result is a limited, even parochial response to PEM, one that is divorced from mainstream economic development.

Similarly, The World Bank has incorporated its Nutrition Unit into a larger entity, the Human Development Department. The Nutrition Section at UNICEF carries on but has largely abandoned protein-energy malnutrition in favor of initiatives on the micronutrients plus breastfeeding. PEM is now pretty much the responsibility of the Health Section, which has numerous other concerns, as well.

The tendency to define protein-energy malnutrition as primarily a health issue and to organize policy responses to it under a health rubric is a mixed blessing. The tendency may seem bizarre when the referent is "hunger." Yet PEM has a strong health component shaped by the body's failure to derive full benefit from nutrients consumed because of infectious disease, parasitic infestation, and other health states. Whereas "hunger" implies consumption deficits only, nutritional status a` la PEM is understood to reflect the interplay of consumption and morbidity.

That said, health interventions alone are clearly an insufficient response to PEM. UNICEF (and WHO) correctly point out that other UN agencies— FAO, WFP, and UNDP especially— come at the problem in appropriate ways that are complementary to their own approaches in the sense both of going beyond health and— in the case of UNICEF— of addressing macro as well as micro (community) conditions. In effect, comprehensiveness in the UN system is achieved by means of organizational and programmatic fragmentation, whereas at USAID and the World Bank, nutrition initiatives are largely confined to the delivery of services, often through health infrastructures, a pattern found in most governments, as well.

Organizing Action Against Hunger

This is a difficult task. In addition to its political problems, hunger poses operational problems by virtue of its being a complex issue, and one that is also structural and derived. Like "poverty" and "development," "hunger" is a big issue for which no single, onedimensional response will suffice. This leaves hunger policy open-ended and hence subject to controversy even within the development community, where focal concerns vary, paradigms and priorities compete, mandates differ, and actors with compatible, even similar, goals find it necessary to vie with one another for scarce resources.

Moreover, hunger is a state of being produced by other conditions while being embedded in them; and these conditions range from the specific (soils, technologies) to the intermediate (markets, income) to the broad (poverty, political economy).

Hunger is so multifaceted in its causality and context that it is not obvious how best to respond to it. The context is every country in the world, and the causality involves everything from agriculture, to international trade, to the internal and external political dynamics of countries.

It is not obvious whether to organize policy to alleviate hunger as a specific goal or to pursue more discrete goals in agriculture, health, and development at large with the expectation that success in these other areas will alleviate hunger as a happy byproduct.

If the decision is to make hunger a focal concern, a breakthrough that hunger advocates would applaud, there is still the question of how comprehensive vs. specific the policy response should be. Specific hunger policies (improving agricultural yields,. reducing post-harvest losses, feeding people in need) have the advantage of directness (do this, get that), in theory at least, and the likely disadvantage of being insufficient to materially change the hunger outcome given other constraints not adequately addressed.

Comprehensive ("multisectoral") approaches have the advantage of being comprehensive and the disadvantage of requiring political and administrative centrality. Not only must a comprehensive strategy to alleviate hunger be reconciled with other concerns (industrial development, for example) that seek similar, if not greater, centrality; like any long-term strategy, it must survive the corroding influence of short-term claims that cannot be ignored (higher wages for the civil service or new military hardware, for example).

Getting a comprehensive plan approved is difficult if the plan is to be authoritative; keeping it intact and on track over time even more so. Moreover, a comprehensive strategy has to be disaggregated into operational components; and these can easily lose linkage, conceptually and in practice, with one another and with hunger itself as other purposes (export promotion, cheap food for urban centers, political patronage) crystallize. When political leaders and ministries end up disagreeing about specific policies and the priorities among them, the fragile consensus informing a comprehensive strategy easily fragments into autonomous components that become ill-connected and even competitive.

This, in effect, is the problem of reconciling big issues of enormous complexity with segmented structures and mandates; and it mirrors over and over again the rational-comprehensive vs. incremental-adaptive approach to decision making assessed in the literature on public administration wherein the intellectual appeal of being comprehensive is thwarted by its operational cumbersomeness.

Appeal of Policy Disaggregation

Disaggregating big issues into operational components is a necessity that reflects how we now think and function. The British tradition of the classically educated Burkean gentleman intellectual— capable of making policy judgments on a wide range of subject matter, has yielded — in the United States, in particular— to modes of training and forms of expertise that are highly specialized. With the explosion of knowledge unleashed by modern scientific inquiry, in tandem with the social spread of educational opportunity, has come the compartmentalization of knowledge. The essence of most scholarship is to learn more and more about less and less. Scholarship has become an industry, with knowledge "exploding" because of the numbers engaged in research. However, as knowledge has expanded, expertise has narrowed. So, too, in the realm of policy and action. As issues— perceived problems, needs, opportunities— have expanded, organizations to deal with them, public and private, have become more numerous, larger and more complex. Similarly, the proliferation of organization has created capabilities previously unknown.

Yet as capabilities have increased, competencies have narrowed. The expansion of organization and of tasks to be performed has necessitated structural differentiation and functional specification. Bureaucracies grow as their responsibilities increase, but this growth is accompanied by segmentation of responsibility. Just as the expansion of knowledge results in its compartmentalization, so the applications of knowledge result in organizational differentiation. Appeals for coordination, even integration, of administrative action speak to the extent to which these values have been compromised in practice. Often they are also asking more than highly differentiated structures with tightly defined mandates are able to provide. Interministerial and inter-agency coordination, repeatedly invoked as administrative virtues, usually become an operational curse for this very reason, as the values of autonomy and control override those of subordination, shared responsibility, and mutual dependency.

Seen in this light, a big issue like hunger collides with our intellectual and organizational disposition to small solutions that are easier to allocate, organize, and manage. Technical assistance, with its emphasis on specific types of expertise, reinforces this tendency to disaggregate.

An important aspect of the hunger dilemma is that there are a number of challenging conditions that must be addressed together if progress is to be made in reducing hunger. This photo provides an illustration of this dilemma. Arid conditions are clearly shown. The central role of women in providing for their families is also indicated. There are no men at the well! Frequently women must spend a large part of their day in bringing water to their household. They also play a major role in farming and in taking care of their children. Efforts to improve their situation must address the reality that they are already overworked, and find it very difficult to respond to well-meaning efforts to improve their situation, but which require additional time.

Striving for Linkage

Notwithstanding the logic of parceling out specific components of the hunger agenda to largely autonomous units of decision and action, doing so has been at a cost to policy coherence, effectiveness, and reinforcement.

Consequently, there is a counter-tendency toward integration of effort, and this entails incorporating hunger/nutrition agendas into more comprehensive units, as at USAID and the Bank. The result is a trade-off. Organizational reform tries to balance the benefits of issue specificity, visibility, autonomy, and clout with the benefits of incorporation, integration, reinforcement, and possible protection from adversaries. Hunger lends itself to the latter approach because it is a derivative issue that reflects other things. One can isolate hunger, or "nutrition," and give it organizational expression of its own; but in large administrative systems this invites conflict over agendas and control, and it also disposes to isolation and impotence.

To illustrate, USAID's Office of Nutrition, for many years an innovator and catalyst for raising visibility and concern for protein-energy malnutrition, nevertheless confined itself (or was confined) to programs directly targeted to the already malnourished or those nutritionally at risk.

The Office of Nutrition was empowered to develop nutrition interventions but not to address the underlying causes of malnutrition. It dealt with manifestations and sought to treat them in laser beam fashion— food supplements, education, social marketing, etc.; it did not deal with poverty and the multiple objective conditions disposing to malnutrition. Hence, it addressed symptoms, not contexts; and it sought to help the malnourished and those at risk, not to change the conditions outside their control that constrained them. All of that, ostensibly, was someone else's responsibility. By dealing with manifestations and offering only palliation, the Office of Nutrition was not really a development agency at all.

One wonders whether incorporating the Office of Nutrition into the Office of Population, Health and Nutrition was intended to bring "nutrition" more into the development mainstream and to encourage a broader and deeper approach to alleviating malnutrition.

If so, the record to date is not very encouraging . Of the 66 separate projects currently being funded by the Office of Population, Health, and Nutrition, only one, the FANTA project, can be said to address malnutrition as a significant, but by no means exclusive, part of its mandate.

Similarly, food aid's relationship to hunger alleviation— now called "household food security"— continues to be more rhetorical than real. This is true in part because other goals have taken precedence (such as "human capacity development," i.e. education) and in part because documenting nutritional improvement in food aid supported projects has proven to be so difficult (thereby producing other justifications such as providing incentives to attend health clinics and schools).

Clearly, linking hunger to other agendas runs the risk of its being lost as a focal concern and otherwise marginalized in the inevitable array of other objectives. In sum, it is difficult for agencies to capture and organize something so multifaceted as hunger. Expertise is more narrowly defined, methodologies and technologies are usually more issue and context specific, and institutional jurisdictions are more focused and compartmentalized.

Put another way, hunger overwhelms organized efforts to respond to it. In turn, hunger policy tends to be buffeted by alternative dispositions— disaggregation and integration, autonomy and incorporation— and to suffer the indignities of bouncing around administrative systems when it is not lost in some corner. Managing the hunger agenda is a taxing and often frustrating enterprise as a result. Although no one is to blame for this state of affairs, there is no easy way out of the dilemma of organizing hunger.

Hunger is being alleviated in spite of these (and other) impediments. The record is spotty, however; and the hunger community has, on balance, been of only marginal significance to the gains made. Four overlapping conditions appear to be the decisive factors.

First, when a Basic Human Needs strategy of development has been pursued and successfully implemented over a decade or more, be it "growth-mediated" (Korea, Taiwan), "support-led" (Sri Lanka, Kerala), or a blend (China, Chile, Thailand).

Options to Responding to Hunger

Hunger is the kind of issue, rhetorically appealing yet organizationally and programmatically elusive, that invites policy confusion, inconsistency, tokenism and displacement. Consider the following five options as they pertain to government policy and the agendas of international agencies:

— Ignore hunger as a focal concern, perhaps trusting that policies pursued for other reasons will impact favorably on it.

— Respond to hunger with a few discrete interventions,

such as child feeding, that are basically stand-alone initiatives.

— Make hunger one of several organizing principles around which a broader policy is defined and organized.

— Make the alleviation of hunger the overriding principle and core objective of development policy, subordinating other policies (e.g., export promotion) to it.

— Incorporate hunger into a still broader agenda such as Basic Human Needs/Human Development informing an overall development strategy.

These options would appear to be levels on a continuum signifying seriousness of purpose; yet as levels they do not necessarily imply effectiveness of results. Levels 3 and 4 do not exist in fact, even though rhetoric might suggest otherwise. Explicit hunger policy tends to bifurcate between levels 2 (where it is often defined as "nutrition" policy) and 5 (where, ironically, it may not be defined at all). Between the two, most programmatic effort against hunger may be found at level 2, whereas the greatest success in reducing hunger and even eliminating it is the distinctive achievement of level 5. (That, at any rate, is the impression conveyed by the development experience of Thailand, Costa Rica, Kerala, Sri Lanka, and perhaps China and Cuba as well as of Korea, Taiwan, and Chile). Sadly, most development in the modern era is concentrated in level 1, as was the development experience of most Western countries, where hunger carried a badge of social stigma and responsibility for dealing with it was left to private charity.

Second, when a protracted rural based revolution results in a major reallocation of resources toward the poor majority (China, Cuba for a time, Iran, perhaps Zimbabwe).

Third, when a competitive political process emerges, giving populist influence to smallholder agriculture and other rural and lower status groups (Chile, Costa Rica, Sri Lanka, the Indian state of Kerala).

Fourth, when political elites forge a social contract with their populations exchanging supports— health, education, employment, subsidized food, etc.— for loyalty.

What stands out here is the primacy of political conditions, the secondary role of economic variables, and the tertiary role— at best— of the applied technical expertise of hunger specialists. Like nutrition planners of the 1970s, those concerned with hunger today often labor where conditions are least favorable for success. It remains to be seen whether, in time, hunger specialists are able to break through the many constraints facing them. The odds are likely to be shaped powerfully by the political environment.

3

Poverty, Migration and Homelessness

According to recent reports of World Heath Organisation anti-poverty rhetoric is widespread, and some indicators of human well-being have improved. However, current conditions are often appalling, trends in many places negative, and future prospects for hundreds of millions of people very bad. In assessing conditions, and seeing what to do, professionals' realities are universal, reductionist, standardized and stable. Those of economists dominate, expressed in poverty thinking concerned with income-poverty, and employment thinking concerned with jobs. Both project Northern, more industrial and urban conditions, concerns and categories onto Southern, more agricultural and rural, realities. Both have force but miss much and mislead. Professional biases have been challenged but they remain deep, secure and distorting.

The realities of poor people are local, complex, diverse and dynamic. Income-poverty, though important, is only one aspect of deprivation. Participatory appraisal confirms many dimensions and criteria of disadvantage, ill-being and well-being as people experience them. In addition to poverty, these include social inferiority, isolation, physical weakness, vulnerability, seasonal deprivation, powerlessness and humiliation.

Sustainable livelihoods are an objective on which most poor people and professionals can agree. Household livelihood strategies often involve different members in diverse activities and sources of support, at different times of the year. Many of these, such as home-gardening, exploiting common property resources, share-rearing livestock, family splitting, and stinting are largely unseen by normal professionals. A sustainable livelihood intensive strategy stresses natural resources management, redistribution of livelihood resources, prices and payments, health, abolishing restrictions and hassle, and safety nets for poor people during bad times.

A paradigm of reversals and altruism demands a new professionalism. The paradigm and the new professionalism put people before things, and poor people and their priorities first of all. The challenges presented are institutional, professional and personal. The policy and practical means to promote and sustain well-being, livelihoods and equity include two complementary agendas, one conventional and one new. Underlying the new agenda is the basic human right of poor people to conduct their own analysis. Four elements in this new agenda are:

— Analysis and action by local people, especially the poor
— Sustainable livelihoods
— Decentralization, democracy and diversity
— Professional and personal change

Reversals and a radical rethink are required if the realities of the poor are to count.

According to the figures presented in Table 1, aggregate percentage improvements have been shown in some of the usual indicators of human well-being over recent decades.

Smallpox has been eradicated from the earth, and polio and guinea worm disease greatly reduced. In little more than a generation, the proportion of rural families with access to safe water is reported to have risen from less than 10 per cent to more than 60 per cent, and the proportion of children in primary school from less than one-half to more than three-quarters. Facts and figures like these can lull one into an impression of laudable achievement.

Table 1: Indicators of Human Well-being in Developing Countries

	All developing countries		*Least developed countries*	
	1960	1992	1960	1992
Life expectancy	46	63	39	50
Infant mortality per 1,000 live births	149	69	170	112
Adult literacy rate	46	69	29	46
Real GDP per capita (US$)	950	2,730	580	880

The downside of the record is, though, stark. Things are less bad than they would have been had nothing been done, and without the efforts of many organizations and individuals. But the glass that looks half full is also half empty; and as population grows the glass gets bigger. Averages conceal adverse income distribution and the condition of underclasses. Some economies are on a downward slide, especially where there is civil war. Malaria and tuberculosis spread again. HIV menaces whole peoples and economies with its insidious spread. Life expectancy in some countries has fallen, with civil disorder, famine and breakdown in government services. Nearly one billion people remain illiterate, and the primary school drop-out rate is 30 per cent. Some 40 million people are refugees or displaced within their countries.

Globally, the number of people conventionally defined as in "absolute poverty" is often quoted as being over one billion, that is between one person in five and one in four, up from an estimated 800 million ten years ago. Scholastic argument about figures will never end.

The danger is that debate distracts from seeing what to do. Aggregation and generalization are tempting and difficult but changes have occurred, as shown in Table 3.

Table 2: Estimate of Population Living in Absolute Poverty

	Number of people (millions)	*Percentage of total population*
Asia	675	25
Sub-Saharan Africa	325	62
Middle East and North Africa	75	28
Latin America	150	35
Total	1,225	23

These trends seem evident: that poverty, suffering and other deprivations are increasingly perceived as diverse; that conditions are moving in different directions in different countries, and for different groups of people; and that for hundreds of millions of people these have a downward momentum and are becoming worse. Poverty, suffering and deprivation seem to be becoming more regional, concentrated more in those countries which are least able to improve conditions, as in many in sub-Saharan Africa; or in regions within countries, as with the three Indian states of Uttar Pradesh, Bihar and Madhya Pradesh with their combined population (1994) of over 300 million.

As the scourge of HIV spreads, the hitherto localized impacts of AIDS deaths will soon be regional: 8 million AIDS related deaths are projected by the year

Table 3

Comparing 1990 with 1970, the poor are still concentrated in rural areas in Asia, but are:

More likely to be	*Less likely to be*
African	Asian and Latin American
Children, urban women and elderly	Other adults
Landless	Small farmers
Living in resource-poor areas	Living in well-endowed areas
Urban	Rural
Refugees or displaced	Settled

2000, the target year of "Health for All". In the longer term, the time bomb of HIV mocks development and makes a fantasy of much current debate about development. With AIDS, as in other ways, the South is more exposed and vulnerable, will suffer more, and will be far more devastated than the North.

Ill-being and early death take many forms; and those which are in the news - genocide and civil wars in Rwanda, Angola, the former Yugoslavia and elsewhere, and the denials of human rights as in Myanmar, Tibet, East Timor and many other places, all demand attention. But much more widely, less conspicuous ill-being and early death prevail. Much of it is hidden or taboo, as with the selective elimination, persecution and plight of females foetuses, girls and women. The enormity of the abuse, sexual and other, of girl children, is still concealed everywhere by the sacred secrecy of the family. Worldwide, and with a concentration in South Asia, there are 110 million missing females, who would have been alive at the sex ratios of the industrial countries. These missing women almost total the population of Pakistan, or four Canadas, or any two together of France, Iran,

Italy, Turkey or the UK, or the combined population of Sudan, Kenya, Uganda, Tanzania, Malawi and Zambia. The scale of the discrimination, deprivation and suffering which underlie these figures beggars the imagination.

The scale and awfulness are the worse because, as never before, the powerful can see so much of what is happening and have power to act. The nightmare foreseen by C.P. Snow in 1959 has come about. Communications have brought us all dramatically closer and have made it easier and quicker to do things. Now we, the rich, sit in our warm rooms and comfy seats and watch the poor die on television, turning them on and off at will.

Frequent viewing inoculates against compassion. There is more insight than ever before, accessible to those who want it, about how to enable poor people to do better, yet many of the same mistakes and misdemeanours persist at every level of interaction. There is more wealth in the world than ever before, and the peace dividend presents a windfall to give. Yet aid declines, and hundreds of millions of the poorest are on a downward slide, to become poorer and more vulnerable.

Poverty and deprivation are functions of polarization, of power and powerlessness. Any practical analysis has to examine the whole system: - "us", the powerful as well as "them" the powerless. Since we have more power to act, it is hard to evade the imperative to turn the spotlight round and look at ourselves. In doing this, rhetoric and concepts can provide a starting point. Our views of the realities of the poor, and of what should be done, are constructed mainly from a distance, and can be seen to be constructed mainly for our convenience. We embody those views in the words and concepts which we use. Two which receive much prominence, and which are much stressed in the agenda for the Social Development Summit are poverty and employment.

Income-Poverty

"Poverty" is used in two main senses: in its first, common usage in development, it is a broad, blanket word used to refer to the whole spectrum of deprivation and ill-being; in its second usage, poverty has a narrow technical definition for purposes of measurement and comparison.In the words of one authority, "...'poverty' has to be given scientifically acceptable universal meaning and measurement."Poverty is then defined as low income, as it is reported, recorded and analyzed, or often as low consumption, which is easier to measure. This is the nor- mal meaning of poverty among economists, and is used for measuring poverty lines, for comparing groups and regions, and often for assessing progress or backsliding within poverty in development.

In much professional discourse the narrow technical definition colonizes the common usage. Income-poverty starts as a proxy or correlate for other deprivations but then subsumes them. The classic pattern in erudite analysis is to start with a recognition that poverty is much more than income or consumption but then to allow what has been measured to take over and dominate. Thus, Montek Ahluwalia acknowledges that "...longevity, access to health and education facilities, and perhaps also security of consumption levels from extreme shocks" are equally relevant in analysis of poverty but points out that he is constrained because:

> "..time series data on all of these dimensions are not available. Data from a series of consumption surveys conducted by the National Sample Survey Organization (NSS) are available, and these data have been used in most of the studies of rural poverty in India".

and which he then goes on to use.

Similarly, Lipton and Ravallionacknowledge the potential breadth of a definition of economic welfare, but then continue: "While recognizing the limitations of the concept of 'economic welfare' as 'command over commodities', we will largely confine ourselves to that definition, in order to review the many important issues treated in the literature that has evolved around it."

The analysis is then narrowed because past discussion has been narrow. What is recorded as having been measured, usually low consumption as a proxy for low income, then easily comes to masquerade in speech and prose as the much larger reality, a trap into which almost all fall, including the writer, from time to time. It is then but a short step to treating what has not been measured as not really real.

Patterns of dominance are then reinforced: of the material over the experiential; of the physical over the social; of the measured and measurable over the unmeasured and unmeasurable; of economic over social values; of economists over disciplines concerned with people as people. It then becomes the reductionism of normal economics, not the experience of the poor, that defines poverty. The pre-eminence of income-poverty seems wrong but it is understandable. Standing back, four reasons can be seen for its widespread acceptance and use as a measure and concept.

First, economists and their concepts still dominate the development discourse. There can be few multilateral or bilateral aid agencies, and few ministries of planning, where economists are not the most numerous profession. Economists' concepts, measures and methods are accepted as the norm in much development practice and policy-making. This is not to undervalue the utility of economic concepts and methods. But it is to note that one way of seeing things prevails, and what is poverty to economists tends to become the normal meaning and measure for other disciplines and professions.

Second, income-poverty is a concept and measure generated and sustained in the cores of power, reflecting and reinforced by conditions in the rich industrial North. Poor people in the North have been mainly urban, in an industrial milieu, and have tended to rely on cash income, whether wages or social security payments; much of their economic status can then be captured in cash income or largely cash based consumption. Projecting and applying this Northern concept of poverty to the South assumes that similar conditions prevail.

Third, poverty defined as income-poverty or consumption-poverty is measurable. Non-monetary flows for subsistence or consumption can, in principle, be given monetary values and conflated into a single scale. This allows comparisons worldwide between the income, or more usually consumption, levels of different households, regions and nations. It also makes possible the measurement and assessment of poverty lines. These provide time series measurements to show how income-poverty or consumption-poverty are changing, and so, how well a government can be presumed to be doing in the reduction of poverty in these senses. The utility of these measures for centrally placed professionals gives them a primacy and pride of place which tends to go unquestioned. What is measurable and measured then becomes what is real, and what matters, standardizing the diverse, and excluding the divergent and different.

Fourth, it is held that the worse-off people are, the more they are preoccupied with income and consumption, with the need to gain subsistence food and basic goods in order to survive. In a recent article, Martin Greeley argued for an income based concept of welfare, and that "...only when absolute poverty [meaning absolute income-poverty] is no longer the core issue should our measure of development encompass a broader agenda of human need."The worse the condition in which people find themselves, then the more justified is the economic reductionism of income-poverty; income-poverty reductionism becomes propoor. Given these four factors and beliefs, it is not surprising to find that income-poverty has some primacy as a measure in the World Bank. A widely quoted statement by Lewis Preston, former President of the World Bank illustrates this:

> "Sustainable poverty reduction is the overarching objective of the World Bank. It is the benchmark by which our performance as a development institution will be measured."

The overarching objective is defined as something which will be measured - sustainable poverty reduction. The World Development Report 1990's approach to sustainable poverty reduction is, it says, twopronged, consisting of "...broadly based economic growth to generate efficient income-earning opportunities for the poor and improved access to education, health care and other social services so the poor can take advantage of these opportunities".In this thinking, income is the end; improved access to education, health care and other social services are justified as means to that economic end. They are not presented here as justified ends in themselves or as a means to enhance capabilities or reduce suffering, or to increase self-respect, fulfilment or other human values.

Social development is a means not an end; the end is economic development. That the World Bank makes sustainable poverty reduction its overarching objective is a matter for celebration. Nor should the narrowness and circularity of the thinking be cause for surprise in an organization which is called a bank, with many economists, and conditioned by the normal economic thinking. But Preston's quite simple statement contrasts with the more complex mission statement of the

Overseas Development Administration, the British Government's aid agency, where social development advisers are relatively more numerous and influential:

> "The aim of our overseas aid effort is to promote sustainable economic and social development and good government, in order to improve the quality of life and reduce poverty, suffering and deprivation in developing countries."

Going beyond economic development, to include social development and good government, and beyond reducing poverty, to improve the quality of life and reduce suffering and deprivation, embodies a much broader set of values. Few would want to deny that measures of income-poverty have uses. They point to one dimension of inequality and inequity, between nations and within nations. But income-poverty is only one dimension among many, and it is suspect because it serves the needs of professionals in the cores of power rather than emerging from the realities of the poor at the peripheries.

Issues of Unemployment

As with poverty, so with employment, the normal professional categories have been applied worldwide. Employment, unemployment, job, workplace and workforce are concepts and categories derived from urban industrial experience in the North. As with poverty, attempts have been made to impose and apply them in the South, including the rural and agricultural South. In his magisterial work on Asian poverty, a quarter of a century ago, Gunnar Myrdal agonized over the misleading preconception of Western economics as applied to Asian conditions:

> "When new data are assembled, the conceptual categories used are inappropriate to the conditions existing: as, for example, when the

underutilization of the labour force in the South Asian countries is analyzed according to Western concepts of unemployment, disguised unemployment and underemployment. The resulting mountains of figures have either no meaning or a meaning other than that imputed to them...The very fact that the researcher gets figures to play with tends to confirm his original, biased approach...the continuing collection of data under biased notions only postpones the day when reality can effectively challenge inherited preconceptions."

And he called for behavioural studies founded on observations of the raw reality.Since Myrdal wrote the above, the informal sector has been discovered and explored, and livelihood has been proposed as a better word than employment to capture the complex and diverse reality of most of the poor. Indeed, livelihood is a larger, more universal and more useful concept for seeing what best to do, encompassing as it does for many of the poor so much more than the employment of a job, which for many is not and can not be a reality. Employment can rather be seen as a subset or component of livelihood.

Reductionist employment-thinking in terms of jobs is, though, not only alive and well but flourishing. The obsession in countries of the North and of elites in the South with employment and unemployment, which affects them and their families, has dominated much of the discussion and writing leading up to the Social Development Summit.

In the background note for the Stockholm Roundtable of June 1994, the third section was entitled "Expansion of Productive Employment and Sustainable Livelihoods". But in the whole section, the word livelihood appeared only twice, in contrast with employment 28 times, unemployment 11, underemployment five, jobs six and workforce four times, all words and concepts derived from, and linked with, formal employment.

Even more marked were the employment, industrial and urban biases of the major document debated at the Second Preparatory Committee for the Social Development Summit in New York in August 1994. In the 6,500 words of the third section, on "Productive Employment and the Reduction of Unemployment", livelihood appears only once but "jobs" features 13 times on one page alone; and the urban industrial bias is reflected in rural and agricultural concerns receiving only four paragraphs out of 48.

Employment-thinking is deep rooted, and livelihood-thinking remains a marginalized orphan. The Society for International Development convened regional conferences on sustainable livelihoods as part of the run-up to the Social Development Summit but it is doubtful whether these will even ripple the mainstream. Whatever happens to the poor, full employment seems assured for normal economists and statisticians as they continue to analyze the available data on employment and unemployment, and to project their categories and concerns onto the raw and rather different reality of most of the poor in the South. Myrdal would be sad to learn how little has changed.

Efforts have been made to offset the biases towards the income measure of poverty and deprivation, and towards an employment measure of livelihood. Those offsetting income-poverty are well known. The World Bank's World Development Reports, since their inception, have ranked countries according to per capita GDP. However, the weak relationship between per capita GDP and human well-being is commonplace. Income distribution is critical. Much of the good life is uncounted in GDP (friendship, love, story-telling, self-sacrifice, laughter, music, health, creativity) and much of the bad life adds to it (insurance claims, security guards, fossil fuel consumption, cutting down forests).

Very different perspectives have been given by UNICEF's annual State of the World's Children which ranks countries according to their under-five mortality rates; by the Physical Quality of Life Index (PQLI) which combines in a single scale life expectancy at one year, adult literacy and infant mortality; the Human Development Index (HDI) of UNDP's annual Human Development Report which combines per capita GDP, life expectancy at birth, and literacy; and by the World Bank itself, with its Social Indicators of Development (1993) which lists poverty indicators such as public expenditure on social services, immunization, and fertility rates. All these show up weaknesses in the correlations between income- poverty and some other deprivations.

Strikingly, the latest Human Development Report shows Sri Lanka, Nicaragua, Pakistan and Guinea all with per capita incomes in the US$400- 500 range but with life expectancies of, respectively, 71, 65, 58 and 44, and infant mortality rates of, respectively, 24, 53, 99 and 135.Whatever the criticisms of these measures and scales, they have been useful for comparisons and for forcing reflection on priorities. Efforts to offset the bias towards employment measures are less developed. Livelihoods are harder to measure than mortality rates, life expectancy or literacy. So they are treated as less real. Labour intensive growth as an objective is designed to increase employment and may indeed do so. But it is not the same as sustainable livelihood intensity where livelihoods depend on a multiplicity of activities and resources.

Realities of the Poor

A person who is not poor who pronounces on what matters to those who are poor is in a trap. Self-critical analysis, sensitive rapport, and participatory methods can contribute some valid insight into the values, priorities and preferences of poor people. We can struggle to reconstruct our realities to reflect what poor people indicate to be theirs. But there will always be distortions. We can never fully escape from our conditioning. And the nature of interactions between the poor and the nonpoor affect what is shared and learnt. The new methods enable poor people to analyze and express what they know, experience, need and want. They bring to light many dimensions of deprivation, ill-being and wellbeing, and the values and priorities of poor people. Three sets of findings provide illustrative insights:

1. *Jodha's Paradox*: Income-poorer but better off: Jodha asked farmers and villagers in two villages in Rajasthan for their own categories and criteria of changing economic status. They named 38 criteria. Comparing data from his fieldwork in 1964-66 with 1982-84 he found that the 36 households which were more than 5 per cent *worse off* in per capita real incomes were on average *better off* according to 37 out of their own 38 criteria. The improvements included quality of housing, wearing shoes regularly, less dependence in the lean season, and not having to migrate for work. Several of the criteria reflected more independence. The reality which these income-poorer villagers presented to Jodha contrasts with a normal economist's reality. They were income-poorer and so, in an economist's terms, worse off; but in their own terms they were, on average, much better off.

2. *Findings from Participatory Analysis*: Analysis by local people using participatory rural appraisal (PRA) methods has shown similar outcomes. In a PRA process in a Pakistan village in April 1994:

   "...the local people did a matrix on their existing sources of income to determine the preferred income source. Interestingly, for me, the criterion 'more income' was the ninth or tenth one listed (out of a total of about 20 criteria). 'More time at home', 'ability to get involved in neighbours' joys and sorrows' were listed earlier...the generally perceived-to-bepreferred source of income (high-paying skilled/manual labour in the Middle Eastern countries, particularly Dubai) did not emerge as victor..., the reason worked out by the local analysts being that it did badly on their social criteria."

   Diverse criteria have also emerged from well-being ranking, one of the methods of PRA. In an economic tradition, "wealth" was originally the criterion by which local people were asked to card sort the households in their community.Repeatedly, when outsider facilitators have tried to focus discussion and ranking on wealth, local people have insisted on using a wider range of criteria as contributing to their concepts of well-being and ill-being, of the good and bad life.Health and physical disability feature strongly.

3. *Participatory Poverty Assessments*: The World Bank has been breaking new ground in its poverty assessments. In the words of Sven Sandstrom these are designed:

   "to help us to address three fundamental issues: Who is poor? Why are they poor? What needs to be done to reduce the number of the poor?"

The Participatory Poverty Assessments (PPAs) conducted under the auspices of the World Bank in Ghana, Zambia, Kenya and some other countries now have the potential for going beyond these questions, to ask: Who defines poverty? Who are the poor as defined within a society by local people themselves? What criteria of poverty or deprivation do they have? What are their priorities? The PPA sponsored by the World Bank in Zambia, using participatory rural appraisal techniques, gave insights into conditions, trends and poor people's priorities with practical implications.

Dimensions of Deproviation

These and other examples illustrate the multi-dimensionality of deprivation and disadvantage as poor people experience them. Deprived people are often thought of as being uniform. The "rural masses" commonly expresses a stereotype. But, if anything, there is more diversity among the poor than among the non-poor. Under extreme deprivation, as Viktor Frankl found in his study of inmates of concentration camps, people react in sharply different ways.

Disadvantage itself takes many forms. Any list of dimensions will be provisional and personal. The eight which follow are an attempt to capture some of poor people's reality, but can surely be improved upon. The first three are among the better recognized dimensions of deprivation:

1. *Poverty* refers to lack of physical necessities, assets and income. It includes but is more than being income-poor. Pov-erty can be distinguished from other dimensions of deprivation such as physical weakness, isolation, vulnerability and powerlessness.
2. *Social inferiority* can be ascribed, acquired or linked with age and lifecycle. It can be socially defined as

genetically inferior or disadvantaged, including gender, caste, race and ethnic group, or being "lower" in terms of class, social group or occupation, or linked with age, as with children and sometimes daughters-in-law.

3. *Isolation* refers to being peripheral and cut off. Poor people can be isolated geographically - living in a "remote" area; isolated in communication, lacking contacts and information, including not being able to read; isolated by a lack of access to social services and markets; and isolated by a lack of social and economic supports.

Five other dimensions, prominent in the realities of the poor and weak, have been relatively neglected by the development professions:

4. *Physical weakness*: Disability, sickness, pain and suffering are bad in themselves. Beyond this, the body is for many their major resource. Professionals, dependent as they are on their brains more than their bodies, tend to undervalue the importance to many of the poor of the asset of a fit, strong body and the liability of a body which is sick, weak or disabled. Repeatedly, in defining ill-being and well-being, poor people mention physical weakness, sickness or disability, both as bad in themselves and in their effects on others. Having a household member who is physically weak, sick or handicapped, unable to contribute to household livelihood, but needing to be fed and cared for, is a common cause of income-poverty and deprivation as graphically shown for river-blindness and now spreading widely in new forms with AIDS. The prominence of disability in the consciousness of poor people in the South is shown by the frequency with which, in participatory social mapping, village analysts spontaneously represent

the disabled as a category. Those who are sick are the concern of health services. Those who are otherwise disabled are numerous, yet neglected. There are perhaps 200 million disabled persons in the South, and probably more than another 200 million adversely affected and impoverished through having to support the disabled. Yet the 1993 UNDP Human Development Report does not include disability in any of its tables. The disabled are among the most unseen and politically powerless, and not only in the South.

5. *Vulnerability*: Much prose uses "vulnerable" and "poor" as alternating synonyms. But vulnerability is not the same as income-poverty or poverty more broadly defined. It means not lack or want but exposure and defencelessness. It has two sides: the external side of exposure to shocks, stress and risk; and the internal side of defencelessness, meaning a lack of means to cope without damaging loss. Loss can take many forms - becoming or being physically weaker, economically impoverished, socially dependent, humiliated or psychologically harmed. For hundreds of millions, vulnerability has increased and so their livelihoods have become less securely sustainable even when their incomes have risen. In most cultures and contexts, patron-client safety nets have weakened, the extended family gives less support, contingencies such as weddings, funerals, brideprice and dowry have become more costly, and effective health services have become less accessible or more expensive or both. More people have moved into insecure environments. More people live exposed to the risks of famine, flood, storm, and some human, crop and animal diseases, than before. War and civil disorder remain widespread. And where there have been past disasters, many are more

vulnerable through the earlier loss of livelihood assets and means to cope. It then takes less to make a famine, as in the current 1994 famine in Ethiopia. For poor people there are often trade-offs between income and security. Income-poverty thinking can neglect vulnerability in seeking to raise incomes. On a huge scale, the Integrated Rural Development Programme in India provides subsidized loans to poor people to acquire assets aimed at raising their incomes. But, as many have experienced, this increases vulnerability: loss of the asset can lead to debt and being worse off than before. At the margin, poor people often prefer a lower income with less risk of debt and dependence.

6. *Seasonality*: The seasonal dimensions of deprivation are under-perceived by professionals who are urban based and season proofed. Yet, in tropical seasonality, many adverse factors for the poor often coincide during the rains - hard agricultural work, shortage of food, scarcity of money, indebtedness, sickness, the late stages of pregnancy and diminished access to services; and indicators such as birthweights, body weights, infant mortality and morbidity all bear this out.
7. *Powerlessness*: The poor are powerless. Dispersed and anxious as they are about access to resources, work and income, it is difficult for them to organize or bargain. Often physically weak and economically vulnerable, they lack influence. Subject to the power of others, they are easy to ignore or exploit. Powerlessness is also, for the powerful, the least acceptable point of intervention to improve the lot of the poor.
8. *Humiliation*: Self-respect, with freedom from dependence, is perhaps the dimension most

overlooked and undervalued by professionals.

Deprivation and well-being have, then, many dimensions. Poor people have many priorities. What matters most to them often differs from what outsiders assume, is not always easy to measure, and may not be measurable at all. If poor people's realities are to come first, development professionals have to be sensitive, have to decentralize and empower, to enable poor people to conduct their own analysis and express their own multiple priorities.

Our knowledge has an advantage with the physical universe and with whatever is microscopic, macroscopic, large-scale or distant from where poor people live. In these domains we are empowered by our linked communications, instruments and science. But their knowledge has an advantage with the local, the social, whatever is continuously observed and experienced, and whatever close to them touches their lives and livelihoods; and they are the only experts on their life experiences and priorities. But our power in the past has overwhelmed their knowledge, hidden their analytical abilities and allowed us to assume that we know what they experience and want. The problem is one of balance between two realities ours which is powerful and theirs which is weak..

Economic Crisis and Cross-border Migration: Case of the Mekong region

Cross-border migration remains an ever-increasing problem in the Mekong region, despite the stunt in economic growth due to the economic and loss of hundreds of jobs in affected countries. Economic disparities within and between countries result in migration when people seek to improve their living standards. Financial difficulty is a common factor in all cases of migration. In Myanmar social and political factors are other forces which encourage people to leave the country. Similarly, in Cambodia political and socio-economic problems lead to migration. Laotians and Vietnamese emigrate largely for economic reasons and to a lesser extent, social concerns.

Of the countries in Mekong region Thailand has perhaps been the worst hit by the economic downturn. In the previous decade, it had made dramatic economic progress and thus attracted much labour from its neighbouring countries. Thailand was both a destination and transit country, and much of the migration that took place within its boundaries stemmed from economic concerns. Its immigrants hailed from every country with which it shares a border and beyond, filtering into Thai soil from Myanmar, Vietnam, Cambodia, Laos and South China.

The economic crisis has brought little change to these trends. As a destination country, Thailand continues to attract a flowing number of immigrants due to the economic opportunities it is perceived to offer. The recession has created a greater demand for unskilled and cheap labourers, even though there is a shortage of work for the Thai people themselves.

Illegal foreign workers, especially under-aged workers, provide a ready supply to this demand – such workers are often very cheap, hardworking and can be controlled by the employers easily due to their illegal migrant status. There are a large number of migrant children working as labourers in construction, factories and the fishing industries.

Some are brought into Thailand to beg and work in the commercial sex trade. 95% of 530 foreign child beggars who were arrested between 1 October 1996 and 31 July 1997 were Cambodians, and 5% were from Myanmar. Gangsters are known to run organised begging and target children under 13 or who are handicapped for this purpose. Extreme abuse is inflicted on these children. There also appears to be a larger number of male child immigrants compared to young girls.

In 1996, the estimate for the total number of foreign illegal child workers was 20% of all illegal workers entering the country, with a male to female ration of 71:29. A recent policy on illegal migration forces migrant workers further underground and renders them more vulnerable to abuse and violations from employers, traffickers and the authorities.

Laos is predominantly a sending country in the migration of child workers. Within Laos, Savannaket province has an especially large number of working children. A preliminary survey reflected that the most vulnerable children are those who cross into Thailand to work illegally. In 1997, it was found that at least 2,400 children went to work in Thailand. Most children who return to Laos afterwards do not return to education, and among them many have evidently been physically abused.

Parents are generally unaware of the situation that their children face on leaving home to go across the border to make a living. They are also ignorant of the possibility of gaining assistance in the event of physical abuse of their children. Evidence of abuse does not prevent continuous migration, however.

Poverty is the most commonly cited reason for going away to work, but by no means is it the main reason. Children say they have nothing to do in Laos since children below the age of 15 are not allowed to work. They are also curious about what life is like in Bangkok. Thai TV, which is televised in Laos, provides a glorified image of Thailand as a whole. This encourages children to cross the river in search of work, with the intention of being seasonal workers.

The shared border between the two countries and also the open nature of the border control enables them to enter Thailand easily. Children are not aware of the risks inherent in illegal migration and are consequently not prepared for the severely abusive treatment many of them suffer in their workplace. The risk of being caught by the authorities deters them from trying to escape the clutches of their employers.

The situation in Cambodia is similar to Laos, although Cambodia is also a destination and transit country in the migration of child workers. The ever-increasing influx of under-aged Vietnamese workers into Cambodia is a particular problem. The issue of identification of Vietnamese children is a significant obstacle in the process of repatriation.

Some Vietnamese families have been living in Cambodia since the '80s, with children entering the workforce at very young ages. Some of the children were born in Cambodian, leading to the contention by Vietnamese authorities that they are more Cambodian than Vietnamese. Since Cambodian officials are easily bribed, it is also relatively easy to gain Cambodian ID cards. Furthermore, there are instances when Vietnamese families living in Cambodia do not want to return to Vietnam.

Simultaneously, thousands of Cambodian children enter Thailand in search of jobs each year. Each month there are about 400 children being deported to their homeland. Their reasons for migration mirror that of child migrants from Vietnam, Myanmar and Laos. Political crises and family disintegration are among other factors that spur a high level of migration of under-aged workers from Cambodia.

Many children speak of middlemen who lure them into crossing the border, with promises of the guarantee of jobs with good wages. Swayed by such stories, these children and at times whole families uproot themselves to seek a new life in the destination country. Some sell their homes and land to pay their way across the border, including the payment of bribes to authorities on both sides of the border. Migrants do not have access to accurate information regarding working life in Thailand, and their eagerness to improve their living standards lead them to make hasty and ill-informed decisions.

There are migrants who are abducted, drugged and sold into prostitution or other exploitative work. Border control between Cambodia and Thailand is very lax and the authorities pay minimal attention to what goes on. Corrupt law enforcement officials aggravate the problem of migration and equally have a part in the exploitation of migrants. Many migrant children encounter a life beyond their imagination in the foreign land. Children tricked into following middlemen may become victims to gangster networks, which administer organised crime in the form of mass begging by young or handicapped children.

Young girls have been made to work as porters, having been drugged so that they are able to manage such heavyweight work. It is common for their wages to be intercepted by middlemen, who assume the payments as a fee for providing employers with cheap labour. In any event, any payment received by children for their services would be low in relation to the inflated prices brought about by the recession. To make up for the cut in the workforce in many industries, employers often expect workers to work overtime for no extra pay or an extremely low wage. Their illegal status and lack of familiarity with the surroundings render working children with no alternative but to succumb to such exploitation.

Cambodian girls have also begun to migrate to Malaysia, legally and illegally. An agreement between the Cambodian and Malaysian governments for 150 young women to work as domestic workers was concluded. Yet, despite their legal entry into Malaysia it has been reported that many of these girls face physical abuse within the household where they work. This creates a difficult situation because concerned organisations in Cambodia and Malaysia are unable to do follow-ups on their situation easily because they work in private homes.

As the recession continues, the number of Cambodian women going into countries such as Malaysia and Singapore as domestic workers is likely to increase. Previously, Filipino domestic workers had been in great demand in these countries, as they are often able to speak English and share cultural similarities to the Malays and Chinese. Prospective employers had to undergo a standard procedure in order to obtain domestic help from the Philippines, a process which cost a lot of money and was time consuming. Given the current economic problems, domestic workers from the Mekong region may prove a much cheaper option.

Children who enter the workforce at such a young age in a foreign country tend to take up potentially hazardous jobs. They suffer psychological, emotional and social consequences, face racial discrimination and are exposed to abuse and life threatening situations. Furthermore, they have no freedom and rights in their alien environment. This poses problems for NGO officials endeavouring to assist children who are victims of abuse in their workplace.

There are a range of inadequacies in existing measures to assist migrant working children who are ill-treated in the workplace. There are no set transferring procedures, nor proper transit houses to shelter children prior to deportation from the destination country. Furthermore, there remains inadequate prevention and follow-up programmes.

There has been a level of cooperation between Thailand and Laos as well as Thailand and South China, in relation to the repatriation process of women and children between these countries. Similarly, there has been some integration between Cambodian and Vietnamese organisations. These occasions, however, do not reflect a general pattern of set practice between the concerned parties. Bilaterally, there is still a lack of formal agreements between countries in the Mekong region. Formal agreements designating a central authority in the country of origin and a central authority in the receiving country is needed. Concerned NGOs in the region nonetheless continue in their effort to help migrant children and assist those who are found in abusive work conditions. This includes a move towards fostering a higher level of cooperation between organisations in these neighbouring countries.

Increased Child Begging Rate

Until recently, the incidence of child beggars was overshadowed by the more visible and voluminous trade in women and children being trafficked for prostitution. But experts see begging as the newest trend in child trafficking throughout the Mekong region.

Until recently, the number of child beggars was dwarfed by trade in some 80,000 women and children being trafficked since 1980 for prostitution. But experts are seeing a rising number of trafficked children used for begging throughout the Mekong region. Since 1997 the number of children caught begging illegally in Bangkok - 95% of them Cambodian - has more than doubled to 1,060.

That they are Cambodian should come as no surprise. Neither should the fact that they ended up in Thailand, still the region's economic hub despite Asia's ongoing economic crisis. Cambodia is limping into recovery from a long period of civil war and many

Cambodians face malnutrition, poor health, and excessive poverty, with little hope for the future. Life expectancy is 53 years, literacy is 35%, and nine-tenths of the population lives int he countryside, still littered with land mines. Cambodia ranks 153rd out of 175 countries on the Human Development Index of the United Nations Development Programme (UNDP), which rates living standards.

Previously a few individuals would come but now it is becoming a business, said Claudia Coenjaerts, Subregional Programme Coordinator for the International Labour Organisation (ILO)' International Programme on the Elimination of Child Labour (IPEC) in the ILO Regional Office for Asia. It is an earning opportunity for more and more criminals, and law enforcers really don't care. It' an easy way to make money, so people at the border wait for the children, to take them away. It is one of the most horrendous forms of forced labour. However abhorrent any trafficking in children, the trade in beggars may be even more sinister than initially thought.

Dr Dominica Garcia of the Jesuit Refugee Service works with children at Bangkok' immigration centre. Recently she treated two little boys aged four and eight who had unnatural deformities. "I hoped I was mistaken", she said, "but these children looked as though they had been mutilated on purpose. Their feet were swollen, some of their fingers appeared as though they might have been hacked off, and there was a clear dent on their skin which could have been the mark of a tightly tied piece of string".

As border officials patrol the rows of silent children, Veng, a strong-looking youth of 15, looks around warily. He is an old Thailand hand, 10 years old the first time he left Cambodia. "I was swimming in the river and a Vietnamese man came into the water and pulled me out," Veng said. "He put something on my face and made me sick, and put me into a taxi and brought me to Bangkok. He taught me how to beg, where to put my cup, how to ask for money. I was afraid but he beat me if I didn't make money. He took it all and kept it and gave me some food but never enough. I was always hungry".

These days Veng crosses the border willingly. Free from his agent, he prefers begging in Bangkok to starving in Phnom Penh. Veng is a trafficked child. According to a just-released ILO report, a trafficked child is one who is recruited and transported from one place to another across a national border, legally or illegally, with or without the child' consent, usually but not always organised by an intermediary: parents, family member, teacher, procurer, or local authority. At the destination, the child is coerced or semi-forced to engage in activities under exploitative and abusive conditions.

Held captive, the children might receive as little as US$0.25 a day in pocket money. But they may hand their agent US$20 or more every day. Some, like Veng, become experienced and escape, striking out on their own. They learn how to avoid the police and may even become traffickers themselves, shuttling between Bangkok and the border, and earning money from the trade. They sleep under bridges, in parks or along highways, with other marginal dwellers. As illegals, they shift around more and may end up in the drug trade or prostitution.

Exploitative Child Labour

According to the ILO report, trafficked migrant children are among the most severely affected victims of exploitative child labour. The report, commissioned by ILO-IPEC from the Institute of Population and Social Research of Mahidol University in Thailand, says children living in a foreign country with foreign customs and language are easily deceived and often treated like slaves. In their isolation, they don't know where to turn for help. They can't use normal channels, and often face discrimination and harassment.

Some are victims of kidnapping or coercion but most trafficked children are sold or given up by relatives. Don, 14, and his 10-year-old sister were asked to go to Bangkok by their mother. "School was finished and my neighbour saw me and wanted to take me", he said. "My parents said I should go because they needed money". Don was spotted begging by Thai police and couldn't escape without leaving his little sister behind. So they both got caught. To help stop this trafficking, ILO-IPEC recently brought together experts from throughout the Mekong region to draft a framework for cooperation and action.

"We will have to see what works and what doesn't", says Ms Coenjaerts of ILO-IPEC. Part of the difficulty is that these children are hidden and invisible, which makes them very difficult to identify. Interventions will be needed both at the national level and the subregional level, aiming to prevent the problem, harmonise legislation, coordinate information and establish bilateral agreements. One way is to prevent child labour at the community level by showing children and their parents the real problems they will face if they go to the city, and by organising community-based surveillance. Families are often lied to by agents and promises of jobs and money are rarely kept. The other approach is through rehabilitation and re-integration once the children return home. Since many children have been forced to lead a criminal existence, reintegrating them into everyday life is not easy.

Given the illegal and fluid nature of the trade, tackling child trafficking has to be a joint effort across borders by governments and non-governmental organisations. But experience on the ground is limited and few organisations work with child beggars, though this may change as the problem grows.

Child labour is at the top of the international agenda. Delegates to the International Labour Conference in June 1998 called for a new Convention which would immediately penalise the worst forms of child labour, the scope of which includes, among others, slavery and practices similar to slavery, such as the sale and trafficking in children, forced or compulsory labour, debt bondage or serfdom. It would reinforce the ultimate goal of the ILO Minimum Age Convention, 1973 (No. 138), to abolish child labour. By concentrating on its most extreme forms, the new Convention would provide immediate protection, paving the way for the longer-term and broader effects of Convention No. 138.

Homelessness

Homelessness is a "revolving-door" crisis. Many people exit homelessness quickly, but many more individuals become homeless every day. During a year's time, four or five times as many people experience homelessness as are homeless on any particular day. Because more families with children than unpartnered people enter and leave homelessness during a year, families represent a relatively large share of the annual population. With 1 out of every 10 poor people facing homelessness at some time during an average year, current policies clearly are not working. Homelessness stems from desperate poverty combined with unaffordable housing in communities too strapped to support their most troubled members.

Personal difficulties, such as mental disabilities or job loss, may increase vulnerability to homelessness, but they cannot explain the high number of people who fall into homelessness every year. And housing market trends indicate that the situation is getting worse rather than better. Current levels of housing costs, coupled with low-wage jobs and economic contraction, could push even the working poor out of their homes. Although the availability of homeless services increased significantly during the past decade, meeting the needs of people once they become homeless is not enough.

A concerted strategy is needed to prevent homelessness, and to end quickly discrete episodes of homelessness if they become inevitable. That strategy must include new housing resources as well as community-building strategies that address the societal factors contributing to homelessness. Each community must work to supply affordable housing, improve schools, and provide support services for those in need. Only strategies that address systemic problems as well as provide emergency relief can eliminate homelessness in this country.

Reasons of Homelessness

Structural, personal, and political factors influence the level of homelessness and determine where it will occur most often. Structural factors that have fueled the problem include:

— Changing housing markets for extremely low-income families and single adults are pricing more and more people with below-poverty incomes out of the market.

— Dwindling employment opportunities for people with a high school education or less are contributing to the widening gap between rich and poor.

— The removal of institutional supports for people with severe mental illness, epitomized by drastic reductions in the use of long-term hospitalization for the mentally ill, are leaving many individuals with few housing options.

— Racial, ethnic, and class discrimination in housing, along with local zoning restrictions that exclude affordable housing alternatives, persists in many areas.

If housing were inexpensive, or people could earn enough to afford housing, very few individuals would face homelessness. But housing costs have risen steadily across the country, and they have skyrocketed in many areas. Further, the inability to afford housing is concentrated among households with incomes below the poverty level,whose members account for the vast majority of people entering homelessness. At the same time, people with little education or job training find it increasingly difficult to earn enough money to raise their incomes above the poverty level, even if they are employed full-time and work overtime.

Once structural factors have created the conditions for homelessness, personal factors can increase a person's vulnerability to losing his or her home.Many factors can make a poor person more susceptible to homelessness, including limited education or skills training, mental or physical disability, lack of family to rely on, and alcohol or drug abuse. But without the presence of structural fault lines, these personal vulnerabilities could not produce today's high level of homelessness.

Public policies may moderate the effects of both structural and personal factors to prevent homelessness. Some European countries guarantee their citizens housing, and many provide supports for families well beyond those available in the United States. Universal health insurance is also available in most European countries. These safety net programs reduce the probability of homelessness, even in places where housing costs are high and wages are low, because they ease the pressure on household budgets.

In the United States, dramatic reductions in federally supported housing over the past 20 years, coupled with the current reductions in safety net programs, place individuals and families squeezed by high housing costs and with few resources at high risk of homelessness. A certain proportion of these people will experience at least a brief episode during which they lack a place to live. If they are struggling with substance abuse, mental illness, or both, and reside in an area where housing is increasingly beyond the reach of low-wage worker households, then homelessness is likely.

Because families are mostly likely to qualify for public assistance programs, they are less likely than individuals to be homeless, or to be homeless for long. Unattached adults are not eligible for most safety net programs, so they are more likely to be homeless and to experience long or repeated spells of homelessness.

In terms of racial and ethnic composition, little difference exists between homeless families and single adults. In US about equal proportions are African American and white, 11 to 12 percent are Hispanic, 6 to 8 percent are Native American, and 1 percent are another race. The high representation of minorities in the homeless population compared with housed people stems from their higher likelihood of being very poor and has no correlation to their race or ethnicity. Geographically, 71 percent of homeless people who rely on homeless assistance programs reside in central cities, 21 percent in suburban or urban fringe areas, and 9 percent in rural areas.

Income and Work

Half of all homeless adults receive less than $300 per month in income, putting them at about 30 to 40 percent of the federal poverty level. In addition, 62 percent have at least a high school diploma, and 44 percent did some work for pay in the month before being surveyed, although only 13 percent held a regular job. Almost half get one or more means-tested public benefits, with food stamps by far the most common type of assistance. Homeless families' welfare eligibility accounts, in part, for the level of income they report; most single people's *ineligibility* for welfare helps explain their very low incomes.

Disabilities

Many homeless adults have physical and other types of disabilities. Almost half of homeless people are having chronic physical conditions. Problems with alcohol, drugs, and mental health among homeless people are well documented and often occur together. Among adults using homeless services, many reported to have a combination of mental health and substance abuse problems (alcohol and/or drugs) within the past year. And several others are having problems with drugs and/ or alcohol problems, but no mental health problems.

Childhood Homelessness

The homeless population includes not only adults but also the children these adults bring with them into homelessness. One-fourth of homeless people are children in homeless families. These children are much more likely than housed children to experience serious difficulties, including physical, cognitive, emotional, and mental problems. Further, childhood homelessness translates into a greater risk of homelessness in adulthood.

Most children living with homeless parents are very young and are therefore physically and emotionally vulnerable in the event of household disruptions. Children living with homeless parents, however, are not the only children affected by homelessness. Three out of five homeless people are parents, and half these parents have at least one child age 17 or younger. But only one in four of these children lives with the homeless parent.

Children of homeless mothers are much more likely to stay with their homeless parent than are children of homeless fathers. Children of homeless fathers typically live with their mothers outside of homelessness. Children not living with their homeless mothers tend to live with relatives other than their fathers or in foster care. A period in foster care is a strong predictor of future homelessness.

Patterns of Homelessness

Societal factors create the conditions within which individual characteristics can lead to homelessness. Of individual factors, extreme poverty (incomes at less than half the federal poverty level) is, of course, the most important predictor.Virtually every study shows that adverse childhood experiences are also strong predictors of homelessness. These experiences include physical and/or sexual abuse by family members and removal from one's home to be placed in foster care or other institutions. Also important are alcohol or drug abuse as a teenager, current alcohol or drug abuse, mental health problems, chronic physical problems, and, for males, incarceration.

Clearly, homeless people's lives differ in many ways. The pattern of a person's homelessness reveals much information about how to intervene and ways to reduce or eliminate such episodes. People who are homeless for the first time and experiencing a single crisis may need relatively simple remedies, such as rental assistance, help negotiating with landlords, or referrals to public benefits or services. Persons with repeated or long episodes of homelessness, however, are likely to need considerably more support for longer periods of time.

The proportion of people displaying a particular homelessness pattern is hard to calculate, because the definitions of homelessness and the type of data used in such calculations differ widely. Using the most common type of data—surveys conducted at a single point in time—about one-fourth of homeless people report being continuously homeless for at least five years, and about one-fourth say they have gone in and out of homelessness numerous times. The rest are experiencing a first or second episode, which has usually lasted less than a year, or in some cases, only a few weeks or months.

Data reflecting longer periods—for example, one year—capture many of the people experiencing short-term crises who leave homelessness as well as the additional people entering shortterm homelessness. People who have weathered many episodes also tend to leave and return, or to leave and be replaced by others.Meanwhile, chronically homeless people remain without a place to live during the entire period. By the end of the year, chronically homeless people will make up a smaller proportion of the homeless population during the year than at a single point in time. Conversely, those with very short spells will account for a higher proportion of the population over a year's time than on any given day.

The experience of the past 15 years indicates that the number of very poor people driven into homelessness for at least short periods has not diminished significantly. Families with children are still a large part of the mix. Over the past 15 years, the resources of the homeless service system, which gives people in desperate circumstances a place to go for help, have also increased. While essential, these services make visible and undeniable the severity of structural factors currently operating to produce homelessness.

Homeless Assistance Programmes

The availability of transitional housing and permanent housing with supportive services for disabled formerly homeless people is growing. With the growth of shelter capacity, the homeless service network was able to serve more people, and more people in desperate circumstances came forward seeking services. Rather than being a self-fulfilling development, the availability of services and the demand among the poor indicate a profound level of need. Changes in emergency food services confirm this interpretation. Emergency food services receive far less government support than do shelter and housing programs. Yet they too grew during the 1990s in response to the greater demand.

Virtually all programs related to homelessness focus serving people who are already homeless.When assistance is restricted to those who are homeless tonight, not much can be done to prevent homelessness tomorrow. Developing capacity to serve those who are already homeless while ignoring prevention does little to change the underlying problems among the very poor. Only policies that expand the availability of affordable housing to people with belowpoverty incomes will ensure stable homes for these individuals. However, policies during the past decade have moved in the opposite direction.

The results of a decade and a half of research to determine what works to end homelessness are fairly conclusive about the most effective approaches. Providing housing helps currently homeless people leave homelessness. It also prevents people from losing their homes. In fact, without housing, virtually nothing else works.Housing often needs to be accompanied by supportive services, at least temporarily, but such services without a housing component cannot end homelessness.

Evaluations of demonstration projects, and the experiences of providers in many communities around the country, also have shown that even the most chronic, most severely mentally ill people can be brought off the streets and can live stable lives, *if* they are supplied with housing. The same is true for families headed by a mother struggling with mental illness. With the appropriate help, even people with extensive histories of substance abuse have left the streets and obtained stable housing.

Furthermore, the evidence shows not only that making these services available works to end homelessness, but also that, for long-term homeless people with substance abuse and mental health histories, these service provisions are virtually cost-neutral.With adequate housing resources, homelessness can also be averted for the many people who approach the homeless service system because they do not know where else to turn. Communities throughout the country that have committed such resources have developed a variety of effective programs to prevent homelessness, including

— Programs that negotiate with landlords and help with bad credit histories;

— Housing trust funds, rental assistance programs, and access to funds that can solve a household's short-term problems, such as paying back rent, security deposits, and other moving expenses;

— Programs that encourage developers to build or renovate attractive, accessible properties; and help managers ensure good maintainence and repair; and

— Programs that help people develop personal and family financial management skills, establish or reestablish good credit and rental histories, and retain housing.

When a community ensures that housing within reasonable price ranges exists, offers its members living-wage jobs, provides quality schooling to develop individuals' capacity to hold good jobs, and offers other supports for families and individuals, people can maintain stable housing. But far too few communities have these resources or are positioned to provide them. The answer? Put simply:

— Rebuild communities, especially the most troubled ones;
— Build more housing and subsidize the costs to make it affordable to people with incomes below the poverty level;
— Help more people afford housing, by providing them with better schools, better training, and better jobs; and Prevent the next generation of children from experiencing homelessness.

Without these basic building blocks of a civil society, we are creating an underclass of persistently poor people vulnerable to homelessness. The costs of this neglect are too high in terms of both individual lives and public dollars for health, mental health, and correctional institutions. It is more effective, more humane, and ultimately more fiscally prudent to invest in prevention and support that leads to self-sufficiency and independence among all residents.

Rights of the Homeless

Thousands of people around the world are living without homes. They live either in shelters or on the streets. In cities, they sleep on park benches, sit on sidewalks, or beg for change in front of stores. Some citizens and business owners would like to control such behaviors. They say shoppers feel intimidated by the clusters of panhandlers who gather near popular stores and restaurants to beg. Shop owners believe their businesses suffer as a result of such loitering. In response, large cities across the world are considering or have already passed civility ordinances. These laws restrict where panhandling can occur, whether people can rummage through garbage, and what hours people can sit or sleep on downtown sidewalks.

Homeless rights activists call civility ordinances attacks on the constitutional rights of the homeless. They say such laws unfairly punish the homeless because they often do not have anyplace to go during the day, making it almost impossible for them to avoid violating the law.

Ending Chronic Street Homelessness

There are mainly 11 key elements shared by many of the approaches successfully reducing chronic street homelessness. Five of these elements, in combination, are essential for the strongest approaches. In addition to these five elements, trigger events is an important catalytic element. Five other elements when present contributed to making an approach stronger. The elements were:

Essential Elements:

— A paradigm shift;

— A clear goal of ending chronic street homelessness;

— Community-wide level of organization;

— Strong leadership and an effective organizational structure; and

— Significant resources from mainstream public agencies.

Catalyst Element:

— Trigger event—capacity to capitalize on triggering events.

Contributing Elements:

— Significant resources from the private sector;

— Commitment and support from elected officials;

— Outcome evaluation mechanisms for program support and improvement;

— Openness to new service approaches; and
— Strategies to minimize negative neighborhood reactions to projects.

Of the five essential elements the most important is a paradigm shift away from traditional homeless program goals and approaches. The old paradigm is that street homeless individuals should be cared for more by charitable, often religious, organizations rather than by mainstream public agencies. The old paradigm relied heavily on emergency shelters, transitional housing, and sobriety-based programs. The old paradigm did not plan, or expect, to end chronic street homelessness.

The new paradigm emphasizes reducing and eventually ending chronic street homelessness through an integrated community-wide approach that includes substantial participation by mainstream public agencies. Part of the paradigm shift is the adoption of an explicit goal to end chronic street homelessness. A second part of the shift is communities recognizing that their existing homeless assistance network is not reducing homelessness and that they had to do something different. Permanent supportive housing programs had to expand, they had to be structured to accommodate people with co-occurring disorders, and clear and simple pathways from the street into housing had to be available. The general homeless service programs may remain, but the new programs, supported with new resources, contribute the most to reaching the goal of ending chronic street homelessness.

The paradigm shift to low-demand permanent supportive housing on a broad scale affects policymakers, funders, program planners, and service providers. The new approaches can be especially challenging for traditional housing developers and social service providers.

For mental health and social service providers, low-demand environments mean they cannot require tenants to use services, and they have to deal with both mental health and substance abuse issues, and do so simultaneously. In addition, tenants may not use their services consistently, thus reducing reimbursements on which the providers may rely.

For housing providers, a low-demand residence means that tenants may not act as predictably as the property managers might wish. For both, the challenges are as much philosophical as financial, in that the new model demands that they conduct business in ways that had formerly been considered not just impractical but wrong.

The most successful community-wide approaches have an explicit goal of ending chronic street homelessness. Some communities have adopted the goal of ending chronic homelessness, which has turned their priorities away from emergency and even transitional programs. They invest heavily in permanent supportive housing and have stabilized or actually reduced the number of emergency shelter beds they support as they work to move persistent shelter stayers and street homeless people into permanent supportive housing.

A community-wide level of organization exists when agencies are working together to end chronic street homelessness. It helps to think about three levels of contact or working together for two or more agencies—communication, coordination, and collaboration. These levels are hierarchical—agencies cannot coordinate without communicating, and cannot collaborate unless they both communicate and coordinate. The hierarchy reflects the extent to which agencies pay attention to other agencies, perhaps change their own ways, and make a joint effort to reach shared goals. These hierarchical terms can be defined as follows:

— *Communication.* Agencies are at the level of communication if they have accurate knowledge of each other's existence, service offerings, and eligible clientele. They will also know how to access each other's services, and may refer clients to each other. They may have shared involvements through meetings, committees and task forces, but they do not have mechanisms in place to support each other's work.

— *Coordination.* Agencies are at the level of coordination if in addition to communicating they support each other's efforts to obtain resources for clients. However, they do not deliberately work to develop shared goals and structure their operations to meet these goals.

— *Collaboration.* Agencies are at the level of collaboration if they work with each other to articulate shared goals, analyze their operations to determine how they may achieve those goals, and make the changes dictated by this analysis. Of course agencies may relate to each other *below* the level of communication—that is, they do not know these things about each other, do not interact in any way, interact negatively, and/or hold inaccurate views of each other. In most communities at most times, most agencies operate toward each other at the level of communication or worse. This is "business as usual"—it takes work to get beyond it.

Collaboration may mean that agency staff members fulfill new roles or restructured roles; colocate, team, or otherwise work together with staff of other agencies; merge money, issue joint requests for proposals, apply together for new money to do new programs in new ways; actively support each others' work; have mutual feedback mechanisms to assure continued appropriate service and program delivery; and/or other mechanisms and activities that reflect a purposeful, well-thought-out commitment to work together to reach common goals. Collaboration can occur between two agencies, or among several agencies. When it extends to include all or most agencies in a community focused on the same population with the same goals, we can call it a strong community-wide level of organization.

Effective Leadership

Strong leadership within an effective organizational structure is crucial in the development of successful community-wide approaches. Ultimately, it is people and not systems that make things happen—especially in the beginning. Individual personality and devotion plays an extremely important role in the development of the homeless assistance systems. In most of these communities, a few people have been such essential players that it would be hard to imagine that without them the system would be what it is today. They have not all played the same roles. Some have been idealistic inspirers who brought public and private resources to focus on the issue of chronic street homelessness and stick with it, although their role in the actual organization of services might have been slight. Some have been socially and politically skilled organizational masterminds who knew what it would take to get an aggregation of programs and personalities to become a system focused on chronic street homelessness. Some have occupied vitally important positions in government agencies and persisted over many years in bringing those agencies to the table, keeping them there, and seeing that agency resources are applied to homeless issues, including chronic street homelessness. And some have been instrumental in bringing about a significant meeting of minds because they insist on cooperation and accountability, yet have a high tolerance for tension and the ability to channel it toward useful outcomes. It is vital to recognize the role played by people who really care, and who have the ability to translate that caring into structures of cooperating individuals, programs, and agencies. Without them the homeless assistance systems in their communities would look far different.

Mainstream Public Agencies

Ending chronic street homelessness requires resources far beyond those commanded by agencies, programs, and networks exclusively focused on working with homeless people. Major commitments of resources are needed from mainstream public housing, health, mental health, substance abuse, welfare and other agencies.

Mainstream public agencies have four roles to play with respect to ending chronic homelessness. These are facilitating homeless people's access to their services, developing specialty approaches, establishing funding priorities, and contributing leadership of various types. Most communities enjoy considerably less mainstream agency involvement, and could benefit from increasing the effectiveness of such partnerships.

Getting mainstream public agencies to the "homeless" table takes planning, persistence, and sometimes power. It also often takes being able to present the case for their involvement as a mutually beneficial situation in which mainstream agencies are able to serve "their own" clients better by joining forces with the local homeless assistance network.

The mainstream agencies whose own missions coincide most closely with the goal of ending chronic homelessness, and hence the ones that will have the greatest incentive to work with homeless assistance networks toward that end, include housing and community/neighborhood/economic development agencies; health, mental health, and substance abuse agencies; and to an increasing extent, corrections agencies.

Involvement of the Private Sector

In addition to governmental agencies, private businesses and foundations are often mainstream organizations making significant contributions to reducing street homelessness. Many of the communities have been promoting central city redevelopment. In the past many downtown businesses and developers have had a kneejerk reaction against providing services to their neighborhood's street homeless people, fearing that services would attract more homeless individuals. However, in many other communities, businesses and their associations took leadership roles in programs providing services to help end street homelessness.

Foundations and Nonprofit Organizations

Organizations such as the United Way, which address a wide range of community needs, have the potential to make significant contributions to a community's efforts to end chronic homelessness. In Columbus the United Way helps fund supportive housing for Rebuilding Lives. In Columbus United Way also supports emergency shelter and other CSB initiatives including Rebuilding Lives. In Boston the United Way funded $4 million of emergency shelter, transitional housing, and support services; cash, and in-kind donations from businesses, religious and civic organizations totaled over $3.6 million; and over 50 foundations contributed over $7 million. Cash donations from individuals to programs are also substantial, totaling an additional $12.5 million.

Support from Elected Officials

Commitment and support from mayors, city and

county councils, and other elected officials can be a significant contributing element in the progress of community-wide efforts toward reducing chronic homelessness. Mainstream city officials and business leaders plays a seminal role in initiating collaborative programs to end homelessness.

State and national political environments also have a significant impact on community approaches to reducing chronic street homelessness. This may be especially true at the state level, which requires a wider mobilization of support than city or county initiatives. Many state assemblies and governors would not follow the examples of California and Massachusetts in making large fiscal commitments to programs to end homelessness. Winning support from elected officials for state and other mainstream funding of programs to end homelessness is greatly facilitated by demonstrations of positive outcomes and cost effectiveness. The potential savings from innovative programs may be demonstrated by developing good estimates of how much homeless persons are costing the public through conventional emergency services and law enforcement programs.

Openness to New Service Approaches

Ending chronic street homelessness requires new approaches to homeless service delivery. It requires new ways of helping people (such as harm reduction), new ways of providing old services (such as housing first), new agency relationships (such as joint provision of mental health and substance abuse services, or agency mergers), and new investments in effective approaches (such as permanent supportive housing). It can also involve redesigning service systems to create better matches between people's needs and the services they receive.

One such shift involves reserving emergency shelter

and other forms of short-term assistance for those with acute needs who are homeless for the first time or as the result of a crisis, while those with chronic needs receive longer-term supports and permanent housing. Reducing chronic street homelessness also results from effective outreach and engagement strategies, especially those that are able to link people directly to housing. Finally, new approaches to prevention can prevent people with chronic disabilities from becoming homeless in the first place.

Building Sustainable Livelihoods

For many of the poor, livelihood seems to fit better than employment as a concept to capture how poor people live, what their realistic priorities are, and what can help them. "Sustainable" then refers to the longer-term and "livelihood" to the many activities which make up a living. On sustainability, it is a common prejudice among those who are not poor that poor people inherently "live hand-to-mouth" and take the short-term view. But, in practice, again and again, they show tenacity and self-sacrifice in trying to take the longterm view and safeguarding the basis for their livelihoods. Small farmers with secure rights invest their labour in land-shaping, terracing and creating fertile micro-environments; in harvesting water, silt and nutrients; and in planting and protecting trees.

It is now a widespread finding that, as soon as food shortage threatens, poor people eat less and worse in order to protect their livelihood assets in the bad times to come.It is less the poor, and more the outsiders, who take the short-term view - contractors who cut the forest, officials fixated on the financial year and politicians who cannot see beyond the next election. On livelihoods, the strategies of the poor are usually diverse and often complex. They can be compared to those of hedgehogs and foxes, after the saying of Archilochus that "The fox has many ideas but the hedgehog has one big idea". Full-time employees in the industrial world and industrial sectors are hedgehogs, with one big idea, a single source of support. Those poor people, often powerless, desperate or exploited, who have or can have but one survival strategy are the same - slaves, bonded labourers, outworkers tied to single supplier-buyers, beggars, some vendors, prostitutes and some other occupational specialists.

But most poor people in the South, and more now in the North, are foxes with a portfolio of activities, with different members of the family seeking and finding different sources of food, fuel, animal fodder, cash and support in different ways in different places at different times of the year. Their living is improvised and sustained through their livelihood capabilities, through tangible assets in the form of stores and resources, and through intangible assets in the form of claims and access.

Fox strategies are rarely fully revealed by conventional questionnaire surveys. Schedules construct a standardized, short and simple reality, and investigators' incentives are to record less, not more. Much that matters is liable to be left out.

The ingenuity and opportunism of poor people, and the diversity and complexity of their strategies, can be illustrated by case studies and the accounts of social anthropologists and others.Even within the same village, different social groups of the landless can have completely different strategies.

Strategies and sources of food, income, support and survival include:

— *Home-gardening:* (Both rural and urban) and the exploitation of micro-environments. Six studies in Indonesia reported the proportions of household income deriving from home gardens as variously 10-30, 20-30, over 20, 22-33, 41-51 and 42-51 per cent, while another Indonesia study found the proportion higher among the poor, providing 24 per cent of their income compared with 9 per cent for the well off.

— *Common property resources (CPRs):* Fishing, hunting, grazing, and gathering in lakes, ponds, rivers, the sea, forests, woodlands, swamps, savannas, hills, wastelands, roadsides.... for any of a vast range of fish, animals, fodders, wild foods, fibres, building materials, fuel, fertilizer, medicines and much else.

— *Scavenging*: (Mainly urban) and gleaning (mainly rural), including traditional rights and access to private residues (buttermilk, crop residues as fuel etc.)

— *Processing, hawking, vending and marketing*: Including produce from home gardens and common property resources.

— *Share-rearing of livestock*: Where livestock are lent for herding in exchange for rights to some products and/or offspring. The core of a livelihood can be expressed as a living, with people, tangible assets and intangible assets contributing to it. The tangible assets commanded by a household are *stores* such as food stocks, stores of value such as gold, jewellery and woven textiles, and cash savings in thrift banks and credit schemes; and *resources* such as land, water, trees, livestock, farm equipment, tools and domestic utensils. The intangible assets are *claims* which can be made for material, moral or other practical support, and *access*, meaning the opportunity in practice to use a resource, store or service, or to obtain information, material, technology, employment, food or income.

- Transporting goods with a horse, donkey, mule, cart, bicycle, or head or backloading.
- *Mutual help*: Including small borrowings from relatives and neighbours.
- *Contract outwork*: Weaving, rolling cigarettes, making incense sticks.
- Casual labour and piecework especially in agriculture.
- *Specialized occupations:* Barbers, blacksmiths, carpenters, prostitutes, tailors
- *Domestic service*: Especially by girls and women.
- *Child labour:* Both domestically (collecting fuel-leaves, twigs, branches, dung, collecting fodder, weeding, herding animals, removing stones from fields and ticks from livestock...) and working in factories (making matches, candles, fireworks...), restaurants, people's houses.
- Craft work of many sorts.
- Mortgaging and selling assets, future labour and children.
- *Family-splitting*: Including putting out children to others.
- Migration for seasonal work in agriculture, brick-making, urban construction.
- Remittances
- Seasonal food-for-work, public works and relief.
- Stinting in many ways, with food and other consumption.
- Begging
- Theft
- Triage: especially with girl children and weaklings.

The point of this incomplete list is to illustrate.

Often, an individual or a household engages in many livelihood activities such as these over a year. This does not fit in with any concept of "employment" in "a job". Individuals and families diversify and complicate their livelihood strategies in order to increase income, reduce vulnerability and improve the quality of their lives.

A similar pattern is shown by "the third agriculture".The first, or industrial agriculture is standardized and simple and the second, or green revolution agriculture has high-yielding packages in controlled conditions. The third agriculture, which provides support for some 1.9 to 2.2 billion people is complex, diverse and risk-prone. Farmers working within complex, diverse and risk-prone farming seek to reduce risk and increase food and income by complicating, diversifying and, where labour is available, intensifying their farming systems, adding to their enterprises. They multiply the internal links and flows within their farming systems, for example through aquaculture, composting, cut-and-carry for stallfed livestock, multiple cropping, agroforestry, home-gardening, and the concentration of nutrients, soil and water in micro-environments such as silt deposit fields and protected pockets of fertility.

For these realities, of the strategies employed by most of the rural poor and many of the urban, sustainable livelihood fits better than employment as a concept. Employment, in the sense of having an employer, a job, a workplace and a wage is more widespread as an aspiration than as a reality. Where economic crisis and structural adjustment cut urban jobs, the proportion of foxes can be expected to increase. Moreover, however much poor people may seek employment and educate their children in the hope that they will find a secure and remunerative job, for most such a job is not a realistic prospect. Even in the North, the classic concept of a single employment is being challenged and portfolio, fox, livelihoods are becoming more common.

In identifying actions, then, it makes sense to shift thinking from labour intensive growth towards sustainable livelihood intensive change. This is not to argue against growth, or against a strategy of labour intensive growth, but to qualify and complement it. For labour intensity and sustainable livelihood intensity, though overlapping, are not identical. As a concept, labour intensity links with employment. A sustainable livelihood intensive strategy goes beyond employment to stress:

— *Natural resources*: Sustainable management of natural resources, especially common property resources, and equitable access to them for the poorer.

— Redistribution of private and public livelihood resources to the poor.

— *Prices*: Marketing, prices and prompt payment for what poor people sell, and terms of trade between what poor people sell and what they buy.

— *Health*: Accessible health services for the prevention of disease and for prompt and effective treatment of disabling accidents and disease.

— *Restrictions and hassle*: Removal of restrictions on livelihood activities otherwise used to hassle and exploit the poor.

— Counter-seasonality and safety nets for poor people at badtimes, mitigating seasonal stress and enabling them to conserve their livelihood assets.

To conclude, deprivation and well-being as perceived by poor people, and sustainable livelihoods as a shared goal of outsiders and the poor, question the degree of primacy often attributed to income-poverty. The realities of the poor are many and particular. They can experience and agonize over acute tradeoffs between different dimensions of deprivation and well-being. What they value and choose often differs from what outsider professionals expect. Income matters, but so too do other aspects of well-being and the quality of life - health, security, self-respect, justice, access to goods and services, family and social life, ceremonies and celebrations, creativity, the pleasures of place, season and time of day, fun, spiritual experience and love. If development means good change, it is so much more than economic growth and income; it is also these and many other aspects of well-being and quality of life, as poor people experience and wish them.

Anti-poverty Action

Anti-poverty Action has often been justified to the rich and powerful by appealing to enlightened selfishness: this has stressed mutual interests and the bad impacts of poverty, suffering and deprivation on those who are better off, and on the North as a whole. The strongest argument was perhaps that of the Brandt Commission, that the North had an economic interest in economic growth in the South. To the extent that reciprocal non-zero sums exist or can be found, they must be welcomed. But such arguments do not always hold up.

Well-meaning casuistry about mutual interest, argued during the development decades to justify helping the poor, can prove a shifting sand. To rely on arguments about mutual material interests is to risk loss of support if they do not exist. Ethical arguments are stronger, surer and better. The prescriptions which follow are founded not on self-interest on the part of the rich and powerful, which may or may not be served, but on the values of common decency, compassion and altruism.

The differences between top-down reductionist definitions and objectives, and poor people's realities present development professionals with challenges which are institutional, professional and personal. The challenges are paradigmatic: to reverse the normal view, to upend perspectives, to see things the other way round, to soften and flatten hierarchy, to adopt downward accountability, to change behaviour, attitudes and beliefs, and to identify and implement a new agenda; in sum, to define and embrace a new professionalism.

This new professionalism and its paradigm stress reversals, decentralization, local diversity and complexity, and empowerment.

The Institutional Challenge

Professionals, whether in NGOs, government departments, training institutes and universities or donor agencies, have been slow to see that the fine words "participation", "ownership" and "empowerment", by and for the poor, demand institutional change "by us". Participation "by them" will not be sustainable or strong unless we too are participatory. "Ownership" by them means non-ownership by us. Empowerment for them means disempowerment for us.

In consequence, management cultures, styles of personal interaction and procedures all have to change. One indicator of the orientation of an agency is the composition of its staff. Middle-aged economists, often Northern and male, still dominate international development organizations and the development discourse. In contrast, social anthropologists, social development advisers and psychologists remain few. Modest increases in their numbers are patchily achieved: numbers of social anthropologists and sociologists working in their professional capacities for the World Bank are hard to estimate but they are outnumbered by their economist colleagues by perhaps between 20 and 50 to one.In contrast, the ratio of economists to social development advisers in the Overseas Development Administration of the British Government is of the order of three to one,still high, but dramatically lower than in the Bank. Gains in the numbers and influence of non-economist social scientists are also vulnerable.

The International Potato Centre earlier demonstrated the big contributions social anthropologists could make in agricultural research but has now reduced their number. Astonishingly, the International Crops Research Centre for the Semi-Arid Tropics (ICRISAT) is reported to have no anthropologists at all.The institutional challenge for all development agencies is to become learning organizations.It is to flatten and soften hierarchy, to develop a culture of participatory management, to recruit a gender and disciplinary mix of staff committed to people, and to adopt and promote procedures, norms and rewards which permit and encourage more open-ended participation at all levels. Project procedures, textbooks and training all require revision. Topdown targets, drives to disburse funds fast, rewards for big spenders, and rushed visits, meetings and decisions have all to be restrained and reversed.

The Professional Challenge

The professional challenge is paradigmatic and profound. Normal professional orientations, concepts, values, methods and behaviour reinforce the dominance of the North and of whatever is industrial, capital-intensive and "sophisticated". Its magnetic force repeatedly reasserts itself. Small successes in reversing it are vulnerable to flipping back again to the norm. In the CGIAR, for instance, farmer participatory research, painstakingly established by a small number of social and natural scientists, is threatened by the current "infatuation with biotechnology as a top-down cure-all".

The challenge is to learn to see things the other way round, to appreciate and grasp that other reality, of local people. In the words of the recent vision paper for the

CGIAR it is "...to reverse the chain of logic, starting with the socio-economic demands of poor households"in order to identify appropriate research priorities. But such reversals are impeded by normal professionalism, by disciplinary specialization and by the nature of worldwide upper-lower interactions between those who are dominant and those who are subordinate.The stronger the dogmatism and drive of the upper (the World Bank task manager, the senior official, the knowledgeable professional...) so the more he (most are men) is likely to be misled.

As with the remarkable story of the misperceived ecological history of the Guinea forest- savannah mosaic, professional and bureaucratic misbelief is perpetuated by the politeness and prudence of those who know another reality: "Villagers, faced by questions about deforestation and environmental change, have learned to confirm what they know the questioners expect to hear."So the prudent poor and weak perpetuate the fantasies and fallacies of the powerful and strong. All power deceives.

The professional challenge is to review and reorient normal professional concepts, values, methods and behaviour which serve "our" purposes and, instead, enable the poor to express their reality. The new professionalism entails recognizing the extent to which "our" reality is generated by our training, interactions, power and central needs, and then revising and reversing many normal concepts, values, methods and behaviours.

The Personal Challenge

The personal dimension is as paramount as it is perversely overlooked. Again and again, in the experience of Participatory Rural Appraisal, the behaviour and attitudes of outsiders have been the key to facilitating participation, to enabling people who are poor and weak to come together and express and analyze their reality. Yet the personal is scarcely on the development agenda at all.

Psychologists and psychotherapists are rare among development professionals and, where they are found, tend to be in other than their specialized roles. It is, though, obvious to the point of embarrassment, that individual personality, perceptions, values, commitment and behaviour are crucial for institutional and professional change. The personal challenge applies in all social spheres. It is not limited to professional work. For example, men can feel personally threatened by feminism and the focus on women in development. For these imply changes in roles and relationships both at work and at home. And they can raise ethical questions about limits to inter-cultural tolerance, as with dowry, female genital mutilation and selective abortion.

The personal challenge can be expressed as the paragon new professional. She is committed to the poor and weak and to enabling them to gain more of what they want and need. She is democratic and participatory in management style, is a good listener, embraces error and believes in failing forwards, finds pleasure in enabling others to take initiatives, monitors and controls only a core minimum of standards and activities, is not threatened by the unforeseeable, does not demand targets for disbursements and achievements, abjures punitive management, devolves authority expecting her staff to use their own best judgement at all times, gives priority to the front-line, and rewards honesty.

For her, watchwords are truth, trust and diversity. And throughout this paragraph she can also be a he. Much of the challenge is to give up power. It is to enjoy handing over the initiative to others, enabling them to do more and to do it more in their way, for their objectives. This has its own satisfactions, in seeing how well and how differently people do things and what they achieve.

The need is for those with power to learn to value and enjoy these satisfactions.

Well-being and Livelyhoods

This analysis reframes and shifts the balance of objectives of development: from reducing income-poverty to diminishing deprivation and enhancing well-being; and from increasing employment to sustaining livelihood. Development then demands and generates diversity, as deprivation is so much more than lack of income, livelihood is so multifarious and dynamic, and well-being as people experience and desire it has so many dimensions. Equity also applies but now more to what poor people themselves define as priorities and strategies, and less to what we suppose they ought to want.

To support and achieve these objectives there are two agendas: one with elements that are current and familiar even it is often convenient to overlook parts of it; and a new one based on the paradigm of reversals. For completeness, both are presented but the first in brief.

1. *A Current Agenda:* An updated and amended current agenda overlaps with, qualifies and adds to the two-legged orthodoxy of the World Bank of labour intensive growth and basic services with its add-on of safety nets.This agenda includes:

   i. *Peace and equitable law and order:* these have primacy as pre-conditions for sustainable well-being. The horrors of Rwanda are an extreme example and civil disorder has spread since the end of the Cold War. Much more widespread is the lack of the equitable rule of law to provide justice for the poor and powerless.

   ii. *International terms of trade:* given the dominance of greed and selfishness in the Western democracies, it is unlikely that anything much will be done about this until powerful people change and exercise extraordinary leadership. This requires altruism, meaning that the powerful must value non-material rewards and act against their own narrowly defined material interests for the sake of others.

iii. *Debt relief and good aid to debtor countries* (but not including the United States or other rich debtors). The need for these is so widely recognized that no more will be said.

iv. *Domestic macro-economic policy:* this includes livelihood intensive growth. Domestic macro-policy in all countries should be informed more by the realities of the poor as they experience and express them, and less by the realities supposed for the poor by the powerful. Few would now deny that, had structural adjustment programmes been oriented in this manner from the start, much suffering would have been averted.

v. *Redistribution*: redistributive policies from the rich to the poor, whether through assets such as land or through taxation, deserve revival and restoration from the limbo to which neoclassical orthodoxy has consigned them. Redistribution, for example of land, has been found again and again to be efficient as well as equitable.

vi. *Rights and information*: the poorer people are, the more they need, and can gain from, secure rights and information about those rights. This includes the credible abolition of rules and restrictions which empower officials to extort bribes, and organization and legal support to ensure effective justice.

vii. *Infrastructure and access to basic services*: this includes health, education, water, transport, credit and marketing. These are well recognized but access by the poor remains crucial and is often neglected and weak or non-existent in practice.

viii. *Access to affordable basic goods:* the ILO basic needs list did not include access to affordable basic goods yet they matter much to poor people and are quite often beyond their reach, especially those who are rural and more remote from urban centres.

ix. *Safety nets*: safety nets, the third, sometimes lame, policy leg of the World Development Report are vital for many of the poor.Food-for-work and famine relief often come too late, after people have lost or been forced to dispose of livelihood assets. Some professionals and organizations still see food aid only as famine relief and not as a livelihood-sustaining safety net to help poor people avoid becoming poorer. For sustainable livelihoods, the vulnerable poor need safety nets.

2. *Reversals and Altruism—the New Agenda*: The new paradigm is people centred, participatory, empowering and sustainable. These nice words are more deeply embedded in the reflexes of paper and speech-writers than in the mental frames and personal behaviour of those who write the papers and read out the speeches. For the paradigm demands reorientation, an upending of much of the normal upper-lower, North-South dominance. It combines reversals and altruism: reversals to stand the norm on its head, to see things the other way round, to enable the poor and weak to express their reality, and to put that reality first; and then altruism, to act in the interests of the poor and powerless. The paradigm of reversals and altruism stands as a challenge for the Social Development Summit.

The reversal of logic is fundamental. Instead of starting with the analysis of central professionals, the logic starts with the realities of the peripheral poor. Policy is not deduced and driven centre-outwards, with distant assumptions about effects on the poor, but induced and drawn up from the experience and analysis of those who live local realities and know what happens close to them. Nor is the argument that this should be the only logic: it is complementary. But the scales are so weighted against it that, unless it is put first and kept first, nothing like a good balance and mix of logics will ever be achieved.

A key point for healthy sceptics is the cost-effectiveness of this agenda. Good things which poor people want and which have not been done because they have not been recognized can have high pay-offs. Many measures which make a big difference to poor people have low financial costs. Rights, security, the rule of law, information, access, changes in procedures, removals of restrictions, polite behaviour by officials, timing actions for the right season, timely delivery, providing diverse "baskets of choices" (of crop varieties, trees, uses of credit and so on) - these are examples of actions which can have low financial costs and high benefits to well-being. The key is identifying such measures and then implementing them. The paradigm of the new agenda has four pillars. Each will be illustrated with a few of its potential practical implications.

i. *Analysis and action by local people, and putting first the priorities of the poor*: central to the paradigm is the basic human right of poor people to conduct their own analysis. People centred development starts not with analysis by the powerful and dominant outsiders - the "North", uppers and professionals, but with enabling local people, especially the poor, to conduct theirs.In the past five years innovations in approach and methods, some of them known as participatory rural appraisal (PRA), have contributed a new repertoire which has proved powerful and popular, when well used, in enabling poor people and communities to undertake their own appraisal, analysis and action. Putting first the priorities of the poor can refer to whole communities which are poor but equally to those who are disadvantaged the poor, weak and marginalized, whether women or a social or economic group - within communities. To find, convene and facilitate groups of the disadvantaged demands commitment to the analysis of difference.The outcomes can include awareness and action by these groups, joint action with outside agencies and feedback into policy.

PRA approaches and methods are now being used in over 40 countries with a wide range of applications including natural resource management, agriculture, health and nutrition, and poverty programmes. PRA methods have been used in participatory poverty assessments (PPAs) sponsored by the World Bank and bilateral donors in Ghana, Zambiaand Kenyaenabling poor rural and urban people to analyze their conditions and to express their own values, definitions of well-being and priorities, in short, to present their realities. Some practical implications are:

— Experiential training: those with experience in participatory approaches and training are mainly in NGOs. The spread of PRA and similar approaches requires special field based training which is still in short supply for both NGOs and government. The multiplication, personal development and deploy- ment of good trainers is a key to realizing the potential of participatory approaches.

— Local priorities and practice: putting people first, and poor people first of all, generates local priorities requiring local differentiation. PRA-type approaches and methods can thus reinforce and support decentralization and local diversity.

— Participatory poverty assessments and policy: PPAs give potential for poor people's problems and priorities, and their definitions of well-being, to have direct impact on national policy.

ii. *Sustainable livelihoods*: economic growth usually generates niches for new or enhanced and diversified livelihoods, and the resources for services. But economic growth can also destroy livelihoods. Policies can also be livelihood intensive without economic growth. To search for and implement livelihood- generating and supporting policies is a priority. It is especially so in countries where economic growth is difficult. Some practical implications are:

— *Secure rights*: secure rights to land, water and trees encourage and support long-term investment by families. Secure rights to common property resources provide a basis for sustainable management by communities. Secure rights of ownership, access and use are fundamental to the sustainability of livelihoods which rely on natural resources.

— *Removal of restrictions which hamper and harm:*

for example, effective removal of restrictions on urban informal sector activities can reduce the insecurity, anxiety and humiliation of poor artisans, vendors and entrepreneurs, and the petty rents they otherwise have to pay to officials. Or abolishing restrictions on the cutting and transport of trees from private land increases farm-gate values for trees, encourages tree planting and protection and so enhances livelihood security by allowing trees to become savings banks for small and poor farmers.

— *Access to effective health services*: the livelihoods of most poor people depend on their bodies. Health and quick, effective treatment, especially for disabling accidents and sickness, matter more to them than to the less poor. A livelihood cannot be sustained if its main asset is the body, and that is sick, damaged or disabled. Health services for prevention and prompt and effective treatment of accidents and sickness, and for rapid recovery, are basic for sustainable livelihoods for the poor.

iii. *The three Ds*: decentralization, democracy and diversity: reversals require decentralization with transfers of power and democratic modes of operation. Together, these make space for diversity and local fit of action to need. The basic principle is that of subsidiarity, that every activity should be carried out as low down as feasible. Complementing this, ownership and accountability are reframed.

Ownership shifts downwards. At a high level, this was presaged in the World Bank's Wapenhans Report "Effective Implementation: Key to Development Impact"which recommended a shift of ownership from Washington to national capitals; in the Bank's responsewhich endorses partnership and participation; in the Report of the Participation Learning Group of the Bankwhich outlined and recommended practical actions for the participation of the poor; and in the final publication which followed, The World Bank and Participationwhich presented an agreed action plan by the Bank. The implication for all development organizations is that at every level ownership is pushed down, handed over and fostered. Beyond this, participation at the community or group level is then not "their" participation in "our" programme but our participation in theirs; and participation by the poor is not only in the design and implementation phases of projects but also in identification, monitoring and evaluation, and policy formulation. Accountability is reversed. Downward accountability is to the poor and weak. It is to those who have been described in the World Bank as "primary stakeholders: those expected to benefit from, or be adversely affected by, Bank supported operations, particularly the poor and marginalized".So professionals are responsible to their clients: health workers to the sick, agricultural researchers and extensionists to farmers, NGO workers and officials to poor villagers, slum dwellers and others among the primary stakeholders who are or might be touched by their decisions and actions. Some practical implications are:

— *Procedures*: many procedures for central control impede decentralization and diversity. In the World Bank, for example, changes made or contemplated in the legal framework, and procedures for procurement and disbursement, will support decentralization, subsidiarity and participation.

— *Appraisal, action, monitoring and evaluation*: these all shift downwards and become more participatory and more diverse. In particular, poor people and communities conduct their own monitoring and evaluation, using their own baselines and indicators to reflect their own concepts of ill-being and wellbeing and their insights into causality, enhancing their understanding and ownership, and holding agencies to account. Poor people then monitor and evaluate the programmes and actions of development professionals and organizations.

iv. *Professional and personal change:* the key to the new agenda is as obvious as it is neglected. To an extraordinary degree, we development professionals abstain from looking at ourselves as people. The subject is almost taboo. Yet who we are, where we go, how we behave, what we are shown and see, how we learn, are deceived, and deceive ourselves, the concepts we use, the language we speak, what we believe and, above all, what we do and do not do - these so obviously affect all other aspects of development and development policy. It is bizarre that psychology, psychotherapy and management learning scarcely exist in development studies or practice. As a matter not of evangelism but of analytical rigour, it would seem that it is we the profes- sionals, the powerful and the influential, and those who attend roundtables and summits, who have to reconstruct our realities, to change as people, and enable and empower others to change, if the new paradigm of development is to prevail. Some practical implications are:

— More participatory management in development organizations, including multilateral and bilateral agencies, NGOs both Northern and Southern, research institutes, training colleges and institutes, government departments in headquarters and in the field, and universities, entailing the adoption of participatory personal styles and interactions.

— Interactive learning to replace unidirectional lecturing and teaching as approach and method, both in teaching and training institutes and in universities and colleges. This entails a shift from top-down teaching to learning which is shared, lateral and experiential.

— Experiential learning from poor people, meaning that those who are powerful step down, sit, listen and learn. One initiative is the German Dialogue and Exposure Programme in which senior politicians, officials and academics engage in unhurried learning in the field from individual poor families. PRA also has been a means to enable outsiders to facilitate and gain insight from the analysis of poor local people both rural and urban. The practical implication is that agencies authoritatively set aside time for field experiential learning for their staff so that they, directly, as people, can see, hear and understand that other reality, of poor people, and then work to make it count.

4

Begging: An Anti-social Behaviour

It is inappropriate that begging is defined primarily as a problem of anti-social behaviour and placed alongside serious problems such as drug dealing and drunken yobs. The vast majority of beggars and street drinkers are homeless, many of them are in fact rough sleepers and all of them are vulnerable. Street homeless people suffer from high levels of unemployment, poor skills, low incomes, poor housing, high crime, bad health and family breakdown; few if any are in their situation by choice. Personal crisis and the traumatising nature of homelessness combined with difficulties accessing essential services often means that they are unable to escape their predicament.

Research by the Joseph Rowntree Foundation on the links between begging, rough sleeping and the selling of the *Big Issue* in Glasgow and Edinburgh found that most interviewees had a family background characterised by disruption and trauma. Almost half had been in residential care or foster care and over a quarter reported drug or alcohol misusing parents. A number of interviewees, particularly women, reported being abused as children. Those who had substance dependencies had developed these early on in life as a means of coping with traumatic experiences.

Homeless people's involvement in crime is for the most part low level and lifestyle relatedand many are hidden victims of crime with a frequency which would not be tolerated amongst the wider population. Processing vulnerable street homeless people through the criminal justice system not only criminalises them but is a costly and inappropriate means of tackling the problems that they face.

A study by the Revolving Doors Agency of people with mental health and multiple needs who fall through the net of health, housing and social care and who come into contact with the police, found that the police have more contact with this group than social services. The study estimated that the annual cost of this group's arrests was greater than the annual costs to emergency services, community health services or social services, with the cost of police arrests totalling £218,955.

The study indicated that early intervention and effective referral could shift the cost of services used by this group away from expensive crisis services – the police, accident and emergency and temporary housing – towards a more appropriate way of supporting this group – primary care, community mental health services – and that this was likely to improve their quality of life.

Police officers have themselves expressed a desire to get beyond enforcement, which is essential in some circumstances but largely inappropriate for dealing with the range of low level nuisance offending undertaken by most street homeless people. Research has indicated that engaging homeless people through partnership working, early intervention and the provision of appropriate support services is a more effective means of addressing the problems surrounding street homelessness.

All begging is wrong and it is a problem that must be tackled head on but it is a primarily a problem of social exclusion and those most damaged by the experience of begging are people who beg. It is essential that we identify the reasons why people beg (for example substance misuse, difficulties with benefits and the a lack of alternatives to street life) and address these problems.

Despite efforts by government and the voluntary sector there remain significant gaps in service provision for vulnerable homeless people and in practice begging and street homelessness can reflect an absence of appropriate support services.

Begging is for the most part non threatening and is mostly a passive activity. Where it is accompanied byaggressive or violent behaviour there exist the legislative tools to tackle these problems.Research by the former Rough Sleepers Unit in 2001 found that in a survey of members of the generalpublic 52% said that they gave to beggars; specific questions about begging in the British Social Attitudes Survey showed that the majority of the public think that beggars genuinely need help. When asked how best to deal with the situation, more supportive policies such as access to housing education, training and employment, garnered the most enthusiasm. Less than a quarter of people feel that arresting people for begging in public is an appropriate response.

Little is known about the reasons why people beg with children and it is essential that the phenomenon is better understood if we are serious about tackling this problem. However research has shown that people who beg with dogs do so for a number of reasons including company and security and it is misconceived to suggest that they simply use their pets as an aid to begging.

A recent report by the IPPR entitled *Them and Us* highlighted the potentially negative impact of a criminal conviction on an individual's life chances and opportunities for social inclusion. Making a begging a recordable offence will burden an already vulnerable people with a criminal record creating a further obstacle to their reintegration into mainstream society.

Aggressive Panhandling

Panhandlers are a permanent part of any rural and metropolitan scene. Some are known by business owners and the police because they are often suspected of theft, fencing, and related illicit activity. While spending much of their time on the streets, most are not homeless. Many of these individuals are persistent and often belligerent. They concentrate on areas of high pedestrian traffic, such as downtown business districts and public gathering spots such at city bus and train stops. For some, panhandling is only one survival tactic sporadically used along with other opportunities for income, including virtual panhandling, theft, and the selling of personal possessions, plasma, drugs, government issued vouchers, and other illegal goods and services.

"Panhandler", like "tramp", is still too easily taken to mean colorful indigents forced to degrade themselves by asking strangers for money. Sometimes, even now, that is precisely what it means. At others time, however, it can mean anything from the behaviour of the mentally disturbed released to the tender mercies of care in the community, to fraud, to simple extortion. Panhandlers can be crippled by alcohol or drugs and seeking money to fund their habits. They can be genuinely homeless teenagers. Or they can be crooks, pure and simple, who have realized that there is an easy, tax-free profit to be had in public sympathy. Whatever the case, it is the phenomenon of aggressive panhandling, for whatever reason it arises, that disturbs the public.

"Aggressively" means behaving in a hostile manner. "Coerce" means to force or bring about by force or threat.

"Harass" means to irritate or torment persistently. "Hound" means to pursue relentlessly and tenaciously. "Intentionally block" means to walk, stand, sit, lie, or place an object in such a manner as to block passage by another person or a vehicle, or to require another person or driver of a vehicle to take evasive action to avoid physical contact. "Intimidate" means to frighten into submission or obedience. "Solicitor" means a person who asks for money or goods as a charity, whether by words, bodily gestures, signs or other means. "Threaten" means to express an intention to inflict evil, injury or damage.

A person "aggressively coerces, threatens, hounds, harasses or intimidates another person" when:

— The solicitor's conduct would cause a reasonable person in the position of the solicitee to fear for his or her safety; or

— The solicitor intentionally blocks the path of the solicitee; or

— The solicitor persists in following the solicitee closely, and continues to demand money or other thing of value after the solicitee has rejected the solicitation by words or conduct.

The following facts, among others, are relevant in deciding whether a reasonable person would have cause to fear for his or her safety:

— the solicitor's making physical contact with the solicitee; or

— the proximity of the solicitor to the solicitee; or

— the duration of the solicitation; or

— the solicitor's making threatening gestures or other threatening conduct, including closely following the solicitee.

A few panhandlers are part of locally organized efforts to solicit money. These individuals usually stake out territory in high-traffic areas such as freeway ramps, with cardboard signs that say "Will Work For Food." They often are temporarily residing in cramped quarters that offer room and board in exchange for proceeds from daily solicitation. The words "Get a Job" usually have no meaning to aggressive pan-handlers! Many panhandlers go about their business in a passive manner, making a request or holding out a cup with coins. Others are much more aggressive, making loud, sometimes repeated demands, or persistently following the pedestrian down the street after a request has been denied. Additionally, some beggars chose to beg in places that are particularly intimidating such as near ATM machines or by confronting motorists at red lights, washing their windshields without consent and then demanding payment.

This aggressive begging places the economic and social functions of the streets and other public places at risk. Where aggressive panhandlers assemble, people are likely to feel unsafe. If people feel threatened in a particular place they are likely to avoid the area in the future, resulting in a decline in business and community life, as well as making the area ripe for more serious crime. In short, panhandling can be a direct threat to community life and the economic vitality of an area.

Anti-panhandling ordinances are laws which make it illegal to "aggressively beg" for money, but it does not prohibit politely asking for money. These laws makes aggressive panhandling a fourth-degree misdemeanor punishable by a $250 fine and/or six months in jail. It targets those who intimidate others while asking for money. They also prohibit beggars from approaching those in vehicles and from begging within 20 feet of a check-cashing business or an automated teller machine.

Although some courts have deemed panhandling to have some constitutional protection as "speech," communities have substantial leeway in devising regulations on how and where panhandling may occur.

Despite press stories of "genius" level panhandlers who receive hundreds of dollars, the average take is $7.00 per month. Experiments by Berkeley students in a homelessness class found that in a "jaded" city like San Francisco the take was very low: under $4.00 in one day. In a city unused to panhandlers, like Thousand Oaks, a student received $20.00 in a few hours. On what are the fruits of panhandling most often spent? Tobacco, alcohol, or drugs. Let some former homeless people who have panhandled tell you about it.What can the homeless who are not into the panhandling scene, do to get back into the work force? The chances for these people are slim to none, due to them often having no fixed address or home phone number, lack of proper identification, and a multitude of other employment obstacles. They often find themselves forced to panhandle, walk flyers, and some times transport stolen goods and drugs for fencing operations that prey on the homeless, all because of their basic needs for clothing, food, and shelter. And, what can they do to raise their already lowered self-esteem and sense of worth, both of which need to be at peak level during those one on one sessions with a job interviewer? There is an alternative to a life of living on the streets and being used by and bounced between one day labor service to another.

Methods to Reduce Aggressive Panhandling

The trouble is, bans on public urination, lounging on the streets, and aggressive panhandling are not enough to carry urban civility much further. The significant gains of recent years are bringing people back to the streets, but there are still large parts of Seattle where ordinary citizens feel unsafe. Here is what additionally can be done to lower crime rates by emphasizing misdemeanor order maintenance:

— Enforce strict limits on beer and fortified wine sales in high-crime areas and the districts around them. Bills in the state legislature this session would strengthen these restrictions.

— Make the parks safer by issuing park exclusion orders against repeat lawbreakers. These orders would prohibit use of a park, or of a list of at-risk parks, by certain individuals.

5

Child Beggars and Ragpickers

It is now the 21st century. In the 20th century we were unable to end poverty and its most visible phenomena, homelessness. We were unable to house, feed and adequately clothe all of our people. Today many of our children roam the streets beaten and bruised. There is a sense of deep despair amongst the homeless and those who have worked in the trenches trying tofind solutions while the nation continues to spend exorbitant amounts of resources caring for the displaced in Asia, Europe and Africa. At home the refrigirators are empty,in places there is no running water, homeless people are dying in the streets of all our cities and our children are killing each other.

In the absence of a consistent, comprehensive, flexible and compassionate national policy addressing the challenging, complicated, and multi-layered needs of the homeless — especially the needs of people who end up on the streets with severe disabilities and are panhandling for survival has been an unsurrmountable challenge.

In India, where the presence of beggars is part of life and the response to a beggar is straightforward: you give, you don't give, you shoo the person away, you ask that they watch or wash your car — there is contact and exchange of some kind. In the U.S. the human responses to the presence of *poverty in your face* are somewhat more complex. The widely varying responses are politically motivated, law enforcement-based, spiritual, compassionate, or fascistic - is that thing under the blanket an eyesore, a human being,expendable, or maybe invisible? Each person, depending on class,culture, history, race, education, and political affiliation, has a different response, and this might be the root cause of our quandry. We cannot find consensus as to how to end poverty and homelessness and respond to its most visible prodigy, the panhandler.

People who beg for survival or to feed their addictions or supplement their mediocre wages are seen as the failures of this great country., lets write them violations until misdeameanors become felonies and put them in jail where we seem to be warehousing everyone who seems like a threat to this great society. Whether to criminalise them or to allow them the right to beg, sleep, lie, or sit in our streets has been at the heart of calm and heated debates in the history of the United States, going back to when Europeans began settling in US. The presence of beggars in the street of U.S. cities is as old as the United States of America itself.

For a moment, let us suspend the 20th century and look at the next, knowing that we will have the resources needed to address any issue, however entrenched, with the great wealth that has been created in recent years. Depending on our spiritual, intellectual, political, and economic values, we will push for different responses in public policy as well as different community responses. We could either go in the direction of higher levels of criminalisation or treat the presence of homeless people, including panhandlers, as a public health and housing issue. Knowing that we will see more people begging as the gap between the rich and the poor increases in the next 10 years, now would be the time, with the coming of the first election of the new millinium, to engage the candidates on this particular issue.

Street Children

Street children are the casualties of economic growth, war, poverty, loss of traditional values, domestic violence, physical and mental abuse. Every street child has a reason for being on the streets. While some children are lured by the promise of excitement and freedom, the majority are pushed onto the street by desperation and a realisation that they have nowhere else to go. In many countries, street children are named after their main survival activities. For example, vendors, street gangs, juvenile prostitutes. What is obvious is that street children are poverty-stricken and their needs and problems are a result of wanting to meet basic needs for survival. Street children go through the struggle of providing themselves with basic things such as food, shelter, health and clothing. Providing targeted interventions that meet the needs of street children requires an understanding of who they are, what they need, what they do and how they can be identified.

A street child may be:

— a 'child of the streets', having no home but the streets. The family may have abandoned him or her or may have no family members left alive. Such a child has to struggle for survival and might move from friend to friend, or live in shelters such as abandoned buildings.

— a child 'on the street', visiting his or her family regularly. The child might even return every night to sleep at home, but spends most days and some nights on the street because of poverty, overcrowding, sexual or physical abuse at home.

— a part of a street family. Some children live on the sidewalks or city squares with the rest of their families. Families displaced due to poverty, natural disasters, or wars may be forced to live on the streets. They move their possessions from place to place when necessary. Often the children in these 'street families' work on the streets with other members of their families.

— in institutionalized care, having come from a situation of homelessness and at risk of returning to a homeless existence.

Typical Age and Gender of a Street Child

The typical age of a street child varies from place to place. In developing countries children as young as eight live completely on their own. In developed countries, street children are usually over the age of twelve. The proportion of girls among street children is reported to be less than 30% in developing countries and about 50% in many developed countries. There are a number of reasons why there are fewer street girls:

— Fewer girls may be abandoned by their families. Girls are often socialized to be submissive and caring and therefore they tend to have fewer behavioural problems as compared to boys. Since girls have fewer behavioural problems, they have less conflict with their families and do not need to leave their home. Families might get rid of girls by other means.

— The authorities or individual members of the community may pick up girls on the street more quickly.

— Street girls may be less 'visible' to researchers or educators. Some street girls disguise themselves as boys to protect themselves from harassment by the police, welfare workers, employers and other street children and others may only appear on the streets at night.

Girls on the street have more difficulties and are often overlooked by street educators. Street girls are looked down upon in many societies and are easily exploited. They usually have less economic opportunities than boys and are given less money than boys for similar activities. Educational opportunities are denied to them and street educators usually engage street boys in various activities while paying little attention to girls. It is important to seek and work to improve the situation of street girls because by doing so, the educator would be:

— Ensuring that young girls and boys have equal opportunities.

— Boosting their low self-esteem. They may then participate in income generating activities and thus break the pattern of vulnerability.

— Ensuring that street girls have improved nutritional status.

— Helping minimize the possibility of early unwanted and high-risk pregnancies by providing them with information about sexual and reproductive health.

— Ensuring the return in investment into future generations, as young women with some education tend to ensure that their own children are educated.

Reasons why Street Children Live on Street

The reasons why street children live on the street vary. However, there is one explanation that holds true for both developed and developing countries - poverty. Most street children go onto the street to look for a better way of life. The following are some of the common reasons:

— *To earn money for themselves and support their families.* Street children work on the streets to earn money for themselves. Some children need to work to support their families. Some children may have been denied a chance to go to school or have dropped out of school and have nothing to do. They can earn money by begging, carrying or bearing, car washing, drug trafficking, juggling, performing music, running errands, scavenging, sex work, shoe shining or vending.

— *To find shelter.* In overcrowded households, children may decide to leave home to make room for younger siblings and elderly family members. Others are on the streets because they do not have an alternative. They may have become separated from their families during civil unrest or their parents/ caretakers may have died from illnesses such as AIDS or killed during armed conflict. Other children may have nowhere else to go when they are released from institutions such as a jail or a detention centre.

— *To escape from family problems including rejection.* Many children feel that living on the streets is better than coping with problems in their homes. These problems can include conflicts with parents, physical or sexual abuse or neglect. Some children are forced to leave home by their families because the family does not approve of a child's behaviour or its consequences, e.g. pregnancy, homosexuality or substance use.

— *To escape from work demands in the home.* In many cultures, children are expected to participate in routine family tasks. At times the demands on children may be more than they can take. This leads to the child feeling that he or she is a slave or a servant. Such children leave home in search of freedom from adult demands.

— *To escape from a children's institution.* Street children may feel that children's homes are 'like prisons'. They cannot adjust to rules after experiencing the freedom of the streets. At times the personnel in these institutions may abuse children.

Problems of Street Children

Street children have a greater burden than other poor children who are supervised by adults. Their problems could be grouped into three classes: social, physical, and psychological.

Social problems

— *Poverty and illiteracy.* They lack basic resources to sustain a healthy living. They usually have no financial means to buy decent clothing (which may be necessary in cold places), and no money to buy food, which is crucial for their development. Because of the costs of services most street children cannot afford to go to school. Even where schools are free, many children cannot afford to buy uniforms, shoes and books. Street children live in places where they are not adequately protected from the environment. They rarely have access to facilities that they need for hygiene and sanitation, such as toilets and clean and safe water supply. They are therefore more vulnerable to health problems resulting from poor sanitation.

— *Discrimination and lack of accessible resources.* When the community makes plans, it does not take into consideration the street childrens' plight. Street children tend to be excluded from participating in most of the activities and facilities of other children. This is one reason why street children often do not have access to medical, educational, recreational and vocational resources. They face problems such as lack of vaccinations; poor health, illiteracy and they cannot acquire skills needed for finding jobs.

— *Violent Environment*. The street is an unprotected environment and street children are exploited frequently. In some places, street children may even face the possibility of physical injuries or death from violence. Common sources of violence are: the police, gangs, drug syndicates, those who operate commercial sex businesses, death squads, other street children, families and sexual partners.

— *Stigmatization*. Society usually perceives street children as difficult children who are out there to cause trouble. In general, the public thinks that street children are uncontrollable and violent, have substance use problems, have no morals, have lost all the ability to feel emotions such as love and that they turn into terrorists and revolutionaries. They tend to be unsympathetic to the street childrens' plight. This negative attitude may be a result of the society's inability to care for its people.

Physical problems

— *Lack of adequate nutrition*. Even though some street children can usually get enough to eat, they do not have nutritious diets. This leads to malnutrition, anaemia and vitamin deficiencies.

— *Injuries*. Injuries may be caused intentionally (including injuring self while intoxicated or when depressed) and unintentionally, e.g. due to use of tools which have been designed for adults. The rate of injuries is usually higher for male than for female street children.

— *Sexual and reproductive health problems*. Sexual and reproductive health problems affect both girls and boys. However, street girls are more vulnerable to physical and sexual abuse and exploitation. Common sexual and reproductive health problems include sexually transmitted diseases, HIV/AIDS, unwanted pregnancies and unsafe abortions. Pregnant street girls do not receive adequate antenatal care.

— *Common diseases.* Street children experience many common diseases such as tuberculosis, skin diseases, dental problems and parasitic diseases which can be prevented easily if these children have enough resources and their basic needs are met.

Psychological/mental problems

— *A Stressful Past.* Many situations and events that pushed these children onto the street in the first place (like natural disasters, man-made disasters, exploitation and conflicts) may have a lasting impact on their well being. For example, the family conflict that pushed the child onto the streets continues to deprive the child of emotional and material support for years afterwards. When the child has his or her own baby, neither the new parent nor the baby will have the benefit of the previous generation's support.

— *A Transitory Lifestyle.* Street children in some large cities move frequently from district to district or between cities. Sometimes they do this by choice, but at other times they are forced to move to hide from the police, welfare authorities, gangs, and drug syndicates. This type of lifestyle leads to problems of social isolation and loneliness and difficulties in developing emotional attachments to special individuals.

— *Mental Health.* The stresses that street children experience make them vulnerable to emotional problems, psychiatric disorders and learning difficulties. They do not receive adequate care for these conditions.

— *Substance use.* Many street children are involved in harmful use of psychoactive substances. This can lead to overdose, increase the chance of accidents, violence, unwanted pregnancy and unprotected sex. Over time, the continued use of substances can lead to complications such as brain and liver damage.

Survival for Street Children

Survival for street children means obtaining food, clothing and shelter, and protecting themselves against violence and other forms of abuse. It depends on:

— *Personal strengths*: The child's resourcefulness (the ability to solve problems quickly and efficiently with available resources), and resilience (the ability to recover from shock, depression, and other difficult circumstances) determine his/ her survival. Resourcefulness and resilience would depend upon the child's creativity, hard work, intelligence and concern for one another.

— *The peer group*: Peers are individuals who share common interests and needs. Peer groups tend to be homogeneous in age and gender. The peer group has a strong influence on street children because of the child's need for acceptance, belonging and protection. The group often determines the process of change, socialization and development among street children by providing emotional and material support.

Street children often help in one another's survival. They often join together to form emotional and material support networks. The networks can range from a simple circle of friends to an organized, business network. Experienced street children teach new comers how to survive. Members of the group share food, clothing, shelter, information and psychoactive substances.

— *Chance factors:* An important thing that determines the mode of survival is the people whom the child meets on the first day away from home, whether it is a group of car washers or drug traffickers. Being new to the situation he or she does not know that there are other ways of surviving on the street.

— *Exploiters:* Street children may have to do many unhealthy or dangerous things to survive. Other street children, the police, and the adults who run the sex and drug trades may easily victimize them.

— *Other support mechanisms among street children:* These mechanisms could be related to trade or activities in the streets and tend to be hierarchical. For example, there may be a leader and a spokesperson. The roles of group members can vary depending on their strengths and weaknesses. The members tend to protect each other in the face of gang wars, police arrests or other risky situations.

Problems of Child Ragpickers

According to UNICEF, ragpicking is one of the worst forms of child labour, and falls under the street children category. The concept of street children and the definition of the term *ragpickers* appear to have undergone modifications over time. Initially, ragpickers were considered those children who literally work and live in the street, known as *children on the street.* Today, the denotation of ragpickers has been extended to include those working in the street but living with their families in homes, slums, squats, etc., known as *children of the street.* This study includes both cases, whether they belong to the "of the street" or "on the street" category. Ragpickers, also known as 'garbage pickers,' live on the street, in slums or shanty areas, and he/she makes a living from sorting, collecting, and selling waste metal, rags, containers to the local junkyards or garbage collection centres. Past studies indicate that, while none of the ragpickers were found to be malnourished, they had very poor health due to the consumption of unhygienic food and to working in an unhealthy, polluted environment. They are particularly vulnerable during the rainy season, when most of them suffer from diarrhoea and scabies, and in winter when they suffer from colds. The nature of the ragpickers' work, collecting rags from the garbage dumps and waste bins, is of course hazardous. They are highly exposed to tetanus and other infections caused by cuts from sharp metal pieces, broken glass, and other materials. The risk of falling ill is very high since they operate in unhygienic, polluted areas, and consume dirty or unhealthy food and water.

Besides the physical exertion and risks associated with the collection of rags, which they usually perform from early morning to late evening, such activities do not allow time conducive to recreational activities and/or proper psychological and physical development. These children are generally deprived of love and education, considered two essential elements in the development of children, and are at high risk of being exploited by others, especially people running junkyards and adult bandits that exploit and/or abuse them criminally or sexually. Based on the assessment of previous studies on the situation of street children and ragpicking, ragpickers can clearly be identified as being subject to one of the worst forms of child labour. The following study therefore intends to explore the situation more comprehensively to fully describe the nature and extent of the issue.

Child ragpicking differs from other forms of child labour in that it belongs to the street children category. Although in some cases the term 'street children' may not be considered appropriate to describe them, ragpickers do work on the streets, and many of them even live on the streets. Still, data shows that a large number of ragpickers live with their families, either in their own homes or in rented houses, or in slum areas.

Child ragpickers can be grouped into two categrory:

(i) child ragpickers "of the street"

(ii) child ragpickers "on the street."

These two categories are defined as follows: Children *of the street* refers to children who live in the street and children *on the street* refers to children who only use the street as their working place or social hangout but live with their families.

Almost a third, and by far the largest portion, of the child ragpickers live in rented houses, while a significant portion of them live in junkyards or in the streets. Almost all girl ragpickers come under the "on the street" category, living mostly in rented houses or slums. Comparatively, the majority of boys are "of the street," living in NGOs or in the streets.

The history of ragpickers is closely linked to the history of street children. Onta describes how street children have been universalised as a new category in the last decade, although, she argues their history begins with the history of the beggars.

Beggary is perceived as a morally wrong activity and beggars are believed to be cheaters who take from the society without contributing in return. As a result, society scorns beggars, and consequently, beggars have had to turn to other options for survival. As the market of recyclable materials has increased, a number of children involved in begging turned to ragpicking.

The term ragpickers is now more specifically applied to those persons who collect rags or recyclable materials that can be sold for money. These materials, which are usually gathered at dumpsites, riverbanks, street corners or in residential areas, are mainly plastics, bottles, cardboard papers, tin, aluminium, iron, brass, and copper. Most ragpickers collect plastics as well as tin or aluminium products, while paper goods rank low on the list. Under the "other" category, iron is the most common material collected because it can be found easily, while other valuable materials like brass and copper are harder to find.

The price ragpickers get for their goods varies according to the quality of the materials. Tins, bottles, and papers are not worth much, so they prefer not to collect these materials. However, higher-price materials such as copper, brass, and aluminium are hard to find, and may be assumed to be the product of theft. Thus, plastics and polythene are the easier and most commonly collected materials.

The type of materials gathered also depends on the amount of experience of the ragpicker. Newcomers prefer to pick easy-to-find materials such as plastics and bottles, while older ones tend to be more selective and prefer to collect relatively more valuable goods such as metals and gudiyas over tins, bottles, or papers.

All-season ragpickers rely only on ragpicking for their survival. However, ragpicking is a seasonal occupation, winters being more productive and summers more slack. In the rainy season, materials are wet and dirty and collecting them is very difficult because of the rain and mud. The materials they do collect often end up being sold at a lower price at the junkyards because of the state they are in. This means ragpickers may go hungry more frequently during this season. Some of them may borrow money from the junkyards to survive, which puts them in a situation of debt bondage, as they have to work for the junkyard owner until the loan is paid back. Others resort to begging or criminal activities to make up for the lack of revenue during that season. A small portion of the ragpickers work seasonally. They live at home and work as ragpickers in the winter while they do other work in the summer. A few part-time ragpickers attend school and work as ragpickers during vacations.

Working long hours is vital for ragpickers. Their earnings are directly related to the amount of items collected, which depends on the number of hours they work. On average, as stated previously, ragpickers work about six hours per day although children from the younger age group tend to work slightly less than those aged 10 years and above.

More particularly, the large majority of ragpickers work five to eight hours, though almost a third of them work less than five hours per day. Very few of the children spend more than eight hours per day working, and the number of hours worked is comparable among boys and girls in the different age groups.

The question naturally arises as to what the children do with their earnings. The simple answer is they spend all the money on food and fun, especially children of the street, who live day-to-day and are not concerned with future needs. This makes them more vulnerable in days where earnings are low because they fail to collect rags or they fall sick. However, most of them have specific reasons for wanting to spend all their earnings in a day, namely:

i) they do not have access to safe shelter where they can put away their money

ii) they cannot open bank accounts because they do not have citizenship certificates

iii) they may be exposed to looting from adults (junkies or street people) if they keep the money with them

iv) when they have money leftover, they tend to share it with others in the group who have no money for food.

According to key informants and focus group discussions, several children who live with their family support them with their earnings. However, most ragpickers have little money to share, and do not send it to their families.

There are genuine reasons why ragpicking is considered one of the worst forms of child labour. The risks related to the children's health and physical development, as well as the hindrance this work places on their education and psychological development, make ragpicking a particularly adverse occupation for children. This section considers the issues related to health and hunger, use of substances, involvement in crime, and fears.

Staying hungry is common among child ragpickers for various reasons. The children of the street, who have no home or guardians taking care of them, usually spend all their earnings in a day, and therefore have no means of survival for days where earnings are insufficient. As for the ragpickers in the "on the street" category, most come from families who are living in precarious economic conditions, and where overall earnings may be insufficient to feed the family.

Falling sick is another common phenomenon among child ragpickers. Most are not aware of the health risks associated with the nature of their work, and are generally uneducated about health. In addition to the physical hazards of ragpicking, such as wounds and cuts inflicted by glass or metal pieces, ragpickers are subject to illness due to cold, inappropriate nourishment and exposure to contaminants or bacteria. Apart from food, a majority of the children their money on smoking, alcohol, and drugs. Smoking is quite common among child ragpickers. Furthermore, there is a direct relationship between the age group and the prevalence of smoking: the average number of smokers more than doubles between the 5-9 and the 10-14 age groups, and increases another 33 percent in the 15-17 age group. Clearly, age and sex are direct factors in the incidence of smoking among ragpickers. Similarly, age is a factor in alcohol intake.

As street children, ragpickers are potentially highly vulnerable to drugs, since they are more likely to be exposed to drug addicts and suppliers. In fact, the higher instances of drug usage among ragpickers occurred in Once again, the correlation between age and usage can be clearly observed when it comes to drugs. While none of the younger ragpickers use drugs, six percent of boys in the middle age group confessed to doing so, and the incidence more than doubled for the older children.

Ragpickers' Background

Majority of child ragpickers come from severely deprived families who have no home, are landless or have marginal land. They generally originate from rural areas with road access to urban centres. Most belong to the Dalits and hill ethnic groups who are overall more affected by poverty and illiteracy. Their illiterate guardians, involved in low paid manual labour, usually cannot afford to send them to school, and are less likely to be aware of their children's rights or be concerned with their development.

Family size and structure may also be factors in driving children to leave home, though they may not be primary factors. In fact, it seems that poverty and the prospect of obtaining work in urban centres, where new industries have been introduced, are the main elements that may motivate children to migrate to cities in search of a better lifestyle.

Majority of child ragpickers are migrants. Half of them moved with guardians, while the other half are runaways. Those who migrate with guardians were usually involved in different types of work before they ended up on the street. As a matter of fact, focus group discussions showed that many ragpickers had worked in hotel/restaurants, manufacturing, or as domestic servants. The difficult work and inappropriate wages often compel them to go to the street in search of an "easier" occupation.

Most of the ragpickers fall into one of four categories:

a. those who have left home and ended up on the street,

b. those who came to the city for another job and later moved on to ragpicking,

c. those who were taken to the city and abandoned, and

d. those who live at home but come to the street daily to pick rags.

The reasons for them to leave home and come to the street can be further subdivided into various social or personal situations. The highest percentage of ragpickers reported that they left home due to family problems, stepparent or parental abuse. Parents' migration and poverty are also among the main factors, though peer influence and the attraction of city life are not negligible.The process by which these children become ragpickers also varies, but half of them report having been initiated into this occupation by friends.

Domain of Ragpickers

There are six basic social sectors related to ragpickers. They consist of other street children, local NGOs working for child rights and development, junkyard owners who buy materials from ragpickers, the police, civil society, and people involved in criminal activities with whom the ragpickers may interact.

Ragpickers and other Street Children

Ragpickers only represent a portion of the category of street children. Other street children do other types of work such as street vending, manual labour, workshop work, hotel/restaurant service, etc. Ragpickers often interact with these other children, who may have more street experience than them or could provide them with alternative jobs. Another note should be made here about the relationship ragpickers have with other ragpickers within their groups. The group environment is usually quite positive, and does not display any discrimination. Children from the same group share their earnings or food with each other.

NGOs provide humanitarian help and socialisation support to enhance the rights of street children and other children at risk. They also work for the reintegration of children into their families. Child ragpickers often consider NGO personnel as guardians and NGO locales as home. Many sleep in the NGO common rooms after a day's work. They go there for treatment when they get hurt and sick or simply to hang out when they have had a good day. Many children have benefited from NGO services such as literacy and education, awareness and even guardianship.

Ragpickers and the Junkyard Owners

A considerable portion of child ragpickers report living in junkyard shops at night. In addition to shelter, junkyard owners also often provide loans to children when they need money for food, which they have to pay back by collecting rags for them, as a type of debt-bondage. In fact, the relationship junkyard owners have with ragpickers can often be described as being exploitative. Apart from cheating the children when weighing materials and exploiting them by demanding payment for shelter or food, some junkyard owners also indirectly encourage children to steal materials like metal goods for their benefit.

Ragpickers and Civil Society

The relationship of ragpickers with civil society is very antagonistic. Most people do not trust them and do not even want them in their neighbourhood, feeling they represent the worst characters of society. By contrast, however, most ragpickers have a very lively relationship with marginalised families living in slum communities. They help each other and understand each other's situation, though at times they may encounter problems with local slum dwellers if they are suspected of stealing. As for their impression of society, ragpickers say they would prefer not to re-enter it, as they enjoy the freedom, albeit precarious, of their lifestyle, and regard social life as constrained.

Ragpickers and the Police

The relationship of ragpickers with the police is harsh. As an unwritten rule, police consider ragpickers to be thieves and pick-pockets, and automatically suspect them of crimes. Very few of the children interviewed had not been in police custody. According to them, the police sometimes rob their money, or ask for illegal levy against their freedom. They may even encourage the children to go pick-pocketing and to share the earnings with them. Most children have a strong fear of the police and see them as a danger to them rather than a protector. There is an interesting triangular relationship between ragpickers, junkyard owners and local police. Each group is very knowledgeable about the others, but maintains strongly suspicious and highly negative relations with them.

Ragpickers and Criminals

People involved in illegal activities such as criminals, pick-pockets, drug dealers, and hoodlums, exploit child ragpickers in different ways. Many children are being used as drug peddlers and some as middlemen for commercial sex. Adult hoodlums sometimes force them to steal or pick-pocket. Some street 'dadas' often visit the junkyards to raise 'fees' from ragpickers, and beat them if they do not comply. In addition, several child ragpickers have been sexually exploited and abused by street bandits and other criminals.

Consequences of Ragpicking

Though ragpicking could arguably be regarded as one of the consequences of a dysfunctional society, resulting from a disorganised as well as failed development process, one must also consider the negative impact that the prevalence of ragpicking has on society. The phenomenon of ragpicking has many consequences, both on society and on the children themselves.

On Society

Due to high population growth and rampant poverty throughout the country, the prevalence of under- and unemployment has also been increasing. In many cases, this has led to family disintegration, which may have caused children to leave home to tend to their own survival. This growing tendency for children to end up on the street in urban areas represents a great threat to the development of society.

Though they may be smart enough to survive on the streets, ragpickers are exposed to or are involved in criminal activities, as they are easy targets of exploitation by criminal gangs. Many child ragpickers are actually involved in illicit activities related to alcohol, drugs, and sexual activities. Furthermore, they are more inclined to become victims of drug addiction or prostitution as they work in close proximity with people of this milieu. In the long term, this may result in the spreading of HIV/AIDS, especially in urban centres.

On Themselves

Compared to school-going children, ragpickers have a completely different perspective on life, and a higher sense of survival, co-operation and resourcefulness. Their lifestyle on the street has made them clever in handling conflicts and other difficult situations, and being part of a group has given them a sense of collectivism and responsibility towards others. Yet, most of the consequences of ragpicking on these children's lives are detrimental to the development of their future. Since they have no education or skills their prospect of finding jobs is very low. Most of them are physically weak because of their exposure to diseases and unhealthy living conditions. Child ragpickers do not like restrictions and value the freedom they find in the street because most have experienced violence, abuse or maltreatment. Yet, this often leads to their indulging in delinquent behaviour because they lack a sense of social values or guilt.

Use of Psychoactive Substances by Street Children

Studies have found that between 25% and 90% of street children use psychoactive substances of some kind. The word 'substance' describes any psychoactive material which when consumed affects the way people feel, think, see, taste, smell, hear or behave. A psychoactive substance can be a medicine or an industrial product, such as glue. Some substances are legal such as approved medicines, alcohol and cigarettes, and others are illegal, such as heroin and cannabis. Each country has its own laws about substances. The percentage of substance users among street children varies greatly depending on the region, gender and age. To understand substance use a framework called the Modified Social Stress Model is used. The model explains the complex relationship between factors that affect the onset and continuation of substance use. The model suggests that positive and negative aspects of six vulnerability/protective factors affect the risk of substance use. These are stress, normalization of behaviour and situations (acceptance) of substance use in the community, effects of behaviour and situations, attachments, skills and resources.

Types of Psychoactive Substances

The types of psychoactive substances street children

use can be many and varied and it may be difficult to determine what substances they are using. Substances which are sold on the market can be identified by their generic name. This is the standard name used through out the world. However some substances are marketed under various names known as trade names and others have 'street names'. For example, diazepan is the generic name while valium is a trade name. Diacetlymorphine is a generic name for heroin and 'brown sugar' or 'smack' are some of the names it is called by on the streets. It is important for the street educator to know the general categories of substances and the effects that substances can have on a street child. The following examples of substances in their general categories may not be the ones used generally, they are merely illustrative.

Alcohol. Alcohol is a depressant which inhibits or decreases some aspects of central nervous system activity. Substances containing alcohol include the following: wine, beer, spirits, home-brew, some medicinal tonics and syrups, some toiletries and industrial products.

Nicotine. Nicotine is a stimulant; that is any substance which activates, enhances or increases central nervous system activity. Nicotine is found in the following substances:

— cigarettes, cigars, pipe tobacco, chewed

— tobacco, snuff, nicotine gum, spray, skin

— patches.

Opioids. Substances in this group may act as analgesics (they relieve physical pain) and depressants. They may be synthetic or made from opium poppies (opiates). The following substances are examples of opioids:

— *opiates*: codeine (such as in some cough mixtures), heroin, morphine, opium

— *synthetic opioids*: buprenorphine hydrochloride (Temgesic), methadone (Physeptone), pethidine.

Hallucinogens. Hallucinogenic substances can alter a person's mood, the way the person perceives his or her surroundings and the way the person experiences his or her own body. There are many different types of hallucinogens, some of which are chemically produced and others which are naturally occurring.

— *LSD (Lysergic Acid Diethylamide):* in its pure state LSD is a white, odourless powder. It is usually mixed with a lot of other ingredients. It is often put into capsules, liquids, tablets, and as small spots on absorbent paper.

— *mescaline*: made from the pulp of the peyote cactus.

— *psilocybin mushrooms*: Psilocybin is the hallucinogen found in some mushrooms. It is usually made available as dried mushrooms.

— *PCP (phencyclidine):* this substance was used as an animal tranquilliser.

Cannabis. The cannabis plant grows in many parts of the world. Preparations containing different concentrations of cannabis are consumed.

— *marijuana*: the leaves and flowers of the marijuana or hemp plant.

— *hashish (oil and resin):* these forms of cannabis are made from the resin of the flowering heads of the plant tablets containing THC (Tetrahydrocannabinol, the main active ingredient in cannabis)

Hypnosedatives. The drugs in this group are made synthetically and do not occur naturally. There are a large number of different drugs in this group. All are slightly different, but all subdue the body's nervous system.

— *benzodiazepines*: e.g. alprazolam (Xanax), diazepam (Valium), flunitrazipam (Rohypnol), oxazepam (Serepax), temazepam (Normison)

— *barbiturates*: pentobarbital.

Other sedatives, such as chloral hydrate and methaqualone (Mandrax)

Stimulants. This group of substances activate, enhance or increase central nervous system activity.

— *caffeine*: caffeine has been around for thousands of years. It is found in different amounts in coffee, tea, cocoa, and chocolate. It is also in some soft drinks and in some medicines.

— *coca products*: coca leaves, coca paste.

— *cocaine*: cocaine is produced from coca leaves.

— *amphetamines*: amphetamines are found in prescription drugs and included in some diet pills, as well as in various forms on the street. On the streets in the Philippines they are called *shabu*, a Japanese word for fast/quick, and in Australia *speed* or *goey*.

— *MDMA (Ecstasy):* this substance is a type of amphetamine which has both stimulant and hallucinogenic effects. It can be in the form of a tablet, capsule, or oil which is usually mixed with other substances.

— *khat:* the leaves and buds of a plant found in East Africa, which are chewed or brewed as a drink.

Inhalants. Inhalants include a wide range of easily available products including aerosols, volatile solvents and gases. The following substances can all be inhaled: aerosol sprays, butane gas, petrol, glue, paint thinners, solvents, amyl nitrite.

Other psychoactive substances. Some substances do not neatly belong in any of the categories above.

— *kava:* a drink made from the roots of a shrub, which is used in the South Pacific for social and ceremonial purposes.

— *betel nut:* this substance is the seed of an Asian palm tree.

Street children claim that inhaling through a wet carbon paper, inhaling vapour produced by a mixture of fibre matting and boiling toothpaste, inhaling fumes from burning insects, and inhalation of raw sewerage can produce desired effects. Efforts should be made to learn about the types of substances that are being used by the street children locally.

Methods of using substances

Substances can be used in many different ways. They may be:

— Chewed, swallowed or dissolved slowly in the mouth.

— Placed on a mucous membrane (such as inside the anus or vagina, or nose, or under the eyelid).

— Rubbed into the skin.

— Injected under the skin or into a vein or muscle with a needle.

— Smoked or inhaled through the mouth or nose, or inhaled by placing a bag over the head known as bagging.

The way the substance is taken also influences how fast the substance reaches the brain or other organs. Injecting a substance is especially dangerous because of the risks of infection that are carried through the blood. In particular, sharing needles or other injecting equipment and the way the substance is prepared can spread HIV (the virus that causes AIDS), hepatitis B and C, and other infections because of contamination with infected blood.

Effects of substances on the street child

Any substance can be harmful to a human body if taken in large enough doses, too frequently or in an impure form. The health effects of substances can occur immediately or in the long-term. The effects are influenced by the dose, the method of administration as well as whether the substance is used with another drug. The long-term effects often take a long time to appear and are usually due to damage of body organs. Be aware that some signs attributed to substance use may be due to other conditions, e.g. poor concentration can be a sign of glue sniffing, but it could also be caused by stress or worry about a life event, about pregnancy, or as a result of head injury. Effects of individual substances are presented below:

Alcohol. The effects of alcohol will vary from person to person. Children, young people and women are usually more affected by alcohol than adult men because they tend to have lower body weights, smaller livers, and a higher proportion of fat to muscle. This leads to faster absorption of alcohol in the body.

— *Immediate effects:* These include drowsiness, uninhibited actions, loss of physical coordination, unclear vision, slurred speech, making poor decisions or impairment of memory. Excessive drinking over a short period of time can cause headache, nausea, vomiting, coma and death.

— *Long-term effects*: Drinking large amounts of alcohol regularly over a long period of time can cause loss of appetite, vitamin deficiency, skin problems, depression, loss of sexual drive, liver damage, heart ailments, nerve and brain damage or loss of memory.

Associated health risks: These occur when alcohol is taken with other substances or drugs. Taking alcohol with drugs that depress the body's systems, such as hypnosedatives or cannabis, can increase loss of judgement and loss of physical coordination. Combination with hypnosedatives can lead to coma, respiratory depression (person stops breathing) and death.

Nicotine. Nicotine, the active substance found in tobacco is addictive in nature. Once a street child starts using tobacco, they are likely to continue using it for a long time.

— *Immediate effects*: A person feels alert immediately after using tobacco, and then feels more relaxed a few minutes later. There is also an increase in pulse rate, a temporary rise in blood pressure, dizziness, nausea and reduced appetite.

— *Long-term effects*: These effects may be due to the nicotine or the form in which it is taken. Heart and lung disease, blockage of arteries, high blood pressure, breathing difficulty, cancer of the lung and cancers of the mouth may occur.

Opioids. Substances in this group may act as pain killers and/or depressants. Some are used as medicines while others are illegal. Opium, morphine, codeine (constituent of some cough mixtures) and heroin are derived from opium poppies directly or through chemical processing (opiates), while buprenorphine (Temgesic), methadone (Physeptone) and pethidine are made synthetically (opioids).

— *Immediate effects:* Opioids often produce a detached and dreamy feeling, sleepiness, reduction in the size of the pupil of the eye, nausea, vomiting and constipation. Overdose leads to unconsciousness, respiratory depression (failure to breathe) and death.

— *Long-term effects:* The main danger is the development of dependence and the chance of overdose that can cause death. Tolerance and dependence can develop quickly.

Associated health risks: Opioids may be injected into the body. Injecting the substances with a needle that is not sterile or is shared between users can transmit blood borne infections including HIV, hepatitis B and C, and may result in septicemia (infection in blood).

Hallucinogens. These substances can alter a person's mood, the way the person perceives his or her surroundings and experiences his or her own body. A user may also hallucinate.

— *Immediate effects*: The immediate effects are those of change in perception and in the awareness of things happening inside and outside one's body. Things may look, smell, sound, taste, or feel different e.g. seeing colours, lights, pictures. 'Bad trips' may also occur. The term refers to unpleasant and disturbing feelings e.g. panic, fear, anxiety, confusion and alteration in the sense of reality. The nature of the experience is partly determined by the setting in which the hallucinogens are taken.

— *Long-term effects:* Many users report getting the experiences first obtained under the influence of substance, days or even months after they have stopped taking the substances. These experiences are called 'flash backs'. Regular use of hallucinogens can decrease a user's memory and concentration and can result in depression and other mental health problems. PCP is particularly likely to cause lasting mental health problems.

Cannabis. Cannabis may make a user euphoric at first, and then relaxed and calm. Large doses can change perceptions in ways similar to that seen with hallucinogens.

— *Immediate effects:* feelings of well being, relaxation, loss of inhibitions, loss of motor coordination and loss of concentration. There may be increased pulse and heart rate, redness of the eyes, and increased appetite. Large quantities can cause panic, hallucinations, restlessness and confusion.

— *Long-term effects:* there is no evidence that using cannabis occasionally in small quantities causes any significant long lasting health problems. Regular use over a long time increases chances of dependency, impairment of memory and concentration and may worsen mental problems such as schizophrenia.

Hypnosedatives. These substances are depressants. They make the nervous system less active. Health workers often prescribe them for treating sleep difficulty and anxiety because of their calming properties. There are a large number of different drugs in this group.

— *Immediate effects:* all substances in this group cause effects similar to alcohol. They slow down a person's thinking and movements and decrease the ability to concentrate. They cause 'hangovers', or problems such as slurred speech, sleepiness and lack of coordination after the intoxication has worn off. Low doses reduce feelings of anxiety while higher doses cause sleep or unconsciousness. Alcohol increases their effect. Repeated doses cause other associated health risks because the substance is not broken down quickly.

— *Long-term effects:* regular use of these substances can lead to dependence, and continued heavy use can result in problems with memory, ability to learn, and problems with coordination. Convulsions and delirium can occur when the substance is withdrawn.

Stimulants. Stimulants enhance or increase central nervous system activity. They are popular because they make people feel energetic, self-confident and they decrease the feeling of hunger. They are often used to reduce weight and help people stay awake for work. If too much of the stimulant is taken, the person may become anxious, irritable, suspicious, panicky, and/or threatening to others.

— *Immediate effects:* caffeine in coffee and teas spreads quickly through the body and makes a person feel awake. Too much of caffeine can cause an increase in heart beat, anxiety and upset stomach. The effects of cocaine and amphetamines are similar except that the effects of cocaine last for less time. These are excitement, decreased need for sleep and food. High doses can cause anxiety, panic, high blood pressure, convulsions and aggression. With crack a person usually experiences a brief intense feeling of intoxication and an exaggerated feeling of confidence. The mood then quickly changes to a low feeling and may prompt the person to repeat the dose. Overdose is commoner with crack than with other forms of cocaine.

— *Long-term effects:* coffee and tea may cause anxiety, depression, stomach upset and difficulty in sleeping. Longterm use of amphetamine and cocaine can cause dependence, inability to sleep, irritability, and mental health problems such as feelings of suspiciousness and hallucinations. Similarly, heavy use of khat can result in dependence and physical and mental problems.

Inhalants. Like alcohol, they make a person uninhibited at first and drowsy later.

— *Immediate effects:* Feelings of happiness, relaxation, sleepiness, poor muscle coordination, slurred speech, irritability and anxiety. Hallucinations and fits can occur with heavy use. The most immediate danger to the user is of 'sudden sniffing death'. Death could also occur as a result of suffocation.

— *Long-term effects:* Regular long-term use may lead to nose bleeds, rashes around the mouth and nose, loss of appetite and lack of motivation. Some of the solvents are toxic to the liver, kidney, heart and brain.

Other psychoactive substances. Some substances do not belong in any of the above mentioned categories. Examples are:

— *Kava:* is used in the South Pacific for social and ceremonial purposes. It causes mild sedation and feeling of well being. Heavy use can cause dependence and medical problems.

— *Betel nut:* is often chewed in parts of Asia and the Pacific. Regular use can cause dependence and diseases of the mouth, including cancer.

In many areas, street children use more than one substance at the same or different times. In developed countries, this often includes using alcohol, nicotine, opioids, stimulants, hypnosedatives, hallucinogens and inhalants. Combined use of substances makes the assessment of substances that the child is using more difficult. In addition, it complicates the process of detoxification or withdrawal. Combination of substances increase the risk of overdose and thus the chances of accidents, death, violence and suicide. There are a number of special considerations the educator need to be aware of with regard to substance use. These include malnutrition, mental health and pregnancy.

— *Malnutrition.* Although alcohol has calories and provides energy it can also prevent the absorption of necessary vitamins and other nutrients. In general, a person taking substances can easily overlook the importance of good nutrition. Street children use substances to relieve hunger and this can lead to malnutrition.

— *Mental health.* Alcohol may increase feelings of sadness and isolation in young people who are already depressed. A serious state of depression can also be a consequence of long-term excessive alcohol use.

— Hallucinogens may cause mental heath problems such as depression, with suicide being a risk. They may also worsen a pre-existing mental disorder such as schizophrenia.

— Young people who use substances such as inhalants may like the experience and get relief from their tension. This limits the development of other more constructive coping strategies: For example the use of hypnosedatives can help street children feel less anxious, but they do not change the cause of the street child's anxiety.

— *Pregnancy*. Regular drinking of even small amounts of alcohol during pregnancy can damage the health of both the mother and the foetus. Heavy drinking can lead to miscarriage or foetal alcohol syndrome (slowed growth and mental disabilities in the baby). Alcohol can be passed to the infant through breast milk.

Smoking during pregnancy can reduce the amount of oxygen available to the unborn and may affect the baby's growth and development before, and after birth. This usually leads to low birth weight in the baby. Similar problems may accompany the use of cannabis during pregnancy.

A mother using opioids, hypnosedatives and stimulants exposes the baby to the substance. If the pregnant or lactating mother stops using these substances suddenly the baby will experience withdrawal. Amphetamines may lead to miscarriage and cocaine can cause developmental delays. LSD can increase the chance of a miscarriage and complications during pregnancy. Babies of mothers who use hallucinogens, may be born with physical deformities.

Even though using psychoactive substances may lead to serious problems, many street children use them either because a particular substance adds something to their lives or it temporarily solves a problem. There is a connection between the problems of life on the street and the effects that substances sometimes produce.

Often the substances do not produce the effect the street child wants and they leave the child with even less emotional, financial and health resources than before. Street children in developing countries who use substances often do not fit the stereotype of an adolescent substance user in the developed world who tends to be unhappy, insensitive and disrespectful. Young substance users on the street are often cheerful, affectionate, and respectful of authority. They do not use substances because they reject mainstream society, but rather because they have lost their place in it.

Patterns of psychoactive substance use

Two important factors that determine patterns of substance use in the community are the price and availability of the substances. Street children almost always choose the least expensive and most readily available ones, e.g. inhalants such as glue or petrol. If they decide to drink alcohol, they tend to pick the cheapest beverage with the highest alcohol content. Patterns of substance use vary greatly among street children and may change over time. Some develop a regular pattern of use while others may be quite haphazard. A street child may change his or her pattern of use over time. Use of substances does not mean that he or she will automatically progress to using other substances or to use more intensively. Included under patterns of substance use are experimental, functional and harmful use, abuse and dependant use.

Intoxication. Intoxication is a temporary state that follows the use of one or more substances resulting in a change in the person's alertness, thinking, perceptions, decision making, judgement, emotions, or behaviour. An intoxicated person is more likely to suffer from burns, suffocation, seizure, poisoning, overdose, sudden death etc. They may also be involved in accidents, violence, unsafe sex and rape. Intoxication is highly dependent on the type and dose of substance and is influenced by an individual's level of tolerance and many other factors. It is not always clear when street children are intoxicated as intoxication with different substances has different signs and symptoms. In general, an intoxicated person will have the following common signs; they may be exceptionally sleepy, have trouble in thinking and speaking and talking to them may be difficult. Their eyes may be dilated, they may giggle or laugh inappropriately their mood may switch quickly between highs and lows and they may become aggressive. Even when it appears that a street child is intoxicated, it should be remembered that some of the signs and symptoms may be caused by other physical or psychological states, such as hunger, sickness and emotional difficulties.

*Harmful use.*Harmful use is a pattern of substance use that results in damage to physical or mental health. Most physical harms experienced by street children following the use of substances occur as a result of intoxication, hence health damage can also occur with experimental and occasional use. Other harms result from the way in which the substance is used. Injecting drugs is particularly dangerous because it can lead to an overdose or it may increase the risk of hepatitis, HIV and other infections from contaminated needles and syringes. Smoking substances can result in disorders of the respiratory system and burns. Some substances such as leaded petrol, benzene and coca paste are particularly toxic and can cause health damage in even small amounts. As most street children have not been using substances for long enough it is unusual to see them with disorders such as alcoholic liver disease or smoking related lung cancer or heart disease which occur late in life.

Dependent use. This is a pattern of substance use in which the user has a strong desire to take the substance and can not control its use. Thus substance use gains priority over other activities for the user. Long-term use increases tolerance as their body adjusts to the substance so that the same amount of substance no longer produces the effects. They may also experience physical withdrawal reactions if he or she goes too long without the substance. Users who are dependent may continue to use substances despite very serious consequences. They may spend more and more of their day involved with substances.

Withdrawal. When a person stops taking a particular substance that he or she has been using regularly, he/she may experience adverse effects known as withdrawal symptoms. Unless young people have been using large amounts of the substance for a long time, they rarely need to be weaned off a substance in a medical setting. They can be assessed and managed in other safe places with their cooperation. The most dangerous withdrawals are from alcohol and hypnosedatives, which may trigger convulsions and delirium. In these situations medically assisted detoxification may be advisable.

Consequences for the individual street child. Using a psychoactive substance can have many different consequences. Some of the consequences are insignificant and some are extremely serious. Psychoactive substances have effects on the body of the user as well as consequences on the life of the user and the whole community.

Physical

— Accidents

— Convulsions and coma
— Infections include HIV (especially injecting drug use)
— Malnutrition
— Damage to body parts eg. liver, lungs, nerves etc.
— Cancer
— Death

Psychological

— Restriction of interests and lifestyle
— Depression
— Memory and concentration problems
— Delirium (confusion and hallucinations)
— Psychosis (fixed false ideas; hallucinations; grossly abnormal behaviour)
— Social
— Rejection by peers, family, employers
— Exploitation and violence (including murder) by drug syndicate
— Inability to work and loss of income

Legal problems due to:

— Behaviour under the influence of substances
— Crimes committed to obtain substances

Consequences for the Community

Everyone, including street children, occasionally has conflicts with family members, friends, strangers, and lovers. Like other young people they also want the excitement of taking a risk from time to time. Substance use can sometimes make these experiences unpleasant or even dangerous. Here are some consequences for the family and community.

— Important responsibilities may be forgotten, and disagree-ments can become emotionally or physically destructive.

— Substance users with little income are constantly faced with the problem of finding money to purchase substances. Some of them may steal or use violence to get the money and others might join illegal businesses or the sex industry to earn enough money.
— Activities such as building a fire can become dangerous if the children involved are under the influence of substances because of the lack of safety already present in the situations where they live.
— The demand for illegal substances has produced wealthy and powerful organizations that manufacture and distribute substances in some parts of the world.

Modified social stress model in substance use

The Modified Social Stress Model is a framework which has been used by the WHO street children project to understand the vulnerability to risk behaviour and situations associated with substance use. This model could also be applied to sexual behaviour. The model has six major components; stress, normalization of behaviour and situations, effect of behaviour and situations, skills, attachments, and resources.

Stress, normalization of behaviour and situations and effect of behaviour and situations (the experience of substance use) are viewed as factors that may increase vulnerability. Skills, resources and attachments are seen as factors that may reduce vulnerability to risky behaviour and situations. However, each of these factors has aspects which can increase vulnerability (risk factors) or decrease it (protective factors).

The model serves as a guide to factors which may contribute to street children engaging in various risk behaviours. The basis of the model is this: if many risk factors are present in a person's life, that person is more likely to begin, intensify, and continue the use of substances, and experience related problems. Conversely, the more protective factors that are present, the less likely the person is to become involved with substances.

Vulnerability can be understood better if both risk and protective factors are considered at the same time. Besides providing a conceptual understanding, the framework is useful for planning interventions to prevent or treat problems such as those related to substance use, sexual and reproductive health including HIV/AIDS/STDs, at both the individual (street child) and the community level.

Each component presented in the model can have positive and negative aspects that function as risk or protective factors.

Stress
Effects of behaviour and situations
Normalization of behaviour and situations
Attachments
Skills
Resources

Risk Behaviour — Protective factors increased
Risk factors increase

Stress. Stress is the way a person feels in response to real or perceived stressors. A stressor may be observable, or it may be less visible to others. The more stress a child is under, the more likely he or she is to use substances. Street children often have extremely stressful lives. To understand just how stressful their lives can be, consider the five types of stress that are described below.

— *Major Life Events.* Dramatic events that have a profound effect on the survivors. They include death of parents, abandonment, serious accidents, natural disasters, demolition of home by authorities, war, physical and sexual assaults, and suicide attempts. Street children may use substances after the event to lessen the pain of the event and to help them adjust to their new situation, which is inevitably worse than before.

— *Enduring Life Strains.* The lives of street children are usually filled with long-term problems that are difficult to solve: poverty, denial of human rights, psychological difficulties, illnesses, and lack of educational and recreational opportunities. Rejection or a sense of rejection by family members, friends, school, health or other services, and society in general can also make the street child feel a sense of loss similar to that experienced when someone close to one dies. Using substances may provide excitement, or help in imagining a better future and offer relief from physical pain. Substances are sometimes used to decrease guilt feelings and pain related to providing sex for money.

— *Everyday problems.* Most of a street child's time is spent working on survival issues; finding food, clothes and shelter, and avoiding violence and the police. They often have ongoing conflicts with other street children, merchants and community members or authorities. This daily struggle is tiring and leaves little time for other things. Substance use offers a quick and easy escape from day-to-day problems.

— *Life transitions.* Transitions in life, such as moving neighbourhoods or cities, changing peer groups, or beginning a romantic relationship, are always stressful because they require people to behave in new ways. People may use substances during the transition to reduce their anxiety. If a street child's new friends use substances, he or she may imitate their behaviour in order to be more easily accepted.

Although stressful, some life transitions may result in a positive situation for street children. A family move may bring the street child who stays with his or her family at night into contact with different people who may have a positive influence.

— *Adolescent developmental changes.* All young people go through physical, psychological, and social changes during their adolescent years. These changes are particularly difficult for street children who are becoming adolescents because they have no one to explain to them about these changes. They may not have had access to adequate adult role models and they may not get the opportunity to gradually assume more adult roles and responsibilities or negotiate such roles with parents and other adults. For example, street children may have to find a new source of income after puberty and may be enticed into commercial sexual activities. It can be confusing and depressing for street adolescents to cope with the immaturity of their bodies, especially while they are dealing with adult responsibilities. Street children want to be accepted by their peers even more than the typical adolescent.

Joining in when their companions use substances or engage in other activities that can harm health are ways to be accepted more easily. Sometimes stressful events and situations may be associated with positive outcomes for street children. The change brought about by the event may ease their situation in some cases, e.g. the marriage of a widowed parent may be stressful, but it may improve the family situation. The rebuilding of a community after a natural disaster may bring new educational resources or work opportunities for street children and their families.

Growth and strength that come with adolescence are highly valued by many boys and girls. They may believe that they will not be abused as much, that the smallest members of their community will admire them, and that they may get better jobs. Stressors may lead to a positive outcome in yet another way. If the child negotiates a difficult situation successfully, it may enhance his or her self-esteem.

Careful assessment of the actual positive or negative results of key life events on individual street children, their families and their communities is necessary to understand the full impact of stressful events and situations at risk of substance use. Although many street children seem to possess remarkable abilities to cope with difficult circumstances, some street children may be particularly vulnerable. Understanding what different street children regard as most stressful for them, and how they are dealing with these stresses, is vital for developing specific ways to help them.

Normalization of behaviour and situations. According to the Modified Social Stress Model, a person is more likely to become involved with substances if using substances is considered normal in the person's environment. Many street children live in places where other street children, the adults in the neighbourhood, and even the entire society accept the use of some substances. This makes it easy for them to use substances as well. Factors that encourage a group or an entire society to accept the use of a particular substance include:

— *Legality and law enforcement.* If a substance is legal, it is much more likely to be accepted or normalized in general society. The use of illegal substances that are tolerated by the authorities could be acceptable to many people, including street children.

— *Availability.* The easier it is to get a substance, the more likely it will be normalized, as with the use of caffeine, alcohol, and tobacco which have become normalized in many countries across the globe. On the other hand, restrictions imposed on the manufacture and sale of psychoactive medicines limit their availability and make it less likely that their use will be normalized. The same principle holds for illegal substances. If they are easy to obtain, they are more likely to be normalized. The use of cannabis, which is widely available in some places, is acceptable to many members of the community even though it is illegal. Coca paste is used by many youths in the Amazon basin where it is produced. Volatile solvents, including petrol and glue, are readily available in almost all areas of the world.

— *Price.* The more affordable a substance is, the more likely it is to become normalized within a group of consumers. Substances that are normalized among some street children are the ones that are the least expensive. Glue, solvents, and petrol are cheap in most areas. Crack cocaine has become one of the favourite substances of street youth in the United States, partly because of its low price.

— *Advertising, sponsorship and promotion.* When substances are promoted in a community, residents are presented with the idea that using substances is normal and even desirable. Many promotional campaigns for tobacco and alcohol are designed specifically to encourage their use by young people. These include advertisements and sponsorship to activities at sporting events with celebrity athletes, youth festivals, and at 'rock' concerts. People involved in the drug trade may promote illegal substances in some communities. Street children are easily influenced by advertising, promotion and sponsorships. Without many heroes and successful role models in their own confined world, they often fantasize about the lives of celebrities and look to them for inspiration and direction.

— *Media presentation.* A frequent and positive portrayal of substance use on television, in films, books, comics, and street theatres encourage normalization. Characters are shown smoking cigarettes, drinking alcohol, or taking substances in an atmosphere of excitement, danger, or sex. Equally problematic is the depiction of substance use as a normal, everyday event. Street children, many of whom were raised in stressful or atypical homes, may be easily influenced by what they see in the media because they many not have other sources of ideas and information.

— *Community acceptance.* People tend to accept the use of a substance when the production and sale of the substance is an important source of income for the community. Some street children live in areas where substance production and trade are the major source of income for most of the residents. The leaders of alcohol, tobacco and other drug companies may be important members of the community. In certain slum areas, this is true of even illegal drug traffickers. They are admired by some of the residents because of the money they earn, and because they sometimes provide financial and other services to the residents that are not provided by the government or other agencies.

— *Cultural role.* Substances that have a place in the traditional culture of a society are usually normalized. The use of at least one substance has a cultural purpose in almost every society in the world. In religious activities, some Christians and Jews drink alcohol and some indigenous communities use hallucinogens. In many cultures, alcohol is used to celebrate special occasions such as New Year's Day and weddings. In parts of Asia, opium may be smoked during social gatherings and for relaxation.

Cannabis is used for cooking and socializing in parts of Africa and Asia.

Even when governments make a traditional substance illegal, some ordinary people may choose to continue using it because it is an important part of their traditional lives. Street children, like everyone else in the society, are influenced by the role of substances in their culture.

When deciding whether it is normal to use substances, a person looks at the behaviour of people who are similar to him or her. These people, called a peer group, might find the use of certain substances acceptable in certain situations, even though it would not be acceptable to the general society. For example, it is considered normal in some groups of young people to openly smoke marijuana at musical concerts, although this would not be acceptable to other groups of young people or most of the adult population. The peer group for a street child is usually other street children of similar age who are involved in the same type of work as he or she is. Each peer group has its own unwritten rules about the use of substances. Working children in Mumbai, for example, accept the use of solvents, but they don't approve of sleeping tablets because the effects last too long and they feel too tired to work.

Effect of behaviour and situations. Many street children use substances because the substance adds something to their life such as entertainment, or it temporarily solves a problem. Street children use substances because substances lessen hunger, add excitement, decrease physical and emotional pain, induce sleep, may increase energy levels to work, improve alertness, provide a form of recreation, provide a feeling of belonging to the peer group or may even give the courage to commit crimes. If a substance produces a positive or desired experience for a street child, he or she might use it more frequently. The effect that a substance has differs from person to person, and from occasion to occasion. The exact effect that a particular substance has on a particular individual depends on the user, the substance and the setting.

The User

— The person's physical condition and state of mental health

— The person's expectations about the effect of the substance

— The person's past experiences with substances

The Substance

— The type of substance

— The strength and purity of the substance

— The route of intake

The Setting

— The atmosphere of the occasion

— The physical environment

— The expectations of the group

Attachments

Attachments are personal connections to people, animals, objects and institutions. Having at least one person with whom someone has a close bond and feeling of acceptance has been found to be vital to developing a sense of positive self-esteem. A desire for close relationships can make a street child vulnerable to close relationships with people who can have a negative influence. A street child is more likely to develop strong attachments to other people if:

— He or she spends a lot of time with them

— He or she performs well in that group in any activity

— He or she is consistently rewarded by the group

Street children are less likely to begin using

substances and more likely to stop using them if their strongest attachments are with people and things that are not connected with substance use. Unfortunately, the situation of many street children makes it difficult for them to keep in contact with their families, to succeed at school or work, or to surround themselves with friends who do not use substances. Negative attachments are connections to people or institutions that are associated with substance use, abuse or exploitation such as drug syndicates or peers who use substances. Negative attachments make substance use more likely.

Skills. Skills are competencies. Competencies include physical and performance capabilities such as juggling, vending, craft, and self-defence, and psycho-social skills. needed to deal effectively with the demands of everyday life. These skills are often called psychosocial life skills. All young people need to develop physical, psychological, social, moral, and vocational competencies as a part of their healthy development.

Coping strategies are the cognitive, behavioural and social abilities that help a person manage stress. Competencies become coping strategies when they are used to manage stressful situations, e.g. seeking support from others or retreating in the face of danger. Competencies also help young people prevent health problems and cope with them if they occur. If street children have more skills it is less likely that they will need substances to meet challenges or to cope with problems. If they do use substances, they will have a greater ability to control the amount of use and avoid problems related to substance use.

Children may be exploited because of their age and general vulnerability during the process of skill development. This may include being paid less or being forced to work longer hours compared to other older workers. Under such circumstances, children may use substances to stay awake or to keep up energy levels and then use different substances to sleep or relax. The skills developed to survive on the streets, such as the ability to steal or lie to people in authority, can have a negative side in increasing illegal activities such as drug trafficking. This can result in increased use of substances in the community and by the individual. Lying prevents the development of trusting relationships.

Resources. Resources are used to meet physical and emotional needs. Resources can be inside a person, such as a willingness to work hard, or in the environment, e.g. schools, money, and people who care about the person. Examples of resources are:

— Internal resources.

— Intelligence.

— Capacity to work.

— Education.

— Vocational skills.

— Religious faith.

— Optimism.

— Sense of humour.

— External resources.

— Information.

— Family.

— Other street children.

— Street educators.

— Positive role models.

— Community organizations.

— Educational and vocational training services.

— Health services.

— Employers.

— Recreational facilities.

Even though street children usually have many internal resources, they often lack external ones. Without external resources, it is often difficult for street children to learn new skills that would help improve their lives. They may fail to develop healthy ideas and practices about substance use if they do not have the benefit of resources such as street education and informational campaigns. They also have fewer alternatives to substance use for relieving stress when resources such as recreational and vocational facilities are lacking. Resources need to be accessible and appropriate to street children.

Under the Modified Social Stress Model the likelihood that a particular street child will use substances will change from time to time so that during more stressful periods the child is more likely to use substances; even during periods when changes occur, it is important to look at all six components of the model at the same time to understand what a person might do.

Responsibilities of a Street Educator

The term street educator applies to anyone who is directly involved with street children and responds to their needs by providing support and care. Street education is one of the most effective ways to support street children because it takes place in the areas where they live and work. This can be on the streets, in the places they visit or seek shelter or in the community where their families live. The street educator must serve as the main link between the children and the community which can provide them with their needs. To do this, a street educator must be in direct contact with street children and must recognise the expanded role and responsibilities of the street educator.

The roles and responsibilities can be many and various. Some of them are:

— *Assessment:* obtaining correct and relevant information about the situation of street children and the available resources. This helps in prioritizing the needs and problems of street children.

— *Responding to needs and problems*: responding to the immediate needs and problems of street children within the boundaries of available resources.

— *Teaching/educating*: imparting knowledge, skills and appropriate attitudes to street children to help them in preventing or minimizing their problems and in seeking help when necessary.

— *Community mobilization and advocacy*: stimulating both the street children and the community to take action and adopt workable means as solutions by creating awareness about existing needs, problems of street children and about potential resources. Advocating and supporting the street children's cause can strengthen the political will of the government to provide protection and welfare of street children and family units.

— *Management*: planning, implementing, evaluating activities, identifying and linking different resources within the community and ensuring collaboration with relevant government bodies and other organizations.

To be able to carry out these responsibilities it is important to have or acquire certain characteristics, knowledge, skills and attitudes. Experience of working with street children, basic skills of communication and the ability to share information with street children and information on them with other key people and organizations, e.g. government officials, business people, police etc. and basic skills for documenting their work, will be useful.

It is not always easy to work with street children. Street children often become hardened victims of a society that feels threatened by them. Peer pressure, cultural and working conditions of the street are other difficult issues that you will have to deal with. A major task for effective street education therefore is to establish a working relationship with the street children. For this, you will have to spend time on the street to know the world of street children, so that a trusting relationship can be established. The challenge is how to cope with the limitations that you come across.

To be an effective street educator you need to possess or acquire certain characteristics. You should:

— Have knowledge, skills and appropriate attitudes.

— Have the desire to learn continually. This would involve being aware of your limitations and seeking help when necessary.

— Have integrity, maturity, and a sense of responsibility, patience and sympathy.

— Have determination, enthusiasm and motivation.

— Be creative and resourceful.

— Be able to work in a participatory style and encourage everyone to contribute ideas and make decisions.

— Believe in empowering street children by setting up opportunities for them to recognize and develop their own skills by building self-confidence.

Street educators must possess appropriate knowledge, skills and attitudes to be able to work with street children effectively.

— *Knowledge.* Knowledge relates to information and understanding of facts and principles. Knowledge can be acquired by reading reports about street children, talking to street children and other key leaders in the community, conducting assessments on street children and learning from experience.

— *Skills.* A skill is the ability to do something well. You will need to learn certain skills in order to transfer them to street children. Skills can be learnt through practice and demonstrations.

— *Attitudes.* Attitudes are tendencies to think or behave in a certain way. Attitudes include values and beliefs. They can be expressed in what you say, what you do or do not do, e.g. if you do not recognise the plight of street children and do not believe that they need help, your non-caring attitude can be reflected in the way you interact with them. Attitudes develop over a long period of time and are the hardest to change.

To work with street children the educator have to understand the culture of the street and the ambitions and resources available to the child. To be effective, be flexible enough to accept the realities of working with street children. The educator need to develop the capacity to reflect and relearn over and over again as he/she work with street children. For example, if he/she wish to use peer influence for the betterment of street children, he/she need to understand how peer groups are organized. Influential peers will have to be identified. Look for individuals who can communicate and express the group feelings, needs and aspirations.

— Mobilize the group for action.

— Organize the group and initiate team spirit.

— Produce workable ideas and encourage group members to adopt and maintain skills and strategies.

Establishing a trusting work relationship. The fundamental work of street education is to build relationships with street children that are based on mutual trust, respect and a commitment to personal growth. The process of establishing trust with street children is often difficult because many street children have learned not to trust people. The street educator must come across as a person who is genuinely committed and who practices what he or she stands for. Communication plays an important role in establishing such a trusting working relationship with street children.

Engaging. Engaging is the process of encouraging a street child in having a relationship with you. One good way to start the process of building a trusting relationship is to join in when they play games such as football, pinball, hide-and-seek or in something that they normally like to do. The educator can also join in when street children are working. Help them wash cars, search for food, or carry things. Avoid imposing activities as it would make you appear as an authority figure rather than a facilitator and a friend.

Understanding the world of a street child. Street children are more likely to trust you and spend time with the educator if he/she already know something about their world.

— *Language*: many groups of street children have their own special language, which is not known to outsiders. This special language helps to unite them. Learn some aspects of their language in order to understand them and communicate effectively with them. Using the terms they use can help build their trust in the educator.

— *Community*: knowing the physical and social characteristics of the area or locality where street children spend their time can assist you in your work. The physical characteristics are structures such as streets, sidewalks, markets, theatres, recreational areas, public buildings, and empty spaces. The social characteristics of the neighbourhood include sources of food, danger zones, sleeping locations, work places, and areas for using substances. Once you have made a map of the neighbourhood, you will have some idea of where to go in order to engage the street children. The social characteristics can be marked with a code that is explained at the side of the map.

— *Spending time on the streets*: the next step is to spend time in the places where street children are found. This may be in the park, the market place, or the bus or railway station.

Care for problems related to substance use

In providing care to street children who use substances it must be remembered that the interventions should be a part of healthier life management. This approach may help in reduction of risk behaviours without the need for specific interventions, such as detoxification. The common conditions that the educator will encounter may include intoxication, overdose and withdrawal. These complications can result in behaviours such as anxiety, panic, agitation, anger, hallucinations, confusion and disorientation. At times, street children can be managed by placement in any safe and supervised setting, e.g. a child who is intoxicated with alcohol. Medical assistance may be needed under other circumstances, e.g. detoxification from heavy use of barbiturates, as it is associated with the risk of convulsions and delirium (confusion, hallucinations). The educator may have to respond to intoxication, overdose or withdrawal by providing adequate immediate care and appropriate referral. Noted below is what the educator can do when confronted with the specific conditions:

— *Anxiety, agitation or panic.*

  — Approach the street child in a calm and confident manner.

  — Move and speak slowly and reassure the child. Do not leave him or her unattended.

  - Minimise the number of people attending to the street child.
- *Anger, aggression.*
  - Do not touch the street child unless absolutely necessary.
  - Speak in a calm, reassuring way.
  - Address the street child by name when talking to him or her.
  - Do not challenge or threaten by the tone of your voice, eyes or posture.
  - Allow the street child to talk about his or her feelings and acknowledge them.
- *Altered perception, hallucinations.*
  - Explain perceptual errors
  - Create a simple and uncluttered environment.
  - Place child in well lit surroundings to avoid the possibility of perceiving things wrongly.
  - Protect the street child from harm.
- Confusion, disorientation.
  - Provide frequent reality orientation by asking simple questions.
  - Remove unnecessary equipment to avoid injuries.
  - Provide explanations as to what is going on around the child.
  - Do not leave the child alone.
  - Place child in well lit surroundings to avoid the possibility of perceiving things wrongly.
- *Unconsciousness*:
  - Shake the child and call his or her name. If there is no reaction, check breathing.
  - If the child can be revived, get him or her up and moving.

— If the child is not breathing, start mouth-to-mouth resuscitation.

When faced with a street child experiencing any of the above mentioned conditions, be alert to other physical problems or illnesses that may co-exist with substance use. Street children may also get intoxicated with or may have withdrawal symptoms of many substances. Seek further assistance from a health service. If possible, try to obtain a sample of the substance that has been taken. Health care personnel may want to examine it or may run a test on the sample.

Care during detoxification. The goal of detoxification is to provide safe and humane withdrawal from substance(s) dependence. The procedure for detoxification will depend upon the type, combinations and pattern of use of substances in question. Detoxification for hypnosedatives should occur in a medically supervised setting because withdrawal from these substances can result in death from convulsions and heart failure. If the withdrawal symptoms are not expected to be severe and if there is a person to supervise the detoxification, there may be no need for hospitalization or constant clinical care. Selfdetoxification is possible for solvents, cannabis, stimulants and cocaine. Medical assistance may however be needed to ease the withdrawal process.

Your main role will be supporting the street child before, during and after the detoxification process. Support, motivating and structure are more necessary for street children than adults because of their developmental stage, and their impaired nutritional and general health status. Supporting a street child through withdrawal can be a good opportunity to engage the street child and motivate him/her to participate in further treatment. Support can include:

— Dispelling myths and fears about detoxification.

— Helping the street child to access and use the health system.
— Monitoring the general health of the street child.
— Supporting and involving the street child's family when possible.
— Identifying and supporting other people who can support the street child during and after detoxification.

Referral. After providing the necessary immediate care, refer the street child to another service. When deciding on the service, assess whether the street child requires:

— Intensive treatment in a health facility or treatment centre or a residential environment.
— Sessions of a particular intervention, such as counselling.
— A casual drop-in centre.
— Linkage to a supportive adult or a more functional peer in the local community. A well-developed network of appropriate services can help the educator in getting in touch with services or resource persons who can tell the educators what they want to know. The services required might not exist in the area or might not be child-friendly. Where such a network does not exist and if the educator have the necessary skill, train community members to provide the interventions and support that street children need.

It is also important to prepare yourself and the street child for the possibility of setbacks in the process. Street children need to be aware that if one referral does not work out, it does not mean that the problems cannot be solved. Other options can be tried. Street children might have to use a number of services before they achieve their goals.

Goal setting. Goal setting is an important component of assessment and case management. Goals should be negotiated with the street child. The goal should be specific and observable, and broken up into short-term, achievable targets. Plans should be reviewed regularly, and updated to take into account the changing nature of street life, the current availability of resources and services, developmental issues, and the fluctuating motivation that street children typically display.

Motivating the street child to abide by the action plan. The street educator responding to the needs of street children may sometimes feel frustrated when he/ she is trying to help street children control or stop risky behaviour because they may not change at the desired pace. It is essential to realise that the change process can take a long time and proceeds through stages that are described below on the next page. It would also be helpful to consider these stages in relation to life skills It is necessary to know how to encourage a street child to respond positively to the action plan. Motivational Interviewing (MI) is a technique that can help the educator to achieve this.

— Stages of change and appropriate response.

— *The pre-contemplation stage*: During this stage, the street child engaged in risky behaviour is not considering giving up his or herbehaviour. Try to form a relationship with the child and raise his or her awareness of the consequences of risk behaviour.

— *The contemplation stage:* At this stage the street child begins to think about doing something regarding his or her behaviour. Help the child by discussing the advantages and disadvantages of risky behaviour, and those of stopping.

— *The action stage*: At this point, the street child attempts to stop or minimise his or her risk taking behaviour.

Help him or her develop the needed skills and strategies (life skills). The child will need to figure out the situations (associated with people, places, feelings or things) under which he or she is more likely to adopt risky behaviour. Once identified, these situations can be eliminated, e.g. throwing away equipment like syringes, using condoms during sexual activity, avoiding friends who use substances or finding a job to avoid boredom.

— *The lapse stage*: After trying to take action as described above, the child can resume their risk taking behaviour. This should not be seen as failure, but simply as a part of the process of change. Prepare the child in advance for this stage and then help him or her get through it. When the child is ready to try to stop the behaviour again, help him or her make a more effective plan of action.

— *The maintenance stage*: Now the individual wants to consistently practice the desired new behaviour. Help the street child develop a healthy lifestyle, which might include moving into a safe environment such as home, finding activities that keep him or her off the streets, and spending free time with children or adults who do not encourage or participate in risk behaviour. Encourage the child to make a self-assessment on how well he or she is able to maintain the selected acceptable behaviour by monitoring himself/ herself and by recognizing when he/ she is entering risky situations.

Motivational Interviewing. MI enables the street child to convince himself/ herself about the need to change risk behaviours. It can be used at the time of the initial assessment to increase a street child's readiness to change, and at later stages for reinforcing and maintaining the positive behavioural change. MI does not involve coercion or confrontation.

- *Principles of Motivational Interviewing.* There are five broad principles underlying MI:
  - *Express empathy*: The educator should be able to express acceptance and respect for the street child. This is often done through skillful reflective listening.
  - *Develop discrepancy*: A discrepancy between present behaviour and important goals will motivate change. The child should present the reasons why he or she should change.
  - *Avoid arguments*: Arguments should be avoided because they are counter-productive.
  - *Roll with resistance*: Resistance on the part of the child is a signal to change strategies. Statements that a street child makes can be reframed slightly to create a new momentum towards change.
  - *Support the child's sense of ability to change*: Belief in the possibility of change is animportant motivator, so support the child's hope in the range of alternative approaches available. Acknowledging that the child is responsible for choosing and carrying out personal change can foster his/her self-belief.

Reproductive health problemsamong street children

You will be confronted with street children who have sexual and reproductive health problems including HIV/AIDS and STDs. The health worker should be able to recognize these problems, provide immediate care and refer the street child for professional care. The street child should also be taught to look for these signs and taught how to seek support and supervision from a health care worker.

Abortion. A child who has undergone an abortion or an unsafe abortion may complain of:

— Fever.

— Abdominal pain.

— Abnormal discharge or bleeding from the birth canal.

— A street girl may tell that her menses have not been regular or have stopped.

— The child may be confused.

A street girl needs expert support as she could develop serious health complications. Refer the child to a health facility immediately.

Emergency childbearing. Emergency problems or danger signs in a pregnant street child include:

— Bleeding from the birth canal.

— Abnormal discharge.

— Fever.

— Fits or swelling of feet.

Pregnant street children are at high risk for these conditions. If a street child has these signs, refer the child to a health facility immediately. Sometimes the need to deliver the baby may be urgent. This could be due to a variety of reasons, some of them being that the street girl may not be aware that she has been experiencing labour pains and realises too late. Or perhaps she may not even know what labour signs are. If the educator happen to be confronted with an emergency child delivery situation, stay calm and do the following:

— Preparation.

— Find a comfortable and private place for the delivery to take place.

— Help her to assume the most desired comfortable position.

— If water and soap are available wash hands with soap under running water.

— Put clean cloths under the mother where the baby will be born.

— Do not examine the street girl's birth canal.
— The birth of the baby and immediate care of the baby.
— Let the baby be born on its own.
— Do not pull out the baby.
— Do not push on the abdomen.
— With a clean cloth in your hands, receive the baby.
— Listen for the baby's first cry.
— If the baby cries and looks healthy, place the baby, covered in a cloth, on the mother's body.
— Explain that this is important as the mother's body helps to keep the baby warm.
— Make sure that the weight of the baby does not pull on the cord and that you place the baby on the mother's body without causing a pull on the cord
— Reassure the girl that she has done well so far and that you have requested for transport or help but will stay with her until then.
— Make the mother comfortable.
— Ask her to breastfeed the baby, making sure that the baby's nostrils are not being blocked.
— Record all what you have observed and done during the process and give this information to the health worker. You could give a verbal report as well.
— If possible, accompany the street girl to a health facility especially if no health worker can be found in the area.

Sexually Transmitted Diseases (STDs). If a street child has complaints such as:
— Sores on the genitalia.
— Discharge from the penis or vagina.
— Pain on urinating.

Provide advice on the need for treatment and refer them for appropriate care at a health facility.

HIV/AIDS. Street children affected by AIDS may suffer from frequent infections. In this situation, you may have to advise them on many issues such as nutrition, hygiene, dental care, psychological support and medications. Seek advice from health workers on how you can provide support and care to a street child affected by AIDS. To give you some idea on the extent of the care and support required when a street child has HIV/AIDS, a few issues are addressed below.

Anxiety and depression. When a street child is made aware of his condition he will experience mental problems such as shock, confusion and constant fears about the condition. A child who is anxious will :

— Have no appetite to eat food.

— May feel short of breath.

— Will be shaking and feeling very worried and may be jumpy.

— Experience sensation of the heart pounding.

— Sweat and could feel like fainting.

— Experience difficulty in sleeping and concentration.

A child experiencing depression can express this in the following ways:

— A feeling of hopelessness.

— Feeling tired and lack of energy.

— Finds no pleasure in the surroundings.

— May be irritable.

— Unable to concentrate and has poor memory.

— May be waking up in the morning or have difficulty getting to sleep at night.

Mental health problems such as anxiety and depression could make the child have difficulty dealing with everyday life situations. In the case of depression, it could lead to the child wanting to harm him or herself even to the point of considering suicide. Encourage the street child to express his or her thoughts and feelings. Give them an opportunity to go through the grief by simply talking and listening to them. Although you may not be in a position to provide support beyond this, it is important to find someone who can find the necessary support for the child such as the social worker.

At the beginning of the HIV epidemic, HIV testing was used mostly for clinical confirmation of suspected HIV disease. At the present moment, people are encouraged to attend voluntary counselling and testing services to find out their HIV status. If the test is negative, one can be encouraged to adopt preventive measures to prevent future infections. In the case that the result is positive, individuals and families can be helped to learn to leave positively, access appropriate care and support early, learn how to prevent transmission of the infection to sexual partners and plan their own future and that of their family.

You may come across a situation when a street child wants to know if he or she is infected with HIV and may wish to have an HIV test done. Good counselling will assist the street child to make informed decisions and cope better with the outcome of the test, help him or her lead more positive lives and prevents further transmission of HIV. Although HIV/AIDS counselling is usually provided by trained counsellors, street educators if trained in counselling, are better placed to provide effective counselling, advice and support to street children. Counselling requires good communications skills.

Testing for HIV requires two types of counselling. These are:

— Pre test counselling.
— Post test counselling.
— Pre test counselling

The aim of pretest counselling is to provide information to the street child about the technical aspects of testing and the various implications of being found to be HIV positive or negative: Testing should be discussed as a positive act that is linked to changes in risk behaviour, coping and increasing the quality of life. The main issues to be considered in pre testing counselling are:

— The street child's personal history of risk behaviour or exposure to HIV.
— The street child's understanding of HIV/AIDS including methods of transmission and experience in crisis situations.

Preparing the street child for pre test counselling. A decision by the street child to be tested should be an informed one. Try and get an informed consent from the street child. An informed consent implies being aware of the possible implications of a test result. Prepare the street child by discussing :

— confidentiality and informed consent for HIV testing
— implications of test result whether negative or positive
— ways to cope with knowing the HIV status
— sexuality and sexual practices and
— exploring emotional coping mechanisms and the availability of social support
— explaining how to prevent transmission of HIV
— correcting myths, misinformation and misunderstandings related to HIV/AIDS

Post test counselling. Post test counselling helps to put the street child at ease. Find a quiet place to discuss the results, whether negative or positive. It is important to have the street child repeat the information presented. Give the street child time to reflect on the results and understand the next course of action. Counselling and other support activities should address the feelings of shock, fear, loss, grief, guilt, depression, anxiety, denial, anger, suicidal thinking, reduced selfesteem and spiritual concerns. Therefore, continued counselling and support should also take place to help improve the street child's quality of life as well as to enhance his or her ability to cope and make informed decisions about life choices and ongoing care. The result of the test must be kept confidential only when the need to share it with others arises. These others may include family members, loved ones, care giver or trusted street children or friends.

Care for infected street children must be comprehensive across a continuum. Comprehensive care involves a network of resources and services which provide holistic, comprehensive, wide ranging support. A continuum of care includes care between hospital, home or other institutions of care over the course of the illness.

6

Cyber Begging

Cyber-begging is a mode of fundraising that is carried out through donations over the Internet. The cyber-beggar creates a Web site detailing his or her financial plight in the hopes of attracting donations for his or her cause. Begging for money online in America has already become a business. Yahoo! portal has a category entitled E-Panhandling. There are dozens of them there. CyberBeg portal contains about two hundred of them. The titles of cyber-begging sites presumably start with such words as save, rescue, help, or give, send, pay, lend.

Cyber-beggars do not ask money to buy a piece of bread, they need money for goods and services. A lot of them need to pay their debts. They beg to clear a credit card debt, to make a breast enlargement operation, to pay for medical care or education, to help a woman to divorce her husband, to make a movie or an album. Beggars ask for various sums of money: from several cents to a million dollars. Most likely, they ask to send them as much money as you can via the PayPal system.

Wired magazine wrote that the first person to launch a cyber-begging site was a woman named Karyn Bosnak. Her website was called Save Karyn. It is possible to cast doubts on her championship, although her success is obvious. She had a credit card debt of over 20 thousand on June 23, 2002. Karyn Bosnak decided the following for herself: all I need is to get one dollar from 20 thousand people, or two dollars from ten thousand people, or five dollars from four thousand people. As a result, people transferred thirteen thousand dollars to the woman, she added some of her money and paid her debt on November 10th, 2002. As you can see, it took her less than six months to do away with her problem. Karyn has been saved. Now she patronizes other beggars, claiming copyright for her idea.

New York Times confirms that the e-panhandling epidemic was launched together with Save Karyn website. Therefore, the date of June 23, 2002 can be considered the cyber-begging birthday. If a webmaster of a begging site provides his or her full name, as well as the detailed description of a trouble, this site will enjoy great popularity amid benefactors. It goes without saying that if a benefactor-s problem has something in common with the one of a cyber-beggar, a webpage will be even more popular.

Kimberly Smith, the mother of five children, was inspired with Karyn Bosnak's success. She decided to launch Save Kimberly website. She asks visitors a dollar or two for settling her debt — over 25 thousand dollars — and for buying a house for her family. Despite the fact that there were a lot of touchy stories and children's photographs on the website, Kimberly Smith has not had an opportunity to enjoy her success yet. However, Michel Huang managed to obtain $3300 (with the help of cyber-begging) for a breast enlargement operation. As she said, a so-called donor, who wished to remain anonymous, gave her $1200.

Another popular e-panhandling site Help Me Leave My Husband, which was launched by someone named

Penny in August of 2002, brings the profit of $75 per week. Two thousand dollars have already been collected, while twelve thousand are needed. Canadian woman Jennifer Glasser suffers from Lyme disease. She tries to collect money with the help of her site Help Jennifer. She needs to pay the debt to her mother ($32 thousand), to undergo the fourth stage of her medical treatment ($64 thousand). To crown it all, she needs $450 of monthly spending. Save Jennifer site was opened in August of 2002. For the time being, Jennifer has collected about $5.5 thousand ($3.5 thousand were donated by one person). Kellie Cudaback-s success with her site Save Kellie is very humble v five dollars (her husband left her the debt of $20 thousand).

All those sites claim to be true and serious. By the way, cyber-beggars donate money to each other sometimes. This is something like a mutually beneficial promotion. Of course, there are people, who wish to promote and advertise e-panhandling sites. Steve Donohue, for instance, created the webpage called SaveMeSites. This page is meant to help e-panhandling sites to have better banner exchange systems, or to obtain better search engine indexes. It goes without saying that there are lots of jokers among cyber-beggars. You may find a man, who asks people to make him richer than Bill Gates. Someone else begs for money to buy a new guitar, or a Hummer jeep ($120 thousand) and so on. There are swindlers too, for everyone knows that real beggars often work for criminal groups. The same happens online v the Internet is the mirror of the society, although we will not dwell upon this subject here.

The people used to donate their funds to salvation armies, Greenpeace activists, and other charitable organizations. Now those people are ready to give away their money to someone that they have never seen before. Experts believe that cyber-beggars get more and more talented every day, making their websites more technical, making their stories more touchy. On the whole, the e-panhandling business prospers and flourishes before your very eyes. Cyber-beggars evoke compassion and sympathy with professional sincerity, so to speak. Of course, the ground for online beggars is a lot more fruitful in rich America at the moment.

The musical artist known as Shela is the owner of SaveShela.com. She is currently asking for donations on her Web site to help pay off debt incurred from writing and recording her music. She says at first she was "embarrassed by the thought of begging for money online," but says that she does not consider herself a beggar.

"There are plenty of open-source project Web sites that ask for donations to keep their site running, and they provide services like help and advice," she says. Her advice, she says, would be for potential musicians who are looking for advice on breaking into the music industry. The Web site also offers an outlet where people can promote their music.

Shela, who lives in Toronto, says it was a mixture of frustration and her experience working with the Internet that led her to the idea of starting her personal fundraising site. As a computer hardware instructor she was "aware of how powerful a tool the Web could be." A tool she hopes will help her music career off the ground.

Funds are donated to Shela either through the mail or Paypal, an online payment service that makes transactions through credit cards. "I have not listed myself as a charity," she says, an action that would require certain registration and guidelines."It is a simple gift. Anyone can give a stranger a gift right?"

Shela says her feedback has been very positive. "I have been waiting for my first hate e-mail, but it hasn't happened yet." "I am still getting started, but I have gotten $169 U.S. dollars and $100 Canadian," she says. "Over the past few weeks my average daily site traffic has grown 800 percent and I have received seven new donations." It has also been, according to Shela, a success in another way.

Shela says she has dreams of making the site bigger and better, eventually adding a "streaming radio station" that would play MP3s submitted by donors and aspiring musicians. Most importantly, she says, she hopes to pay off the debt, which is a huge roadblock on her road to a music career. "Just the possibility of being free from debt sooner with the help of generous people is enough to keep trying," she says. "At the very least, I will have a Web site with a fair number of people coming back to hear my work, and that is exciting in itself."

7

Features of Indian Beggars

According to Hindu believes Lord Shiva once ran his household by a mere income of scalpings collected by begging among *rishis* and *sadhus*. Have the times changed! Now it is extremely difficult even for full time beggars to make good of two meals. Not so long ago in India, on Saturdays and Mondays every beggar who showed up at the door was given a measure of rice or juvar. The *guru-bhakta* who went worshiping to the temple on Thursdays, got a handful of goodies and money.

The beggar community feels that due to the increase in mankind's selfishness and small-mindedness, they are not able to make a living. The government through its policies has not helped them either. "Like prostitution, begging is oldest profession on earth. Although varying by geography and the times, begging is universal. We have heard that even richest countries like America have beggars in one form or another," is the argument of the beggars. The intellectuals for long have been intrigued by mankind's attraction to living by panhandling. Why do able bodied, working people take up begging? Why do Bengali refugees return to starving Bengal after assisted relocation? Why have we failed to settle vagabond tribes like the Bhils and Mogalayas? It is not easy to give up the skills of earning a livelihood. Even if you protect a prostitute in an *ashram,* the social reformers opine that she does not forget her easy life and in some form or another resumes old habits.

It is very difficult to generalize how and where panhandling begins in the life of a beggar. Some inherited from their ancestors. There are all kinds of beggars whose period of begging spans from five minutes to fifty years. A boy was begging for peanuts on the street, but when someone offered him money, he refused. "I like peanuts," he said ran away - his needs being very specific. The eight year old of a maid-servant who was instructed to play outside was begging the passers by for small change and bought candy.

Generally, the elderly, the disabled, and the unemployed take to begging. Folks who were robbed during their pilgrimage, temporarily beg to return home. The lepers and destitute graduate to this profession. From beggars who cry in front of you asking for food to entertainers who beg with the help of pets and children, most homeless fall into the category of beggars with more or less the same yard stick.

Just like lawyers, administrators and athletes, the beggars can be very professional. They guard their constituencies with great care. It is common to fight over territories. The beggar who beggars in front of Ganesh hotel cannot go and beg in front of Krishna hotel! When an unassuming new comer from a village stuck out his hand in front of the temple, he was chased away and had to go to Saibaba ashram for shelter. Although the beggars do not have an association or union, they unite to defend their sources of income. While the beggars of the temples, churches, and mosques need not travel, the beggars of shops and households have to wander a lot.

The beggars have to care about their attire just like

actors and performers. People who beg in the name of the religion have to grow beard, wear saffron clothes and ash. The fortune teller *Bhils* wear peacock feathers and other make-ups. The *Budabudakis* who do not know about their next meal, but can tell customers what lies in the decades to come wear *Zari* Rumal, and apply ash on the forehead to give them a holy look.

Devadasis wear turmeric powder, flowers, and kumkum. The transvestites (impotent men dressed as women) have altogether different, yet distinct style. They are clean shaven and apply fashionable cosmetics. They have acquired artificial feminine postures and dances. The beggars who use animals for fund raising have to decorate their pets, too. They have to buy caps for the monkey, jingle bells for the cow, and decorative clothing for the bull.

The beggars have to master the art of begging just as they have to master the art of dressing up. They realize that it is very difficult to refuse a hungry man begging just as you come out of a popular restaurant. While a woman begs in the name of her husband who is in the death bed in a hospital, it is not uncommon that the husband is begging in his wife's name on the next street. A pregnant woman will say that her previous child has died, and she needs money for the funeral. Her heart-rendering appeal fetches good money, yet nobody knows if any of her six children has died. An entire family will beg saying they lost everything in the floods. The children and women in scanty clothing will be sleeping on the road side and the head of the household blocks the passers-by for small change.

The beggars are fairly well-organized although they not unionized. They view new beggars with suspicion and try to find out his/her depth by typical questionnaires. They have a means of estimating and budgeting income and expenses. A small town beggar has a hard time to raise two to three Rupees per day while a city beggar can easily earn ten bucks.

During the festivals, they could earn as much as thirty Rupees. For commoners, this may look like a paltry sum, but we have to understand that the beggars do not have any expenses. No rent, no groceries to buy. The leftovers from the hotels is their dinner; else every beggar typically has a godmother who never refuses food for him/her. The roadside food courts typically provide discount prices to beggars. They travel in buses which have friendly conductors, without tickets and they always know that temples/churches/railway stations can be used for toilet and sleeping. Since they do not have a safe place to keep money, they carry with them all the time.

The beggars need protection just like everyone. They especially need protection of their savings and begging zones. Often there are these self-style beggar leaders who enforce the rules. There is no rule to pay him money for his leadership. You can provide a hot cup of coffee once in a while. There are even beggar gangs whose leader takes a bigger share, but distributes among the members. The team of blind men and the team of transvestites belong to this category. The beggars at the railway stations and bus stands are usually dominated by thugs who run begging rackets. There are these *goondas* who liberate beggars from rehabilitation centers and send them back to the streets for begging.

The beggars never make short of the family life. They tie a sari across in the choultry and convert it into a bedroom. Like western cultures, they have complete equality of sexes in the beggar community and the woman can choose and change her partners. When husband and wife go begging separately, sometimes they run away with their other lovers. Many times the husband goes after his wife whom he misses a lot. There was a husband who cut off his wife's nose so she doesn't run away again. The children become independent by the time they are eight. In addition to begging, they take to pick-pocketing, stealing of shoes in temples, and petty thefts at the market place. Many professional thieves hire the beggar children as their assistants, informants, and to peddle stolen goods. If the police catch these kids, they are sent to government remand homes or religious centers, but it is not of much use. They have to take to the streets as that is only means of survival.

The beggar colonies are breeding grounds for the anti-social elements. They live a very unhygienic life style, cooking, sleeping, and defecating in the same area. In our society most people give to beggars more to earn *punya* rather than out of feelings for the beggar. It is not uncommon to see a housewife toss a coin through a window to the beggar after the husband has chased him away. As long as we do not shun this fast track to heaven, no law or reform can stop the profession of begging.

8

Means of Tackling Begging

People who beg are amongst the most damaged and vulnerable people in our society. The vast majority are homeless; they suffer from a combination of poor skills, low income, poor housing, bad health, substance misuse and family breakdown. Few, if any, are in their situation by choice. Personal crises and the traumatising nature of homelessness combined with the difficulties accessing essential services such as healthcare and drug detox services prevent them from escaping their predicament.

Using methods of enforcement to deal with begging is wrong because it criminalises an already vulnerable section of our population increasing their contact with the police and criminal justice system. This is not only a costly and ineffective means of tackling what is essentially a symptom of deprivation, but it is unlikely to address the root causes of begging and may have the effect of exacerbating the problems facing people who are first and foremost in need of a helping hand. There is no doubt that begging is a problem that must be tackled head on, not because people who beg are criminals, but because they are caught up in an activity that is dangerous, damaging and humiliating and are trapped in a cycle of poverty and deprivation. Theirs is a plight that cannot be ignored. The question is not whether we should tackle this problem, but how.

The solutions to begging must be based upon principles of compassion and methods of positive engagement. Methods that empower people by providing them with real and positive choices and by giving them the support necessary to help them overcome the difficulties that they face.

Reality of Begging

The vast majority of people who beg are homeless in one form or another; many are in fact rough sleepers and all of them vulnerable. Evidence of their vulnerability is stark and overwhelming. The overcrowded, cold, damp and unsanitary conditions of homelessness are highly conducive to physical and mental ill health and there is evidence of a growing subculture of drink and drugs.

Research has shown that nearly one in fifty of homeless people have TB; at least one in five homeless people suffer from mental health problems. Four out of five homeless people interviewed for a Crisis report released last year were addicted to either drink or drugs Often an individual will have a combination of all of these problems. These are shocking statistics and yet they tell only part of the story.

Homelessness is both a cause and a consequence of severe trauma and personal crisis, with 33% of homeless people citing relationship breakdown as one of their reasons for first sleeping rough. Loneliness and isolation is common and results in one in four ex-homeless people being unable to sustain a tenancy. People who beg do so out of need, not greed. The monetary benefits of begging are slight and the risks of street life are high. Rough sleepers, for example, appear to be up to 15 times more likely to experience assault than the wider population and 35 times more likely to be victims of wounding.

Despite the stories that are sometimes circulated in the press the reality is that a person begging is lucky if they end their day with ten or twenty pounds in takings. This money will be spent on food, tobacco and for those who are victims of substance misuse, alcohol and drugs.

Most people who beg describe their experience as degrading and uncomfortable and are desperate to get out of their situation but lack the skills, confidence and support to do so; they are trapped by their problems into a downward spiral of dependency and deprivation. Despite the efforts of many people in government and the voluntary sector, we are light years away from having the necessary support and services to help vulnerable homeless people to deal with the problems that entrap them.

The most obvious example of this is the issue of substance misuse. It is a widely acknowledged fact that many people who beg suffer from this problem but accessing detox services remains extremely difficult, with many in the homelessness sector reporting a genuine lack of services and appropriate support.

Similarly, for those people who are forced to live their lives on the street there are few practical alternatives to their lifestyle. Employment is often an unlikely option as an immediate solution and many activities that we take for granted – visiting a friend's home, having a hobby, going to the pub, or joining a club – are out of bounds for those who live on the streets. Homeless people themselves often speak of the frustration that they feel when they are faced by whole days with nothing to do, nowhere to go and no way to move on.

Enforcement as a Means of Tackling Begging

To punish someone who needs help is fundamentally wrong; using methods of enforcement to tackle begging is unjust, unworkable and a waste of public resources.

Where an individual is violent this behaviour must be dealt with through the criminal justice system. However begging is for the large part a low level nuisance and beggars are in practice far more likely to be victims of serious crime than they are to perpetrate it. People who beg do so as a strategy for survival rather than as a means of illegally accumulating wealth or with any particular intent to harm or cause offence. Rather than seeing begging as a crime we should see it for what it is; a cry for help.

Dragging beggars through the criminal justice system is counter productive. A criminal record that will make it even more difficult for them to find work and housing, giving them a fine that they will not be able to pay or insisting that they carry out a community sentence that they will not be able to fulfil is not a way forward. All of these supposed solutions to begging fail to address the underlying causes of the problem, often they make it worse. If someone begs because of substance misuse, then providing them with help to overcome their addiction is the most effective way to tackle the problem; punishing them for begging is not.

Both police and magistrates have in the past expressed frustration at the futility of tackling begging through the criminal justice system. Many recognise that there are far more effective ways of solving the problem and their failure to make full use of existing legislation, much of which provides a range of punitive measures, is testimony to this.

The criminal justice system is already overstretched with 5,600 men, women and children being sentenced in Criminal Courts every day in England and Wales. Adding even more beggars to these numbers will place an increased and unnecessary burden upon the system.

The cost of processing people in this way is high, both in police time and taxpayers' money and it is wasted if the real reasons why people beg are not addressed.

Finding solutions to begging

So what are the solutions to begging? The first step must be recognition that begging is not in and of itself a criminal behaviour, and as a consequence should not be treated as such. People who beg are first and foremost extremely vulnerable individuals who need our help and support.

Within this framework we would suggest four steps need to be taken in order to deal with the problem of begging:

1) Put in place the necessary and appropriate support and services to enable people who beg to overcome the problems that they face: access to accommodation, detox services and primary health care, to name three.

2) Build upon and improve methods of engaging with people on the street that do not involve the police authorities. Beggars need the opportunity to do something about their predicament. For some years now we have had "outreach teams" whose task it is to go out on the streets and engage with people sleeping rough. Their role should be extended to include beggars; they should be provided with appropriate resources.

3) Create genuine alternatives to street life: places where they can feel welcome and safe, where they are given the opportunity to start to rebuild social networks, their skills and their self-esteem; places of learning that cater for different levels of need and different levels of ability; places where people can begin to address their problems at their own pace and in their own time and where they will be

provided with support and encouragement for their efforts.

4) Involve beggars in tackling the issue of begging and give them a say in developing solutions: people who beg understand better than anyone the causes and the consequences of begging.

Begging raises the question of how we deal with some of the most vulnerable people in our society. There is urgency to the task that we face. Begging is unacceptable and should not be allowed to exist; but the hope is that in seeking to address it we recognise the issue for what it really is, a symptom of deprivation and social exclusion, and seek to tackle these problems first. Surely the answer lies in compassion not coercion, in engagement not enforcement.

Feeding the Poor

Most people, probably in the developed world, embrace the charity view in one of two incarnations. On one view being charitable is wholly voluntary, while on the other to whom we are charitable is wholly voluntary. According to the first variation, we have no duty of any kind to the needy. According to the second, traceable to Kant, we have an imperfect duty to help people in need. However, although we ought to be charitable to some degree, there is no particular person we are obligated to assist, and certainly no particular person can expect, let alone demand, our assistance.

Despite their differences both views hold (a) that no particular person can demand or expect charity and (b) that governments cannot legitimately coerce us (e.g., via taxation) to be charitable. Moreover, although the third view holds that we morally ought to be charitable, we can fulfill that imperfect duty without helping anyone who is starving. We could, instead, help the unemployed in our neighborhood, support a literacy program, or give to Planned Parenthood. Some who hold the third view might claim we are duty bound to meet greater needs before meeting less substantial ones. However, since there are pressing needs close to home, likely we could satisfy any imperfect duty of charity without helping any of the world's starving. Thus, on both charity views, people who fail to contribute to famine relief might be stingy or morally short-sighted, but they would not necessarily be immoral.

Most of us think feeding the starving would be good even if it is something that we do not do. We think it is good because (a) we think it relieves human suffering and most accounts of morality hold that (b) relieving human suffering is at least permissible and perhaps morally required. Hardin disagrees. He thinks that (a) is false, and therefore concludes that we should not feed the starving.

Both the duty and the charity views, Hardin claims, assume that our ability to feed people is boundless. It is not. "A nation's land has a limited capacity to support a population and as the current energy crisis has shown us, in some ways we have already exceeded the carrying capacity of our land". Given these limitations, some countries are like overcrowded lifeboats. Their land cannot support the current population—and certainly not future generations given current population growth rates.

Although feeding these starving people may temporarily keep more of them alive, in the long run, it will increase the population to the point where we can no longer feed them, even if we wanted. That will increase suffering and endanger future generations. That is why assistance is morally wrong.

Here's an example to illustrate Hardin's point. At the time of Hardin's writing in the early 70s, India had a population of 650 million people. Despite the large number of people dying from starvation, its population was growing at a rate of 2.6% per year. At that rate, India's population would double every 27 years. The problem was even more acute in Colombia, Ecuador, and Pakistan which had annual population growth rates of greater than 3 percent. At that pace, their populations would double every 21 years. If those countries were unable to feed their current populations, how could they possibly feed a population twice or four times that size—even with massive assistance from more affluent nations? Hence, although our initial impulse is to feed the starving, we should not. We should recognize just "how wrong generosity can be".

Obligation to Feed the Starving

The claim that we have a strong obligation to assist the starving takes two broad forms, reflecting one's general theoretical framework. The first claims that we have a positive obligation to ease suffering and promote happiness; hence, we should assist the starving. The second claims people have a right to food, and that right undergirds our obligation to assist them. Of course rights, absent compelling obligations or duties, are effectively empty. That is why even those who claim that people have rights to food will claim that the relatively affluent have a strong correlative positive obligation to assist those in need.

Hence, although the distinction between these two positions is theoretically intriguing, and could well have *some* practical significance, for present purposes we will collapse them and simply talk about the strong obligation to assist the starving. Those who claim the relatively affluent have this strong obligation must, among other things, show why Hardin's projections are either morally irrelevant or mistaken. A hearty few take the former tack: they claim we have a strong obliga-tion to aid the starving even if we would eventually become malnourished.

On this view, to survive on lifeboat earth, knowing that others were tossed overboard into the sea of starvation, would signify an indignity and callousness worse than extinction. It would be morally preferable to die struggling to create a decent life for all than to continue to live at the expense of the starving. However, most who think we ought to feed the starving will claim, or imply, that *if* feeding the starving had the terrible consequences Hardin predicts, then we should not feed them. Therefore, most who reject Hardin's neo-Malthusianism must show that the projected consequences are at least implausible, if not demonstrably wrong.

Developmental Alternative

Most discussions of world hunger state or imply that (a) starvation is caused by a shortage of food in a region, (b) which is itself usually caused by a natural disaster (drought, floods, etc.). Given these assumptions, we then ask: (c) what, if anything, should we morally do to help people escape the effects of the famine? If we assume someone should assist them (d) we must decide "*who* is responsible for providing this help".

Jean Drèze and Amartya Sen argue that this way of framing the issue mistakenly treats hunger as a naturally induced phenomenon unconnected to the social, political, and economic institutions within which it arises. They claim this is a mistake—even when thinking about a farmer who owns her own land. The farmer's ability to obtain enough food depends not only on the size and quality of her land, a normal rainfall, and her hard work, but also on the actions of others. Will people living upstream dam up or pollute the water flowing through her land? Will they permit their animals to overgraze the land so there is no grass for hers? Will others sell her the supplies she needs: seed, animal feed, and farm equipment, etc.? Will others buy her products so she has money to buy the supplies she needs? Will they pay her a fair price? Will they assist her if some disaster interferes with her crop or prevents her from harvesting it? Unless these and other factors are satisfied, then all the land and hard work in the world will not suffice to feed her family. That is why when families lack adequate food, the reason may have little to do with the general availability of food in the area.

History supports this armchair reasoning. During the 1974 famine in Bangladesh, the amount of food per capita was the third highest during a ten-year period:

This finding was duplicated within the regions of the country worst hit by the famine. "One of the famine districts (Dinajpur) had the *highest* availability of food in the entire country, and indeed, all four of the famine districts were among the top five in terms of food availability per head". The problem, Drèze and Sen explain, is that the families had insufficient "entitlements" to food. These "entitlements" are determined not only by what the person can produce, but also what they can buy and what is made available to them.

This shows why we cannot determine the causes of either episodic or endemic hunger by simply asking whether the country's overall level of food has declined. We must determine whether the people have sufficient entitlements to food. Of course the overall availability of food is one factor determining people's entitlements. Although some detractors claim it is the single most important factor, most researchers agree with Drèze and Sen that its significance is often overemphasized.

Moral Implications

This developmental perspective requires that we explore broader questions about the political, social, and economic relationships within and between countries. But this does not obviate the need to answer the moral question: what, if anything, should those of us in affluent nations do to help impoverished countries and individuals, especially those facing episodic or endemic hunger? It just slightly changes it. We should now ask: "Are we obliged to insure that they have adequate food entitlements?" That requires us to ask several derivative questions: do we have obligations to encourage (or coerce) their governments to enhance their entitlements? Are we obligated to establish ongoing trade relations with these countries to enhance their citizens' entitlements? Do we have obligations to send food or to help distribute food when the country cannot do so on its own?

Although the developmental perspective does not resolve these moral questions, it has prescriptive implications. Minimally it obliterates any simple version of Hardin's argument. Conversely, seeing why Hardin's argument fails elucidates significant features of the developmental perspective.

Hardin claims that a country's ability to feed her people depends solely on its land's ability to produce sufficient food. Developmental theorists counter that the land's fertility is far less important than are her (a) internal economic and political strength and her (b) transnational economic and political agreements. These reveal how heavily dependent we are on others—both within and between countries. They show that no person and no country is wholly self-reliant. For example, while a few of the world's smallest and least prosperous countries import goods valued at only ten percent of their Gross National Products, the average country imports goods equivalent to one-fourth of its Gross National Product. Most European countries import goods valued at greater than one-third of their respective GNPs. Although these countries do not directly feed their people, their people are nonetheless well fed. After all, they have material goods and human skills to trade for food and other essential goods.

Morever, Hardin's projections, like those of Malthus before him, have turned out to be wildly mistaken. In the early 70s he projected that the world's population at the turn of the century would be 6.6 billion. It was, in fact, slightly more than 5.8 billion. And India, which, according to Hardin, had a population growth rate of 2.6% in 1973, had a rate of 2% by the turn of the century; that is projected to decline to 1.2% by the year 2015. There are surely limits to how many people the land can support, but we are not approaching those limits at the breakneck speed Hardin claims. It is not enough to know that his projections fail. It is crucial to understand why they fail. The explanation for their failure reveals significant facts about the nature of hunger, and suggests potent strategies for its control—if not eradication.

Population trends are best explained by the "demographic transition theory," (DTT) a sociological theory around since long before Hardin first advanced his views on hunger. According to one prominent formulation of DTT, population trends move through four distinct stages. In the first, the combination of a high birth rate and a high death rate produce a steady population. In the second stage, death rates decline while birth rates remain high, leading to high population growth rates. In the third, birth rates decline more rapidly than death rates; consequently, population rates increase but at a much slower pace. In the final stage, population becomes stable as low birth rates parallel low death rates. We have long since past the first stage, and the declining population rates worldwide suggest that most of the world has passed the peak of the second stage.

Even those undeveloped countries still in the second stage are ambling toward the third, while countries in the highly developed West are already comfortably settled into the fourth. In these later stages population growth rates stabilize even while death rates decline. That shows that we need not "let 'em starve" to control population growth. General economic development can propel countries into these latter stages in which people have no reason to have large families and heightened reason to have smaller ones.

Although it does not explain all perturbations in population, as a general description of population changes. The demographic transition theory is both theoretically plausible and it squares with the empirical data. Its theoretical plausibility is clear: impoverished people have strong incentives to have large families, especially in countries with poor medical care. In an environment with high infant mortality rates, people can reasonably expect to have surviving children only by having many of them. Having more children means having more hands to feed the family, either by working in the fields, or working in neighboring cities to supplement the family income. They are also the aged person's only source of income in countries without a social security program.

Conversely, relatively affluent countries do not have high infant mortality, nor do its citizens need children to supplement the family income or to care for them in old age. Such countries also have high educational attainment. Although education may enlighten students about the scope of the population problem, its most powerful influences on population growth are indirect. First, post secondary education delays marriage and consequently decreases the number of children any woman can bear. Second, it opens new vocational opportunities for women of childbearing age. Third, people with higher educations tend to have higher incomes, and are thus less likely to need children to provide old-age security. Fourth, in states with compulsory education, the child cannot substantially contribute to the family finances; instead, they drain economic resources. Fifth, states with compulsory education are more likely to have social security for the elderly. All these factors are even more important in tightly knit traditional societies in which individuals are sustained not primarily by the nuclear family, but without extended family and social groups.

These factors collectively explain population growth rates. They predict that as long as people remain uneducated, lack economic security, and live in a country with high infant mortality and no social security, then they will have large families. Conversely, as health care increases, infant mortality decreases, and governments fund social security programs and establish compulsory education, then birth rates will decline even as death rates decline. These theoretical predictions have been borne out time and again by epidemiological facts.

The difference in population growth rates between countries is dramatic. In 1998 rates in the lowest developed countries averaged 1.9%; in medium developed countries, 1.6%; and in the highest developed countries, .6%. Finally, the Human Development Index (a compilation of factors reflecting health and economic well-being) has increased worldwide over the last quarter century. This trend almost perfectly parallels the decline in the number of people starving. The DTT is a theory well established in fact.

Hence, we have compelling theoretical and empirical evidence that Hardin's proposal would likely have a result opposite of that predicted. That's not quite right. Aid that simply kept the starving alive and did nothing to change their overall well-being, might well have his predicted result. It would arguably prolong the second stage of transition, and increase suffering.

However, immediate food aid and medical assistance, coupled with developmental assistance to enhance economic security, lower Infant Morality Rates, and improve the educational attainment of its citizens would remove incentives for large families and replace them with incentives for smaller ones.

Since Hardin's position is both theoretically and empirically flawed, we are left with two basic options. As we stated at the beginning, however, we take the charity position to be the default. That is, if the claim that we have a strong obligation to assist cannot be defended, then we should conclude that assisting is morally permissible but not morally obligatory. Whether that strong obligation can be defended is what we will now determine.

The most familiar ground for claiming that we have a strong duty to assist is simply that, if we can alleviate people's suffering or prevent their dying at little personal cost, then we morally ought to do it. This seems especially plausible when those in need are in no way responsible for their own plight. Since the overwhelming majority of those who are seriously undernourished are children who are paradigmatically innocent and vulnerable, then their need would arguably demand our assistance. In this world we are mutually dependent. We live in the conditions which constitute the "circumstances of justice".

Although some people, and especially children, are more vulnerable than others, all of us were and are dependent on others. None of us is—or could be—wholly self-sufficient. Most of us recognize that our parents had to care for us lest we die. But that is only the beginning of the debt to our predecessors. Our abilities to speak a language, to read literature, to appreciate art, to live in cities, to travel the world, and to purchase the goods we want and need arose only because of the efforts of those who came before. "It is of grace and not of ourselves that we live civilized lives". We are likewise dependent on our contemporaries, both near and far.

Of course someone influenced by Adam Smith might think that people's behavior benefitting others is really just disguised or redirected self-interest. The best evidence suggests a biological basis for altruistic tendencies. Had others acted solely out of their own interest, wholly indifferent to us and our vulnerabilities, most of us would not be alive. Had they largely ignored our vulnerabilities, we might be alive, but in a substantially diminished condition.

Nations, like individuals, are also vulnerable. In the distant past, countries may have been relatively self-sufficient. No longer. Now every country is vulnerable to others' actions. As the earlier data on global imports indicated, we heavily depend on other countries's trading with us.

Indeed, the more developed a country's economy, the more dependent she is on others, although in many respects she may have immense power that masks that vulnerability. For example, the powerful economies of the United States, Japan, and Western European cannot survive without imported oil and raw minerals that drive their respective industries.

Our global economy makes our mutual dependence clear. In such a system, responding to the pressing needs of distant others is morality's way of acknowledging our reciprocal vulnerability, our common humanity. It reflects the fact that we now globally live in the circumstances of justice. Or, to use a different model, reciprocal caring is a form of moral insurance.

Protecting the Vulnerable

Robert Goodin offers an intriguing and powerful variant of this argument. He argues that our obligation to assist the vulnerable is not a unique positive responsibility, but is rather a general moral duty that ungirds all special role responsibilities. On the common view of morality, special obligations are especially potent and arise entirely from our voluntarily assumed obligations. However, Goodin argues, this voluntarist model cannot explain the presence, content, context, form, or strength of our obligations to family and friends, duties of gratitude, or even our obligations arising from promises, contracts, and role or professional duties. The entire panoply of special rights is far better explained as arising from others' vulnerability in relation to us. "It is vulnerability, however engendered, that plays the crucial role in generating special responsibilities".

The voluntarist model cannot even adequately explain the presence—let alone strength—of out duties to keep promises. For promises where nothing is at stake are only minimally binding—and then only for purely consequentialist reasons. At other times, we are obligated to fulfill other's expectations when they are especially vulnerable to us, even without an explicit promise to help them. This obligation is even codified in the legal doctrine of estoppel.

If Goodin is that right that we have this general duty, then we should help those who are especially vulnerable to us, particularly when we can assist them at relatively little cost to ourselves. When others are especially vulnerable to the actions of entire groups, then those groups bear a special responsibility to help.

This account, if plausible, would bolster the

common view that we have an obligation to save the vulnerable, especially since we can collectively and individually assist them at relatively little cost to ourselves. And the fact is, we can save the lives of many. According to Bread for the World, the United States could halve the number of its own and the world's hungry with an investment of $6 billion a year, just slightly more than $20 a person.

Even if this estimate were inflated by a factor of two, we can, through concerted action, largely end world hunger by investing $100 per US citizen, per year, with the amounts diminishing over time. And with the cooperation of the rest of the developed world, we could, with the same contribution, likely end hunger and go some distance toward generally improving the lot for the more than billion people who are currently living in poverty—on less than $1 per day. It is difficult to imagine what argument could be mustered to suggest that (a) this investment is not worth that cost or that (b) any tolerably decent human being would not be willing to pay that cost. It would be, in Goodin's words, just the fulfillment of our collective and individual responsibilities.

However, the argument need not stop here—although often it does. Our mutual interdependence and the extreme vulnerability of the poor paves the way for a second, potentially more potent, argument—an argument that, if sound, shows why even a libertarian would claim that we have an obligation to assist the starving.

Responsibility in the Real World

Most discussions of world hunger ask simply whether the relatively affluent should aid the starving. They imply or assume that the starving are relatively distant, and, in some important sense, wholly independent of us. Even Drèze and Sen often speak this way: they speak of the "problems" of famines and chronic hunger and the "need" (not requirement) for "public action". However, this understates our relation to the malnourished, not only within our country, but throughout the world. It assumes that we are in no way responsible for their plight. Yet if these assumptions are false, then we arguably have a potent "negative" obligation to assist them—to rectify the wrongs we helped create, the suffering we sustain, and the inequalities from which we benefit.

According to most moral theories we have especially strong negative obligations not to cause harm. If we subsequently harm someone, then we have a potent obligation to undo that harm, and, in some cases, even to make recompense for our misdeeds. We have reason to think that those of us in affluent nations are partly caused the plight of the undernourished, that we actively sustain their impoverishment, and that we benefit from their diminished condition. If *any* of these claims are true, then we have not only the "ordinary" positive obligation to assist the vulnerable, but also a negative obligation, arising from the harm that we caused and/or sustain. If all are true, then the negative obligation would be very strong.

The relevance to world hunger is clear. We are voracious consumers. Because we want fresh fruits, coffee, and spices—and we want them at a minimal cost—we bring it about (cause) or support (sustain) efforts to convert an area's most arable land's from growing staples for the locals to growing niceties for us. Sometimes this is devastating to the local poor (even if desired by the local rich), especially if the demand for these luxuries abates, as it often does. Further, in our quest for cheap goods, we financially reward those businesses engaging in exploitative hiring practices in the

Third World, thereby partially causing the suffering of the vulnerable. We also politically support the international borrowing and resource privileges that burden democratic regimes with debts generated by former dictators, and that allow those dictators to legally abscond with the country's natural resources. Although we may occasionally complain about these (and other related) practices, the fact that we support them through our consumption and political decisions shows that we sustain the impoverishment of the worst off, and are thereby partial causes in their continuation.

Even if we do not actively support the systems that harm the impoverished, most people in the Western world benefit from the poor's predicament and do nothing to stop it. In that way we are causal contributors to their deprivation. Some might claim that our causal role—and our moral responsibility—are diminished since we simply failed to stop the harm. In other contexts, however, we recognize that inaction can causal harm. If a state fails to properly educate or provide affordable health care to its children, then the government has caused their illiteracy or ill-health; if a government fails to have an emergency system for coping with natural disasters, then it is responsible for deaths they could have prevented. And if we fail to stop as assault on a third party, especially if the cost or risk of intervening is minimal, then most of us will say that our inaction contributes to any harm befalling the victim.

These three arguments give us reason to think that we have a negative responsibility to ensure that the poor of the world are fed. However, these arguments, though powerful, are not certain. Does this give us a reason to do nothing? Of course not. We should act on the best evidence we have. The degree of epistemological certainty we require before acting depends on the relative costs of action versus inaction. Before assessing criminal penalties—where the costs to accused criminals are enormous—we reasonably demand very strong evidence of their guilt. However, under most circumstances, we do not use nor would we countenance such an exacting standard.

We should employ the same standards of evidence when (a) accepting praise, (b) holding others responsible for harms they partially cause, sustain, or could remedy, and (c) accepting responsibility for similar harms we partially cause, sustain, or could remedy. We use a more relaxed standard of evidence when accepting (and expecting) praise for our successes and when attributing blame to those who harm us. We should use the same standard when determining responsibility for our actions or inactions. If we do, then we will recognize some causal responsibility for the plight of the impoverished in our world. And, if Goodin is correct—that we needn't be causally responsible for harm to have a task responsibility for reduce harm—then we should help, especially since we can remedy their condition at relatively little cost to ourselves.

We have a multilayered argument that suggests we have a strong obligation to bolster the wellbeing of the seriously impoverished. First, we have a positive obligation to assist those who are vulnerable to our actions. Second, we also have reason to think we are partially responsible for the suffering of the world's poor, and hence, have a strong negative obligation to stop further harm. Third, we could feed them and ease their suffering pain with relatively little effort. If we do nothing In the face of these arguments, we have reason to think that we are complicitous in the deaths of many people. We might be wrong, but when, with only a relatively small sacrifice, we can avoid the decided possibility that we are accomplices in many people's deaths, then morally we ought to act.

Knowing precisely how to act is more unclear. Doubtless isolated individuals have limited power to remedy these problem. To empower and feed the impoverished we need collective action and a change in global institutions. Specifically, if the arguments in the last section are correct, then our first efforts should be to cease acting in ways that cause or sustain others' impoverishment. Then we should (a) work to bring international efforts to bear on especially corrupt governments, (b) use global resources to promote broad development that will make endemic hunger a painful note from our collective past, and (c) establish systems which effectively respond to episodic hunger.

Likely, though, bare political efforts will not entirely discharge our duties to the impoverished—since we know that governments are unlikely to soon change their ways or give the support they should. Hence, we should also contribute to non-government organizations with proven track records in eliminating hunger, promoting development, and empowering the poor. These contributions will not only assist the needy, they will shows others that we are serious about the need for our governmental and institutional change. The extent to which we should contribute is, of course, controversial—it raises the ever-pressing issue about the degree to which morality can be demanding.

Lord Bauer's Suggestions to Control Beggary

Peter Thomas Bauer is being remembered as the man who opposed foreign aid most trenchantly. He called aid 'government-to-government transfers' and said that they went from the poor of the developed world to the rich of the underdeveloped. Margaret Thatcher was strongly influenced by Bauer – she was instrumental in getting him elevated to the House of Lords in 1982, and reportedly asked Third World leaders at a Commonwealth meeting to 'read Peter Bauer' – but even she did not close down Britain's Office of Development Assistance (ODA). To the bleeding hearts brigade, Bauer's opposition to aid would make him an enemy of the world's poor.

According to Lord Bauer widespread beggary on the streets of India and Pakistan is not a sign of poverty; rather, this widespread beggary exists because the predominant communities in both countries, Hindus and Muslims respectively, believe they earn spiritual merit by giving alms to the poor. This acute observation of his is dated 1965, and is contained in the very first chapter of his book criticising Indian 'planning'. In his words:

"Hinduism and Islam, the two principal religions [of India], encourage begging, since they enjoin their followers to support beggars. Both religions extol the contemplative life, especially that of the religious mendicant, which encourages the emergence of large numbers of both genuine and bogus religious mendicants."

He pointed out that, in India, there were no Sikh, Parsi or Jain beggars – because these communities discourage beggary (a blot on the entire community), encourage selfhelp, and practice collective charity effectively. Among the Sikhs, for example, the Gurudwara hosts a daily *langar* where any poor person is free to eat to his heart's content. But with it comes a positive motivational factor: the same poor man is encouraged to go out, struggle, earn a living, and one day host a *langar* of his own for the poor. There is also a negative motivational factor: if any Sikh is found begging, other Sikhs will come and beat him up! The question: Who is a true friend of the poor and who is an enemy begins to look more complex as we scratch the surface of Third World poverty and look at phenomena like widespread beggary with a more critical eye.

Economics has a lot to do with observation. Great economists have not been abstract theorists – the so-called 'Ricardian vice' is just that: a vice – and Lord Bauer was no abstract theorist. He was a keen observer. His piercing observation on beggary in India and Pakistan has enormous implications if we want to put in place policies that will really help the poor. If the government of Delhi has woken up to the fact that beggary is an industry here, it is time the entire planet went into a huddle to discuss what constitutes the best charity.

The phenomenon of widespread beggary in India is best understood by looking at an example from Nature. The road between Roorkee and Dehradoon passes through a thick forest. At various points along the way, thousands of monkeys hang around waiting for the scraps of food that Hanuman worshippersthrow at them. Does this prove that the forest is poor and resourceless? Or does this illustrate the role of incentives – what psychologists call 'positive reinforcement'. The monkeys have discovered that hanging around by the road is a cool way of getting food. Similarly with beggars. Because civil society gives alms generously, many have found out that beggary is an easy mode of existence. These beggars do not prove that India is poor. Rather, these beggars prove that Indian civil society is rich and generous: indeed, overly generous.

Lord Bauer's observations on beggary mean that global civil society must reconsider charity. And then the million-dollar question will be raised:

Do we need the State to meaningfully help the poor?

Commonly, people are secteing one of the the following ways to help the poor:

1. Pay taxes to the State and ask it to help the poor

2. Take direct action and give alms generously to every beggar on the street
3. Contribute to the Missionaries of Charity or other such organisations actually working to help the poor

Most people overwhelmingly go for the third option. There is no other way to meaningfully help poor people. It is a hard fact that life is a struggle against adverse circumstances for all, and it is every person's duty to himself, his family and his society to help himself and not be a burden on others. This is the only ethic in a free society. Then, the only economic policy that should apply is complete economic freedom – with which comes responsibility.

It is Bauer who first championed economic freedom for the world's poor – at a time when the entire Third World went in for massive state-directed 'development' at the advice of the World Bank and the IMF. These 'architects of failed policy' manufactured permanent poverty in the Third World by aiding corrupt, predatory states which economically repressed entire peoples. It was Bauer, alone, who dissented. As the Third World gives up statism and moves to free markets – and India is definitely progressing in this direction – it is Bauer who emerges as the towering hero.

Any student of Bauer would point out that poor tribals living in the jungles of Central India possess the knowledge to distil *mahua* from a jungle flower of the same name, but they do not possess the freedom to sell this extremely wonderful alcoholic drink. There are countless Indians who can play musical instruments, sing and dance, but because the State has outlawed the nightlife industry, they languish in poverty. Bauer truly appreciated the economic skills of poor people in Africa and Asia. He noted, for example, how, because of low purchasing power, retailers would 'break down bulk' to extremely small portions: in Africa, you could buy matchsticks in pairs; and in India, cigarette vendors regularly sell loose cigarettes. His studies on the rubber industry in Malaya sang praises to the ingenuity of small traders who actually managed to collectively farm more rubber than the colonials.

Thus, Bauer is always to be found blasting what he famously called 'the denial of the economic principle': the fact that 'development economics' considered Third World poor to be sub-human – i.e., something less than *Homo Economicus*. To students of Lord Bauer, this 'denial of the economic principle' is nothing less than a crime against humanity: the construction of a politico-economic system stressing state power by assuming the people to be economically incapable and irrational.

Go to any Third World market and you will see the poorest of the poor bargaining hardest and scouting around most energetically for the best deals – while the rich get easily conned. Notice also that politicians and bureaucrats in the Third World are corrupt, ignorant and that they command not respect, but fear. They possess no 'functional legitimacy': not a single function of State, starting from traffic regulation, is carried out well. It was Bauer who appreciated the poor, and first warned about what economic totalitarianism would degenerate to. It is high time the entire Economics profession stood firm against 'the denial of the economic principle'.

Bauer's appreciation of the economic abilities of the Third World poor had a very direct positive benefit: it led to academic interest in what has since come to be known as the 'informal sector'. It is estimated that, in South Asia, the informal sector is growing much faster than its formal counterpart – and this is living testament to the economic skills of the people: something Bauer was the first to appreciate. His song was a 'fanfare to the common man'.

In India, it is now a horrific truth that the State is a predator on the informal sector. After an aggressive, high-profile campaign by *Manushi,* even the Prime Minister's office has been forced to concede that hawkers, street vendors and rickshaw pullers in Delhi alone cough up 50 crore rupees every month in illegal bribes to police and municipal functionaries. So we have come a long way from 'the denial of the economic principle'. We have travelled all the way to 'the predatory state'. Everything Lord Bauer stood for has been vindicated; while the people in whom Gunnar Myrdal and Amartya Sen placed so much faith are now openly seen as members of Count Dracula's tribe: blood-sucking vampires.

But Bauer did much more than merely appreciate the economic skills of the people: he was the first to stress that they were an economic resource. He strongly opposed Malthusianism in the Third World – the 'population problem' *wallahs* – and this was long before Julian Simon hit the scene.Bauer noted that there was no correlation between poverty and population growth rates. He also said that the First World had quadrupled its population since 1800, but incomes had gone up even more. Bauer's prescription for stabilising human numbers was simple: increased commercial contact between nations and people so that urbanisation and development would occur. This is a very important area where Bauer stands tall: he stood for the freedom of people to reproduce as they deem fit.

In India, Sanjay Gandhi's programme of forced mass sterilisation is fresh memory. In China they enforced the 'one-child norm' because of which an entire generation of Chinese have 'no brothers, no sisters, no cousins, no uncles, no aunts, two parents and four doting grandparents'. In India, on the 50anniversary of freedom from colonial rule, the Parliament of India, in an unanimous resolution, said that population was India's biggest problem: that is, the representatives of the people were saying that their constituents are a 'problem'! This is a Parliament – against the people!

The greatest enemies of poor people are those who oppose free immigration – often under the guise of the 'population problem'. They divide the world into nation-states and expect people to be indentured to their governments. In the world of today, there are just a handful of good governments. A predominant majority of the members of the United Nations are predatory states whose policies keep people poor. It is fairly obvious that, if immigration were free, people would opt to pay taxes to governments of their choice and, in quick time, predatory states, tyrants, rogue dictators and the like would have no taxpayers left. They would be out of business without any 'global cop'. Instead of this happy scenario, in which government itself faces the market test, these anti-freedom forces keep the Third World poor locked in with predatory regimes – which they prop up. And where they go about 'alleviating' poverty.

Are these people – who travel all over the Third World in airconditioned Pajeros – true friends of the world's poor? Or is it someone like Lord Bauer, who carefully studied and reported on the adverse effects of immigration control in Africa when the continent was divided into nation-states?Only those who despise poor people believe in immigration control. They have nightmares about their countries being swamped by the Third World poor. They do not consider these poor people to be resourceful and energetic economic actors who will soon generate wealth for themselves and their adopted homeland.

A great contribution of Bauer is his definition of poverty. Poverty, he said, indicates just one thing: the absence of economic achievement. Then he went on to add: Economic achievements are made in markets. People are poor because they cannot access markets – as in the case of villagers without roads. Or, when they do go to market, the market is not truly open and free, and they are therefore unable to make as great an achievement as they would otherwise have.

According to Lord Bauer "Capital is the result of economic achievement, not its precondition". These are very important words. Every nation that is rich today started off poor – including America. History is full of rags-to-riches stories. Indeed, inherited wealth is often a curse, and the children of rich people often settle down to a life of idleness, luxury and vice. Instead of teaching the truth – that poverty is a motivator – the socialist State is teaching this complete nonsense and thereby destroying the vital *élan* in our youth. Eager, young minds come seeking knowledge. They do not get knowledge. They do not get truth. They are not told how wealth is created by humans – and humans alone. Instead, they are taught that they and their brethren are the 'population problem'; and, further, that poverty is inescapable. They are taught that the future for them and their nation is bleak.

In Lord Bauer's view, the rural people were not 'poor'; they were 'needless'. All that they wanted, they obtained from Nature. Since they had no other needs, they did not work for the market. Bauer's prescription: not aid, not state-led 'development', but the letting loose of traders with 'incentive goods'. A poor villager would see a radio, desire it, and go about energetically climbing coconut trees, harvesting the fruit, selling it in the market, and making enough to buy the radio. Without the radio – without free trade and traders –there were no incentives to work in the market economy. This observation is particularly true of North-East India – the poorest and most underdeveloped region of socialist

India. To develop, the people of the North-East require an internationalised economy. Today, they have to go to Calcutta to shop. They are not 'poor'.

Another of Bauer's great contributions to our understanding of the fallacies of 'planned development' is the unnecessary stress policy makers in the developing world have placed on 'export promotion'. Bauer is the only one who said that countries like India are not poor because they cannot export; they are poor because they cannot produce! The shoddy infrastructure limits the ability of the people to produce. If that was tackled, and the market freed India could become one the world's leading manufacturing destinations. In his own words:

> "Neither in developed nor in underdeveloped economies is there particular merit in directing resources towards exports or import-saving activities instead of simply trying to ensure that they are deployed to contribute most to present or future output. The distinction between activities yielding or saving foreign exchange and other activities becomes material only if the national currency is overvalued in the sense that the foreign exchange earned or saved, expressed in local currency, understates the contribution of these resources to the flow of income. In the absence of an overvaluation of the exchange rate in this sense, any increase in national output makes the same contribution to available goods and services, regardless of destination. Thus it follows that the capacity to export or to import does not set up obstacles for development distinct from those stemming from the limited capacity to produce."

Export promotion is just a racket run by the ministry of commerce. If someone came into your shop and bought, say, a briefcase, would it bother you if he took the briefcase to the house next door or carried it all the way to Singapore? The destination (and the origin) of a good is of no consequence to any market transaction. This understanding of the Third World was a singular contribution of Peter Bauer.

So what was Peter Bauer's *mantra* for the economic upliftment of the Third World? To sum it up: free trade, free immigration, sound money and property rights. He stood for the eternal verities of classical liberal political economy. His emphasis on sound money makes him an honest economist, one who always opposed debasement. Bauer and BR Shenoy are the only economists who opposed the 'deficit financing' carried out to fund Nehru's ambitious Second Five Year Plan. Bauer went on to repeat on many an occasion that India's subsequent balance of payments problems were all caused by this episode of money creation: debasement would be a better word.

The Bretton Woods system that created the IMF and World Bank had envisaged a planet divided into nation states, each with the essential trappings of sovereignty – which included a central bank. Developing countries do not need central banks. Corrupt regimes cannot be allowed to monopolistically issue money and control the allocation of credit. It is time the entire profession of economists came out strongly on this issue. The future of globalisation depends on it. Free trade is not possible without freely tradeable currencies. Globalisation, the freeing of capital flows internationally, and the consequent inability of many Third World central banks to cope, means that the Bretton Woods twins have outlived their utility. They should both be closed down, and open currency competition instituted. Sound money is something Peter Bauer laid great stress on.

Anti-Panhandling By-laws

Over the past several years, cities across the world

have witnessed a tremendous increase in the number of people panhandling. This visibility is generating much public discussion and debate about the causes of panhandling and what to do about it. One popular response among municipal governments is to introduce antipanhandling legislation, which restricts where, when and how one person can ask another for assistance.

The appearance of anti-panhandling bylaws is an issue of great concern for many counties. The existence of anti-panhandling by-laws raises significant questions about the violation of the human rights. Reductions in government support to people in need of income security have created conditions that force people to beg and rely on individual donations in order to simply survive. Antipanhandling by-laws effectively render the social consequences of government policies invisible. They direct our gaze away from the failure and meanspiritedness of government social and economic policies and shift it to individuals. The by-laws blame and punish people for their poverty.

The practice of making poor people the scapegoats for society's social and economic problems is known as "poor bashing". Turning to the criminal justice system for a solution to what is essentially a socio-economic issue stands out clearly as an example of poor bashing. Such discrimination suggests that the rights of the pooresr are less important than the rights of those who have money.

The reasons for panhandling are multifaceted and are connected to issues of income, food security, housing, social programs and wages, among other things. Growing economic and social inequality can be attributed to both decreased income from earnings and the systematic erosion of our welfare state, which no longer provides adequate incomes to citizen in times of need. In the interests of deficit reduction, federal and provincial governments targeted social programs for dramatic funding cuts. Social spending was falsely declared to be "out of control", needing to be reigned in rather than viewed as a building block of a just, caring and compassionate society.

Historically, the role of income support programs has been a means to counter market failures by redistributing income within the country. This is rapidly changing as both programs have been significantly eroded and scaled back through dramatic reductions in funding levels and tightening of eligibility and entitlement.

Local Responses to Panhandling

The presence of panhandlers confronts us with the underside of a free market economy in which wealth and the benefits of economic growth do not "trickle down" to everyone. Some citizens have made it clear that they are not comfortable being confronted with this reality. In response to the presence of panhandlers on city streets, several local authorities across the country have implemented antipanhandling by-laws.

The anti-panhandling by-laws restrict panhandling in different ways. First, they seek to restrict *where* it occurs. Many of the by-laws prohibit panhandling at transit stops and bus shelters, in front of banks and automated teller machines, in pedestrian walkways, and at traffic control signals or parked motor vehicles. In addition, some local authorities' by-laws prohibits panhandling at the entrance of hospitals; and several others specify prohibition in front of liquor stores; and some others prevent it in front of mobile food vendors, such as hot-dog stands.

These specific geographic restrictions reveal some of the stereotyped assumptions about people living in poverty that are behind the by-laws. Prohibiting panhandling in front of a bank or automated teller machine, for example, assumes panhandlers are more likely to be thieves than other citizens. Likewise, making it illegal to ask for money outside of a liquor store assumes a problem of alcoholism.

From the point of view of a panhandler, however, these sites could be considered strategic locations where a non-panhandler has made some kind of financial transaction (for example, buying a bottle of wine or a hot-dog, or withdrawing money from a bank machine) and possibly has some loose change readily available upon request. In other words, they are wisely chosen locations for panhandling.

The by-laws also seek to control *when* panhandling can occur, although it is inconsistent and varies between cities. For example, In Canada the Calgary by-law makes it illegal between 8:00 a.m. to 8:00 p.m.; Saskatoon from 9:00 a.m. to 6:00 p.m., and Vancouver and Winnipeg between sunset and sunrise. Ottawa has an outright ban on panhandling in all public areas, 24 hours a day. The by-laws seek to regulate *the manner* in which panhandling occurs. The Calgary by-law, for example, states "No person shall continue to engage in panhandling...with a person who has refused or declined the solicitation. No person shall, while engaging in panhandling, move to obstruct the passage of, walk next to, or follow the person being solicited."

In Canada, the Criminal Code prohibits obtaining money by force, and aggressive or threatening actions. Thus these by-laws seek to penalize a conduct, begging, that is peaceful and nondisruptive. Contravention of these by-laws can result in a financial penalty, which vary from city to city. Panhandlers in Vancouver can be fined a minimum of $100.00 and up to a maximum of $2000.00. Calgary states no minimum but sets its maximum at $10,000.00 (!). Those in Quebec City can be charged $500.00 while people in Winnipeg can receive a maximum financial penalty of $1000.00. Not only do panhandlers face this financial discrimination, they also risk terms of imprisonment if they do not pay. The Calgary by-law allows for up to one year in jail; Winnipeg allows for up to six months.

These legal sanctions show the by-laws for what they really are: a mechanism of social control. By criminalizing the simple act of asking another for help, antipanhandling by-laws identify a group in society as not deserving of human rights protection. Moreover, the fact (and irony) that these by-laws impose such stiff financial penalties on a population which has no or little income to begin with indicates quite clearly that in no way are the by-laws designed to assist people who panhandle.

Clearly, such legislation cannot provide a disincentive when other social and income supports remain inadequate. What, then, is the rationale for such legislation? At one level, these by-laws are consistent with a historical pattern of "cleaning up" city streets for tourism as witnessed at Expo '86 in Vancouver, the 1992 Earth Summit in Rio de Janeiro, the 1996 Olympics in Atlanta, and at the 1999 Pan Am Games in Winnipeg. For example, although the Winnipeg City Council passed its anti panhandling by-law in 1995, as the Games drew nearer there was a concerted effort to "ensure that 'undesirables' be removed from all areas of the city where the Games will be celebrated...

Winnipeg will appear dressed up, when in reality buildings will still exist behind the pretty murals, while the homeless and other 'vagrants' will only be allowed to emerge when the Games are over and everyone has gone home.This "out of sight, out of mind" attitude is the strategy of choice by city bureaucrats to deal with panhandling.

Arguments to justify the anti-panhandling by-laws fall into three broad categories: the preservation of economic vitality of city areas; the public's right to the peaceful enjoyment of public places; and the eradication of an unhealthy lifestyle. These justifications will now be examined as well as why they are problematic, weaving in public attitudes and opinions garnered from daily newspapers.

Rationale for By-laws

One argument employed to justify antipanhandling by-laws is that they will preserve the economic vitality of downtown areas. It is believed that panhandlers constitute a street nuisance and consequently their presence creates an environment that is bad for business. "...business owners and their employees have a right to be able to conduct their affairs in an environment that is conducive to their continued viability.

Therefore it is necessary to find ways to minimize situations that compromise the ability of business operators to make a living".The assumption behind this position is that people who panhandle may annoy or upset pedestrians who will then stop shopping in downtown areas, resulting in lost business. Further strengthening this argument is a belief that people who panhandle pose a threat to public and private property and therefore must be removed.

While no study exists to prove a connection between the presence of panhandlers and a decline in business revenue, the fear is that: "when the norms of orderly behaviour are ignored...many people stay off the streets when they can or, more dramatically, they 'vote with their feet' by moving to other, safer, nicer neighbourhoods".According to proponents of this argument, city centres will enter a downward spiral, as middle-class people are driven out and a further deterioration of services will occur.

This argument in favour of the by-laws ultimately creates a hierarchy of rights that places the rights of businesses and shoppers ahead of the rights of people living in poverty. This approach maintains that panhandlers threaten the interests of consumers and businesses, while ignoring the fact that the by-law threatens the interests and rights of those who panhandle. Urban cores are a site of social and economic interaction and as such are a good strategic location to publicly request assistance for basic necessities, such as food. Furthermore, although it may be distressing for someone to encounter and interact with a person who panhandles, "we don't have to accept laws that make compassion illegal."

A second argument employed to prohibit panhandling is premised on the public's right to the peaceful enjoyment of public places and, as such, panhandlers constitute an infringement of this right. The City of Ottawa's by-law, for example, states its purpose as "...to provide for an environment free from certain public nuisances which may degrade the quality and tranquility of life".Saskatoon's bylaw gives its purpose as "...to ensure that panhandling does not unreasonably interfere with the use of streets, sidewalks and other public places by members of the public".One assumption behind this argument is that encounters with people living in poverty who are publicly asking for help are not a "pleasant" experience for the non-poor public and thus must be avoided. An op-ed piece in the *Globe and Mail*, for example, reads:

"The truth is, you cannot escape the intrusion of these people and their outstretched hands into your lives. And it is not fair...They have turned an infringement on the public's right to the peaceful enjoyment of our public places into an unsavoury industry"

This argument attempts to establish people who panhandle as "other", as identified with substance abuse, misfortune, dirt and bad smells. The bylaws are designed as a distancing mechanism between the poor and nonpoor. They effectively exclude people living in poverty from being considered as part of "the public" and therefore not equally entitled to enjoy public spaces.

Discomfort at what panhandlers represent and the consequent narrowing of the definition of "public" shifts, in turn, the notion of "citizenship". Take, for example, an op-ed piece in the *Ottawa Citizen* that states: "Public spaces shouldn't contain things that offend a significant number of people, and beggars do. It's time the cops moved them along".

Defining people who beg as "things" is a shift in discourse that is highly problematic and erases people who panhandle right out of the concept of citizenship. It is a use of language that is de-humanizing to people living in poverty. Not only are people who panhandle defined as the "other", whom the by-laws seek to place outside the boundaries of "normal" society, they are no longer considered as human, active, creative, and thinking people.

Justifying by-laws on the basis that panhandlers infringe on the peaceful enjoyment of public space serves as another means of social control and exclusion. By eliminating people who panhandle from the "public", the by-laws control who is in and who is out, who are acceptable as citizens and who are not. Is it that panhandlers pose a danger to public health and safety or is it that we don't like what they represent? Instead of legislating panhandlers out of our consciousness and out of our understanding and meaning of who constitutes "the public", perhaps we need to be disturbed and provoked by their presence, and to direct our anger to the appropriate sources – current economic and social policies pursued by all levels of government.

A final argument in support of the by-laws is that by making panhandling illegal, poor people will be forced to find employment and thereby break a cycle of laziness and an unhealthy lifestyle. This argument supports the idea that the by-laws are actually intended to help poor people. Reflecting this viewpoint, a letter to the editor in the *Ottawa Citizen* states, "While it is tempting to give a few coins to a panhandler...the consequence is that these people will not seek better ways to earn a living and we are unconsciously keeping them in the panhandling ghetto."

There are self-righteous undertones to this argument implying that panhandlers have chosen not to work in favour of the life of leisure that panhandling seemingly provides. As such, this argument feeds into discriminatory assumptions that people living in poverty are lazy and lack ambition.

Underlying the justification of "helping" panhandlers is the strategy of holding them to be entirely responsible for their situation. In fact, the by-laws add further support to the illusion that individuals alone have the power to improve their economic circumstances. They distract the so called "public" from the fundamental issues that contribute to panhandling in the first place, such as inadequate resources to deal with homelessness; lack of social housing; reductions in government supports, and destruction of our social safety net. Panhandlers are held to be responsible for their plight by a society that has opted for a war on the poor instead of a war on poverty.

Panhandling and Human Rights

Anti-panhandling by-laws seek to mask the very

visible manifestation of poverty rather than address it. At best, they succeed in hiding the issues from the general public. At worst, they are an attack on one of the most disadvantaged groups in society. Anti-panhandling legislation fosters divisiveness, and encourages poor bashing as an acceptable public attitude. In her book *The Ugly Canadian: The Rise and Fall of a Caring Society*, Barbara Murphy notes that tough public attitudes in the 1990s are similar to those in Canada in the early years of the century. She asks: "Where did all that caring go? We take pride in our toughness now, not our generous social policies. We warn the poor and the sick to keep their heads up, they've had their innings. The years of compassion are over. Today we're playing hardball."

Anti-panhandling by-laws and the attitudes accompan-ying them underscore this hard line attitude. As this paper has demonstrated, there is another lens through which to view and understand panhandling, and hence, other choices to deal with it than such discriminatory legislation. Poor bashing does not and should not remain an acceptable public attitude or the dominant public discourse.

Placing the anti-panhandling by-laws within a framework of human rights abuse is one viable strategy to counter poor bashing and to eliminate anti-panhandling by-laws from municipalities. Human rights are often perceived as being synonymous with civil and political rights; but the protection of social and economic rights is integral to realizing human rights and ensuring individual freedom and dignity. Indeed, poverty is one of the most critical human rights issue facing today.

Many of the elements in anti-panhandling legislation constitute an infringement of human rights as recognized in the Canadian Charter of Rights and Freedoms. The Charter was added to Canada's constitution when it was repatriated from Britain in 1982.

It consists of constitutionally protected rights that seek to ensure human rights are respected and that inequality is reduced among Canadians. 30 Under the framework of The Charter, anti-panhandling by-laws often infringe on three distinct rights: freedom of expression, the right to equality without discrimination, and the right to security of the person.

Freedom of Expression

Anti-panhandling by-laws seek to penalize conduct that is by its nature peaceful and non-disruptive. As such, they are in contravention of section 2 of the Charter of Rights and Freedoms because they curtail the right to freedom of expression. In other words, the by-laws deny to panhandlers the right to communicate to another person, in a public place, his or her need for assistance. A ruling in a successful constitutional challenge in Massachusetts on this very point also reflected that such prohibition suppressed "an even broader right - the right to engage fellow human beings with the hope of receiving aid and compassion."

In asking for money, a relationship is built between a panhandler and the person she or he is requesting money from. On the flip side of the right to freedom of expression, then, is the right of donors to freely give direct aid to someone in need. The act of giving involves the values of social solidarity, compassion and community building.

Equality Before the Law Without Discrimination

The by-laws deny to panhandlers equality before and under the law without discrimination. They discriminate on the basis of poverty because they have a disproportionate impact on persons who live in poverty. It is only poor people who are being restricted from parts of a city that are supposed to be open to full public access.

Furthermore, the legislation discriminates on the basis of some of the personal characteristics of people who live in poverty (such as homelessness, mental illness and addictions) in that the by-laws will have a disproportionate impact on these sub-groups of persons living in poverty. These personal characteristics are prohibited grounds of discrimination under the Charter.

The by-laws are deny to panhandler's the equal protection and benefit of the law. They aim to distance and separate panhandlers from the rest of the population in public places, by virtue of their activities. The negative consequences of this shift in consciousness about who is included as part of the public has been previously noted. Essentially, this argument seeks to reaffirm that people who are poor and who panhandle are indeed an integral part of our cities and communities and as such, have the right to equal access and use of public spaces.

Security of the Person

The by-laws deny to certain classes of individuals the ability to provide for the necessities of life, including food, shelter and clothing thereby undermining their own personal security. It also undermines individual efforts to deal with poverty. This right is further denied through the imposition of financial penalties and/or terms of imprisonment. Given the financial circumstances that lead people to panhandle in the first place, it is likely that many panhandlers will not be able to pay the fine and may be jailed.

9

Distribution of Beggars (India/States/ Union Territories/Districts 2001)

Distribution of Beggars

States, Union Territories, Districts	*T/R/U*	*Person*	*Male*	*Female*
1	2	3	4	5
JAMMU & KASHMIR	Total	8,635	5,216	3,419
	Rural	5,513	3,263	2,250
	Urban	3,122	1,953	1,169
Kupwara	Total	434	233	201
	Rural	410	224	186
	Urban	24	9	15
Baramula	Total	1,250	826	424
	Rural	861	557	304
	Urban	389	269	120
Srinagar	Total	1,757	1,045	712
	Rural	564	309	255
	Urban	1,193	736	457

Contd.

Contd.

1	2	3	4	5
Badgam	Total	1,099	657	442
	Rural	802	500	302
	Urban	297	157	140
Pulwama	Total	365	214	151
	Rural	338	203	135
	Urban	27	11	16
Anantnag	Total	1,327	770	557
	Rural	989	572	417
	Urban	338	198	140
Leh (Ladakh)	Total	36	19	17
	Rural	29	16	13
	Urban	7	3	4
Kargil	Total	288	129	159
	Rural	283	127	156
	Urban	5	2	3
Doda	Total	136	74	62
	Rural	120	65	55
	Urban	16	9	7
Udhampur	Total	301	156	145
	Rural	194	97	97
	Urban	107	59	48
Punch	Total	153	86	67
	Rural	145	83	62
	Urban	8	3	5
Rajauri	Total	177	103	74
	Rural	166	97	69
	Urban	11	6	5
Jammu	Total	880	578	302
	Rural	265	146	119
	Urban	615	432	183
Kathua	Total	432	326	106
	Rural	347	267	80
	Urban	85	59	26

Contd.

Contd.

1	2	3	4	5
HIMACHAL	Total	2,033	1,147	886
PRADESH	Rural	1,614	885	729
	Urban	419	262	157
Chamba	Total	60	39	21
	Rural	52	35	17
	Urban	8	4	4
Kangra	Total	471	292	179
	Rural	362	229	133
	Urban	109	63	46
Lahul & Spiti	Total	1	-	1
	Rural	1	-	1
	Urban	-	-	-
Kullu	Total	196	111	85
	Rural	149	75	74
	Urban	47	36	11
Mandi	Total	220	125	95
	Rural	181	97	84
	Urban	39	28	11
Hamirpur	Total	106	56	50
	Rural	90	48	42
	Urban	16	8	8
Una	Total	210	110	100
	Rural	159	82	77
	Urban	51	28	23
Bilaspur	Total	108	56	52
	Rural	90	43	47
	Urban	18	13	5
Solan	Total	124	61	63
	Rural	91	43	48
	Urban	33	18	15
Sirmaur	Total	264	148	116
	Rural	221	123	98
	Urban	43	25	18

Contd.

Contd.

1	2	3	4	5
Shimla	Total	258	142	116
	Rural	203	103	100
	Urban	55	39	16
Kinnaur	Total	15	7	8
	Rural	15	7	8
	Urban	-	-	-
PUNJAB	Total	21,200	12,948	8,252
	Rural	8,245	4,700	3,545
	Urban	12,955	8,248	4,707
Gurdaspur	Total	1,401	780	621
	Rural	713	398	315
	Urban	688	382	306
Amritsar	Total	8,438	5,367	3,071
	Rural	2,370	1,364	1,006
	Urban	6,068	4,003	2,065
Kapurthala	Total	362	184	178
	Rural	145	82	63
	Urban	217	102	115
Jalandhar	Total	1,178	714	464
	Rural	308	168	140
	Urban	870	546	324
Hoshiarpur	Total	668	413	255
	Rural	362	213	149
	Urban	306	200	106
Nawanshahr *	Total	190	106	84
	Rural	119	63	56
	Urban	71	43	28
Rupnagar	Total	372	214	158
	Rural	177	92	85
	Urban	195	122	73
Fatehgarh Sahib *	Total	428	284	144
	Rural	156	96	60
	Urban	272	188	84

Contd.

Contd.

1	2	3	4	5
Ludhiana	Total	2,126	1,369	757
	Rural	557	318	239
	Urban	1,569	1,051	518
Moga *	Total	533	313	220
	Rural	318	201	117
	Urban	215	112	103
Firozpur	Total	863	482	381
	Rural	425	205	220
	Urban	438	277	161
Muktsar *	Total	322	199	123
	Rural	164	89	75
	Urban	158	110	48
Faridkot	Total	268	152	116
	Rural	74	42	32
	Urban	194	110	84
Bathinda	Total	624	404	220
	Rural	251	161	90
	Urban	373	243	130
Mansa *	Total	499	289	210
	Rural	292	170	122
	Urban	207	119	88
Sangrur	Total	2,037	1,074	963
	Rural	1,343	684	659
	Urban	694	390	304
Patiala	Total	891	604	287
	Rural	471	354	117
	Urban	420	250	170
CHANDIGARH	Total	425	226	199
	Rural	43	24	19
	Urban	382	202	180
Chandigarh	Total	425	226	199
	Rural	43	24	19
	Urban	382	202	180

Contd.

Contd.

1	2	3	4	5
HARYANA	Total	12,644	8,484	4,160
	Rural	6,637	4,431	2,206
	Urban	6,007	4,053	1,954
Panchkula *	Total	195	120	75
	Rural	61	26	35
	Urban	134	94	40
Ambala	Total	908	598	310
	Rural	337	201	136
	Urban	571	397	174
Yamunanagar	Total	964	555	409
	Rural	361	208	153
	Urban	603	347	256
Kurukshetra	Total	1,070	906	164
	Rural	222	160	62
	Urban	848	746	102
Kaithal	Total	643	460	183
	Rural	421	304	117
	Urban	222	156	66
Karnal	Total	1,389	1,027	362
	Rural	856	660	196
	Urban	533	367	166
Panipat	Total	907	631	276
	Rural	489	391	98
	Urban	418	240	178
Sonipat	Total	620	391	229
	Rural	290	197	93
	Urban	330	194	136
Jind	Total	646	490	156
	Rural	403	297	106
	Urban	243	193	50
Fatehabad *	Total	448	262	186
	Rural	318	184	134
	Urban	130	78	52

Contd.

Contd.

1	2	3	4	5
Sirsa	Total	667	423	244
	Rural	473	315	158
	Urban	194	108	86
Hisar	Total	894	601	293
	Rural	466	298	168
	Urban	428	303	125
Bhiwani	Total	526	347	179
	Rural	400	255	145
	Urban	126	92	34
Rohtak	Total	422	271	151
	Rural	161	105	56
	Urban	261	166	95
Jhajjar *	Total	235	138	97
	Rural	160	92	68
	Urban	75	46	29
Mahendragarh	Total	237	166	71
	Rural	158	103	55
	Urban	79	63	16
Rewari	Total	246	175	71
	Rural	135	78	57
	Urban	111	97	14
Gurgaon	Total	604	315	289
	Rural	457	245	212
	Urban	147	70	77
Faridabad	Total	1,023	608	415
	Rural	469	312	157
	Urban	554	296	258
DELHI	Total	5,247	3,446	1,801
	Rural	202	101	101
	Urban	5,045	3,345	1,700
North West *	Total	744	554	190
	Rural	59	38	21
	Urban	685	516	169

Contd.

Contd.

1	2	3	4	5
North *	Total	341	236	105
	Rural	4	1	3
	Urban	337	235	102
North East *	Total	1,074	889	185
	Rural	15	8	7
	Urban	1,059	881	178
East *	Total	264	150	114
	Rural	8	6	2
	Urban	256	144	112
New Delhi	Total	72	60	12
	Rural	-	-	-
	Urban	72	60	12
Central *	Total	626	211	415
	Rural	-	-	-
	Urban	626	211	415
West *	Total	757	497	260
	Rural	9	5	4
	Urban	748	492	256
South West *	Total	568	337	231
	Rural	94	35	59
	Urban	474	302	172
South *	Total	801	512	289
	Rural	13	8	5
	Urban	788	504	284
RAJASTHAN	Total	46,247	27,280	18,967
	Rural	28,825	15,562	13,263
	Urban	17,422	11,718	5,704
Ganganagar	Total	1,619	925	694
	Rural	734	455	279
	Urban	885	470	415
Hanumangarh *	Total	887	553	334
	Rural	670	408	262
	Urban	217	145	72

Contd.

Contd.

1	2	3	4	5
Bikaner	Total	788	405	383
	Rural	370	173	197
	Urban	418	232	186
Churu	Total	1,263	708	555
	Rural	790	431	359
	Urban	473	277	196
Jhunjhunun	Total	872	477	395
	Rural	592	324	268
	Urban	280	153	127
Alwar	Total	1,545	951	594
	Rural	1,340	831	509
	Urban	205	120	85
Bharatpur	Total	1,084	761	323
	Rural	741	548	193
	Urban	343	213	130
Dhaulpur	Total	764	487	277
	Rural	461	322	139
	Urban	303	165	138
Karauli *	Total	540	369	171
	Rural	459	312	147
	Urban	81	57	24
Sawai Madhopur	Total	925	537	388
	Rural	557	310	247
	Urban	368	227	141
Dausa *	Total	685	449	236
	Rural	570	382	188
	Urban	115	67	48
Jaipur	Total	2,357	1,534	823
	Rural	1,109	699	410
	Urban	1,248	835	413
Sikar	Total	1,289	731	558
	Rural	1,018	565	453
	Urban	271	166	105

Contd.

Contd.

1	2	3	4	5
Nagaur	Total	2,268	1,222	1,046
	Rural	1,796	949	847
	Urban	472	273	199
Jodhpur	Total	2,543	1,370	1,173
	Rural	1,731	907	824
	Urban	812	463	349
Jaisalmer	Total	357	205	152
	Rural	329	188	141
	Urban	28	17	11
Barmer	Total	2,423	1,320	1,103
	Rural	2,289	1,227	1,062
	Urban	134	93	41
Jalor	Total	1,074	590	484
	Rural	873	479	394
	Urban	201	111	90
Sirohi	Total	1,113	619	494
	Rural	927	500	427
	Urban	186	119	67
Pali	Total	1,972	958	1,014
	Rural	1,451	681	770
	Urban	521	277	244
Ajmer	Total	8,459	6,368	2,091
	Rural	919	409	510
	Urban	7,540	5,959	1,581
Tonk	Total	873	408	465
	Rural	657	297	360
	Urban	216	111	105
Bundi	Total	334	189	145
	Rural	265	143	122
	Urban	69	46	23
Bhilwara	Total	1,422	718	704
	Rural	1,160	580	580
	Urban	262	138	124

Contd.

Contd.

1	2	3	4	5
Rajsamand *	Total	1,000	467	533
	Rural	871	398	473
	Urban	129	69	60
Udaipur	Total	1,624	804	820
	Rural	1,347	657	690
	Urban	277	147	130
Dungarpur	Total	1,741	814	927
	Rural	1,595	731	864
	Urban	146	83	63
Banswara	Total	1,512	761	751
	Rural	1,326	671	655
	Urban	186	90	96
Chittaurgarh	Total	1,097	566	531
	Rural	809	393	416
	Urban	288	173	115
Kota	Total	935	513	422
	Rural	433	240	193
	Urban	502	273	229
Baran *	Total	368	220	148
	Rural	272	162	110
	Urban	96	58	38
Jhalawar	Total	514	281	233
	Rural	364	190	174
	Urban	150	91	59
UTTAR PRADESH	Total	120,013	72,317	47,696
	Rural	88,602	51,857	36,745
	Urban	31,411	20,460	10,951
Saharanpur	Total	1,719	1,000	719
	Rural	1,063	583	480
	Urban	656	417	239
Muzaffarnagar	Total	2,272	1,315	957
	Rural	1,472	889	583
	Urban	800	426	374

Contd.

Contd.

1	2	3	4	5
Bijnor	Total	2,278	1,403	875
	Rural	1,698	1,062	636
	Urban	580	341	239
Moradabad	Total	1,791	1,019	772
	Rural	1,301	744	557
	Urban	490	275	215
Rampur	Total	1,328	784	544
	Rural	923	498	425
	Urban	405	286	119
Jyotiba Phule * Nagar	Total	745	420	325
	Rural	521	282	239
	Urban	224	138	86
Meerut	Total	1,304	726	578
	Rural	525	318	207
	Urban	779	408	371
Baghpat *	Total	442	296	146
	Rural	324	230	94
	Urban	118	66	52
Ghaziabad	Total	1,365	809	556
	Rural	593	340	253
	Urban	772	469	303
Gautam Buddha Nagar *	Total	600	370	230
	Rural	327	216	111
	Urban	273	154	119
Bulandshahar	Total	1,888	1,097	791
	Rural	1,118	659	459
	Urban	770	438	332
Aligarh	Total	1,782	995	787
	Rural	1,013	572	441
	Urban	769	423	346
Hathras *	Total	672	419	253
	Rural	501	308	193
	Urban	171	111	60

Contd.

Contd.

1	2	3	4	5
Mathura	Total	3,106	2,201	905
	Rural	1,327	1,021	306
	Urban	1,779	1,180	599
Agra	Total	2,203	1,254	949
	Rural	1,072	678	394
	Urban	1,131	576	555
Firozabad	Total	1,111	663	448
	Rural	551	352	199
	Urban	560	311	249
Etah	Total	1,553	959	594
	Rural	1,062	624	438
	Urban	491	335	156
1Mainpuri	Total	717	482	235
	Rural	536	356	180
	Urban	181	126	55
Budaun	Total	1,739	1,007	732
	Rural	1,333	784	549
	Urban	406	223	183
Bareilly	Total	2,272	1,501	771
	Rural	1,540	1,021	519
	Urban	732	480	252
Pilibhit	Total	939	527	412
	Rural	736	415	321
	Urban	203	112	91
Shahjahanpur	Total	1,458	940	518
	Rural	1,165	742	423
	Urban	293	198	95
Kheri	Total	2,119	1,128	991
	Rural	1,903	1,016	887
	Urban	216	112	104
Sitapur	Total	2,558	1,578	980
	Rural	2,007	1,193	814
	Urban	551	385	166

Contd.

Contd.

1	2	3	4	5
Hardoi	Total	1,897	1,237	660
	Rural	1,595	1,047	548
	Urban	302	190	112
Unnao	Total	1,651	935	716
	Rural	1,375	791	584
	Urban	276	144	132
Lucknow	Total	1,974	1,204	770
	Rural	656	362	294
	Urban	1,318	842	476
Rae Bareli	Total	2,687	1,375	1,312
	Rural	2,402	1,202	1,200
	Urban	285	173	112
Farrukhabad	Total	1,024	637	387
	Rural	864	548	316
	Urban	160	89	71
Kannauj *	Total	864	528	336
	Rural	721	427	294
	Urban	143	101	42
Etawah	Total	599	417	182
	Rural	453	336	117
	Urban	146	81	65
Auraiya *	Total	1,197	913	284
	Rural	1,090	852	238
	Urban	107	61	46
Kanpur Dehat	Total	1,413	868	545
	Rural	1,309	808	501
	Urban	104	60	44
Kanpur Nagar	Total	5,392	3,588	1,804
	Rural	1,358	748	610
	Urban	4,034	2,840	1,194
Jalaun	Total	745	505	240
	Rural	554	374	180
	Urban	191	131	60

Contd.

Contd.

1	2	3	4	5
Jhansi	Total	1,061	645	416
	Rural	615	374	241
	Urban	446	271	175
Lalitpur	Total	307	154	153
	Rural	255	127	128
	Urban	52	27	25
Hamirpur	Total	566	423	143
	Rural	436	335	101
	Urban	130	88	42
Mahoba *	Total	330	227	103
	Rural	254	176	78
	Urban	76	51	25
Banda	Total	1,284	1,018	266
	Rural	860	673	187
	Urban	424	345	79
1Chitrakoot *	Total	715	521	194
	Rural	451	303	148
	Urban	264	218	46
Fatehpur	Total	1,574	1,063	511
	Rural	1,438	983	455
	Urban	136	80	56
Pratapgarh	Total	1,795	1,099	696
	Rural	1,734	1,060	674
	Urban	61	39	22
Kaushambi *	Total	1,033	715	318
	Rural	953	658	295
	Urban	80	57	23
Allahabad	Total	5,465	3,635	1,830
	Rural	2,625	1,436	1,189
	Urban	2,840	2,199	641
Barabanki	Total	2,767	1,497	1,270
	Rural	2,585	1,402	1,183
	Urban	182	95	87

Contd.

Contd.

1	2	3	4	5
Faizabad	Total	1,890	1,221	669
	Rural	1,204	642	562
	Urban	686	579	107
Ambedkar Nagar *	Total	1,637	951	686
	Rural	1,551	897	654
	Urban	86	54	32
Sultanpur	Total	2,833	1,507	1,326
	Rural	2,759	1,470	1,289
	Urban	74	37	37
Bahraich	Total	2,512	1,421	1,091
	Rural	2,323	1,311	1,012
	Urban	189	110	79
Shrawasti *	Total	1,116	672	444
	Rural	1,090	657	433
	Urban	26	15	11
Balrampur *	Total	1,854	1,120	734
	Rural	1,691	1,012	679
	Urban	163	108	55
Gonda	Total	2,136	1,400	736
	Rural	2,083	1,372	711
	Urban	53	28	25
Siddharthnagar	Total	1,304	717	587
	Rural	1,242	686	556
	Urban	62	31	31
Basti	Total	1,539	868	671
	Rural	1,322	723	599
	Urban	217	145	72
Sant Kabir Nagar *	Total	867	512	355
	Rural	828	487	341
	Urban	39	25	14
Mahrajganj	Total	2,054	1,103	951
	Rural	1,833	976	857
	Urban	221	127	94

Contd.

Contd.

1	2	3	4	5
Gorakhpur	Total	2,213	1,357	856
	Rural	1,792	1,098	694
	Urban	421	259	162
Kushinagar *	Total	1,992	1,207	785
	Rural	1,859	1,103	756
	Urban	133	104	29
Deoria	Total	2,276	1,440	836
	Rural	1,590	856	734
	Urban	686	584	102
Azamgarh	Total	4,042	2,133	1,909
	Rural	3,703	1,939	1,764
	Urban	339	194	145
Mau	Total	1,243	661	582
	Rural	1,069	587	482
	Urban	174	74	100
Ballia	Total	2,229	1,281	948
	Rural	2,059	1,213	846
	Urban	170	68	102
Jaunpur	Total	4,010	2,178	1,832
	Rural	3,855	2,075	1,780
	Urban	155	103	52
Ghazipur	Total	1,526	789	737
	Rural	1,452	742	710
	Urban	74	47	27
Chandauli *	Total	1,174	631	543
	Rural	738	384	354
	Urban	436	247	189
Varanasi	Total	2,640	1,734	906
	Rural	1,031	546	485
	Urban	1,609	1,188	421
Sant Ravidas Nagar Bhadohi *	Total	711	376	35
	Rural	623	332	291
	Urban	88	44	44

Contd.

Contd.

1	2	3	4	5
Mirzapur	Total	1,098	537	561
	Rural	978	465	513
	Urban	120	72	48
Sonbhadra	Total	816	404	412
	Rural	733	359	374
	Urban	83	45	38
BIHAR	Total	60,311	30,765	29,546
	Rural	53,370	26,804	26,566
	Urban	6,941	3,961	2,980
Pashchim Champaran	Total	3,689	2,376	1,313
	Rural	3,468	2,262	1,206
	Urban	221	114	107
Purba Champaran	Total	3,044	1,642	1,402
	Rural	2,666	1,451	1,215
	Urban	378	191	187
Sheohar *	Total	436	214	222
	Rural	423	206	217
	Urban	13	8	5
Sitamarhi	Total	2,503	1,120	1,383
	Rural	2,252	1,054	1,198
	Urban	251	66	185
Madhubani	Total	2,425	1,222	1,203
	Rural	2,324	1,166	1,158
	Urban	101	56	45
Supaul *	Total	1,162	629	533
	Rural	1,138	614	524
	Urban	24	15	9
Araria	Total	2,677	1,495	1,182
	Rural	1,805	698	1,107
	Urban	872	797	75
Kishanganj	Total	3,494	881	2,613
	Rural	3,087	719	2,368
	Urban	407	162	245

Contd.

Contd.

1	2	3	4	5
Purnia	Total	3,226	1,097	2,129
	Rural	2,890	967	1,923
	Urban	336	130	206
Katihar	Total	3,988	1,336	2,652
	Rural	3,873	1,274	2,599
	Urban	115	62	53
Madhepura	Total	563	314	249
	Rural	543	305	238
	Urban	20	9	11
Saharsa	Total	703	352	351
	Rural	622	326	296
	Urban	81	26	55
Darbhanga	Total	2,833	1,526	1,307
	Rural	2,634	1,405	1,229
	Urban	199	121	78
Muzaffarpur	Total	3,215	1,497	1,718
	Rural	2,949	1,354	1,595
	Urban	266	143	123
Gopalganj	Total	1,339	807	532
	Rural	1,266	753	513
	Urban	73	54	19
Siwan	Total	1,768	979	789
	Rural	1,623	896	727
	Urban	145	83	62
Saran	Total	1,393	847	546
	Rural	1,118	693	425
	Urban	275	154	121
Vaishali	Total	1,265	797	468
	Rural	1,211	772	439
	Urban	54	25	29
Samastipur	Total	2,784	1,824	960
	Rural	2,612	1,706	906
	Urban	172	118	54

Contd.

Contd.

1	2	3	4	5
Begusarai	Total	1,422	685	737
	Rural	1,381	664	717
	Urban	41	21	20
Khagaria	Total	577	324	253
	Rural	499	279	220
	Urban	78	45	33
Bhagalpur	Total	1,263	727	536
	Rural	995	572	423
	Urban	268	155	113
Banka *	Total	800	462	338
	Rural	784	454	330
	Urban	16	8	8
Munger	Total	470	266	204
	Rural	342	197	145
	Urban	128	69	59
Lakhisarai *	Total	340	190	150
	Rural	319	178	141
	Urban	21	12	9
Sheikhpura *	Total	245	142	103
	Rural	203	122	81
	Urban	42	20	22
Nalanda	Total	1,180	669	511
	Rural	921	539	382
	Urban	259	130	129
Patna	Total	1,885	1,068	817
	Rural	1,034	579	455
	Urban	851	489	362
Bhojpur	Total	958	525	433
	Rural	805	428	377
	Urban	153	97	56
Buxar *	Total	780	373	407
	Rural	729	348	381
	Urban	51	25	26

Contd.

Contd.

1	2	3	4	5
Kaimur (Bhabua) *	Total	619	317	302
	Rural	598	306	292
	Urban	21	11	10
Rohtas	Total	1,371	697	674
	Rural	1,105	546	559
	Urban	266	151	115
Jehanabad	Total	977	595	382
	Rural	908	553	355
	Urban	69	42	27
Aurangabad	Total	1,055	597	458
	Rural	991	571	420
	Urban	64	26	38
Gaya	Total	2,079	1,120	959
	Rural	1,615	874	741
	Urban	464	246	218
Nawada	Total	910	493	417
	Rural	818	443	375
	Urban	92	50	42
Jamui *	Total	873	560	313
	Rural	819	530	289
	Urban	54	30	24
SIKKIM	Total	113	63	50
	Rural	86	48	38
	Urban	27	15	12
North	Total	16	15	1
	Rural	15	14	1
	Urban	1	1	-
West	Total	21	8	13
	Rural	17	6	11
	Urban	4	2	2
South	Total	20	13	7
	Rural	17	10	7
	Urban	3	3	-

Contd.

Contd.

1	2	3	4	5
East	Total	56	27	29
	Rural	37	18	19
	Urban	19	9	10
ARUNACHAL PRADESH	Total	195	105	90
	Rural	130	74	56
	Urban	65	31	34
Tawang	Total	7	5	2
	Rural	7	5	2
	Urban	-	-	-
West Kameng	Total	17	9	8
	Rural	17	9	8
	Urban	-	-	-
East Kameng	Total	10	7	3
	Rural	5	3	2
	Urban	5	4	1
Papum Pare *	Total	32	11	21
	Rural	10	6	4
	Urban	22	5	17
Lower Subansiri	Total	14	8	6
	Rural	13	7	6
	Urban	1	1	-
Upper Subansiri	Total	6	1	5
	Rural	4	1	3
	Urban	2	-	2
West Siang	Total	14	7	7
	Rural	11	6	5
	Urban	3	1	2
East Siang	Total	14	7	7
	Rural	5	4	1
	Urban	9	3	6
Upper Siang *	Total	4	2	2
	Rural	4	2	2
	Urban	-	-	-

Contd.

Contd.

1	2	3	4	5
Dibang Valley	Total	6	5	1
	Rural	3	3	-
	Urban	3	2	1
Lohit	Total	38	24	14
	Rural	33	21	12
	Urban	5	3	2
Changlang	Total	28	18	10
	Rural	14	7	7
	Urban	14	11	3
Tirap	Total	5	1	4
	Rural	4	-	4
	Urban	1	1	-
NAGALAND	Total	552	295	257
	Rural	403	198	205
	Urban	149	97	52
Mon	Total	65	35	30
	Rural	62	33	29
	Urban	3	2	1
Tuensang	Total	123	73	50
	Rural	114	64	50
	Urban	9	9	-
Mokokchung	Total	39	19	20
	Rural	34	15	19
	Urban	5	4	1
Zunhcboto	Total	47	26	21
	Rural	35	17	18
	Urban	12	9	3
Wokha	Total	28	18	10
	Rural	21	14	7
	Urban	7	4	3
Dimapur *	Total	187	96	91
	Rural	92	34	58
	Urban	95	62	33

Contd.

Contd.

1	2	3	4	5
Kohima	Total	38	15	23
	Rural	23	10	13
	Urban	15	5	10
Phek	Total	25	13	12
	Rural	22	11	11
	Urban	3	2	1
MANIPUR (Excl. 3 Sub-divisions)	Total	408	164	244
	Rural	320	120	200
	Urban	88	44	44
Senapati (Excl. 3 sub-divisions)	Total	19	3	16
	Rural	19	3	16
	Urban	-	-	-
Tamenglong	Total	19	12	7
	Rural	19	12	7
	Urban	-	-	-
Churachandpur	Total	26	5	21
	Rural	26	5	21
	Urban	-	-	-
Bishnupur	Total	39	10	29
	Rural	25	6	19
	Urban	14	4	10
Thoubal	Total	63	26	37
	Rural	44	16	28
	Urban	19	10	9
Imphal West	Total	65	28	37
	Rural	30	13	17
	Urban	35	15	20
Imphal East *	Total	120	58	62
	Rural	105	48	57
	Urban	15	10	5
Ukhrul	Total	18	7	11
	Rural	18	7	11
	Urban	-	-	-

Contd.

Contd.

1	2	3	4	5
Chandel	Total	39	15	24
	Rural	34	10	24
	Urban	5	5	-
MIZORAM	Total	95	47	48
	Rural	66	35	31
	Urban	29	12	17
Mamit *	Total	5	4	1
	Rural	5	4	1
	Urban	-	-	-
Kolasib *	Total	6	4	2
	Rural	4	3	1
	Urban	2	1	1
Aizawl	Total	22	11	11
	Rural	9	5	4
	Urban	13	6	7
Champhai *	Total	12	6	6
	Rural	7	3	4
	Urban	5	3	2
Serchhip *	Total	2	1	1
	Rural	1	1	-
	Urban	1	-	1
Lunglei	Total	21	9	12
	Rural	15	8	7
	Urban	6	1	5
Lawngtlai	Total	23	10	13
	Rural	23	10	13
	Urban	-	-	-
Saiha *	Total	4	2	2
	Rural	2	1	1
	Urban	2	1	1
TRIPURA	Total	2,963	1,046	1,917
	Rural	2,595	934	1,661
	Urban	368	112	256

Contd.

Contd.

1	2	3	4	5
West Tripura	Total	1,293	428	865
	Rural	1,033	354	679
	Urban	260	74	186
South Tripura	Total	966	326	640
	Rural	894	306	588
	Urban	72	20	52
Dhalai *	Total	278	117	161
	Rural	265	111	154
	Urban	13	6	7
North Tripura	Total	426	175	251
	Rural	403	163	240
	Urban	23	12	11
MEGHALAYA	Total	555	256	299
	Rural	453	204	249
	Urban	102	52	50
West Garo Hills	Total	272	121	151
	Rural	248	108	140
	Urban	24	13	11
East Garo Hills	Total	47	27	20
	Rural	31	14	17
	Urban	16	13	3
South Garo Hills *	Total	24	9	15
	Rural	13	7	6
	Urban	11	2	9
West Khasi Hills	Total	42	20	22
	Rural	41	19	22
	Urban	1	1	-
Ri Bhoi *	Total	38	17	21
	Rural	35	14	21
	Urban	3	3	-
East Khasi Hills	Total	95	46	49
	Rural	51	27	24
	Urban	44	19	25

Contd.

Contd.

1	2	3	4	5
Jaintia Hills	Total	37	16	21
	Rural	34	15	19
	Urban	3	1	2
ASSAM	Total	31,895	10,517	21,378
	Rural	29,853	9,534	20,319
	Urban	2,042	983	1,059
Kokrajhar	Total	880	311	569
	Rural	827	274	553
	Urban	53	37	16
Dhubri	Total	3,105	847	2,258
	Rural	2,909	769	2,140
	Urban	196	78	118
Goalpara	Total	1,261	371	890
	Rural	1,194	350	844
	Urban	67	21	46
Bongaigaon	Total	1,415	448	967
	Rural	1,314	388	926
	Urban	101	60	41
Barpeta	Total	2,891	758	2,133
	Rural	2,811	736	2,075
	Urban	80	22	58
Kamrup	Total	2,094	770	1,324
	Rural	1,598	486	1,112
	Urban	496	284	212
Nalbari	Total	1,469	446	1,023
	Rural	1,464	443	1,021
	Urban	5	3	2
Darrang	Total	1,984	614	1,370
	Rural	1,946	598	1,348
	Urban	38	16	22
Marigaon	Total	1,099	322	777
	Rural	1,076	312	764
	Urban	23	10	13

Contd.

Contd.

1	2	3	4	5
Nagaon	Total	3,813	1,253	2,560
	Rural	3,597	1,155	2,442
	Urban	216	98	118
Sonitpur	Total	1,425	624	801
	Rural	1,378	609	769
	Urban	47	15	32
Lakhimpur	Total	565	224	341
	Rural	519	206	313
	Urban	46	18	28
Dhemaji	Total	269	132	137
	Rural	255	123	132
	Urban	14	9	5
Tinsukia	Total	425	225	200
	Rural	336	172	164
	Urban	89	53	36
Dibrugarh	Total	440	218	222
	Rural	370	176	194
	Urban	70	42	28
Sibsagar	Total	734	380	354
	Rural	692	360	332
	Urban	42	20	22
Jorhat	Total	793	377	416
	Rural	701	331	370
	Urban	92	46	46
Golaghat	Total	631	277	354
	Rural	539	237	302
	Urban	92	40	52
Karbi Anglong	Total	356	162	194
	Rural	299	134	165
	Urban	57	28	29
North Cachar Hills	Total	69	43	26
	Rural	58	38	20
	Urban	11	5	6

Contd.

Contd.

1	2	3	4	5
Cachar	Total	2,024	628	1,396
	Rural	1,895	585	1,310
	Urban	129	43	86
Karimganj	Total	2,519	691	1,828
	Rural	2,467	666	1,801
	Urban	52	25	27
Hailakandi	Total	1,634	396	1,238
	Rural	1,608	386	1,222
	Urban	26	10	16
WEST BENGAL	Total	129,406	54,868	74,538
	Rural	90,012	34,483	55,529
	Urban	39,394	20,385	19,009
Darjiling	Total	4,094	2,702	1,392
	Rural	989	559	430
	Urban	3,105	2,143	962
Jalpaiguri	Total	4,735	2,448	2,287
	Rural	2,803	1,248	1,555
	Urban	1,932	1,200	732
Koch Bihar	Total	4,645	1,369	3,276
	Rural	4,052	1,251	2,801
	Urban	593	118	475
Uttar Dinajpur	Total	4,586	1,492	3,094
	Rural	3,571	1,032	2,539
	Urban	1,015	460	555
Dakshin Dinajpur *	Total	2,748	910	1,838
	Rural	2,407	739	1,668
	Urban	341	171	170
Maldah	Total	6,554	2,217	4,337
	Rural	6,355	2,110	4,245
	Urban	199	107	92
Murshidabad	Total	15,249	4,989	10,260
	Rural	14,404	4,656	9,748
	Urban	845	333	512

Contd.

Contd.

1	2	3	4	5
Birbhum	Total	5,942	2,679	3,263
	Rural	5,585	2,514	3,071
	Urban	357	165	192
Barddhaman	Total	9,880	4,333	5,547
	Rural	6,524	2,720	3,804
	Urban	3,356	1,613	1,743
Nadia	Total	9,103	3,772	5,331
	Rural	7,311	3,042	4,269
	Urban	1,792	730	1,062
North Twenty Four Parganas	Total	8,120	3,613	4,507
	Rural	4,391	1,704	2,687
	Urban	3,729	1,909	1,820
Hugli	Total	5,238	2,221	3,017
	Rural	3,483	1,248	2,235
	Urban	1,755	973	782
Bankura	Total	3,874	1,954	1,920
	Rural	3,606	1,822	1,784
	Urban	268	132	136
Puruliya	Total	3,704	2,085	1,619
	Rural	3,329	1,888	1,441
	Urban	375	197	178
Medinipur	Total	12,729	5,042	7,687
	Rural	11,213	4,372	6,841
	Urban	1,516	670	846
Haora	Total	5,144	2,155	2,989
	Rural	2,505	804	1,701
	Urban	2,639	1,351	1,288
Kolkata	Total	14,464	7,604	6,860
	Rural	-	-	-
	Urban	14,464	7,604	6,860
South Twenty Four Parganas	Total	8,597	3,283	,314
	Rural	7,484	2,774	4,710
	Urban	1,113	509	604

Contd.

Contd.

1	2	3	4	5
JHARKHAND	Total	16,625	8,543	8,082
	Rural	11,081	5,544	5,537
	Urban	5,544	2,999	2,545
Garhwa *	Total	824	428	396
	Rural	810	423	387
	Urban	14	5	9
Palamu	Total	1,357	690	667
	Rural	1,292	662	630
	Urban	65	28	37
Chatra *	Total	364	192	172
	Rural	350	186	164
	Urban	14	6	8
Hazaribagh	Total	888	465	423
	Rural	597	301	296
	Urban	291	164	127
Kodarma *	Total	221	117	104
	Rural	158	82	76
	Urban	63	35	28
Giridih	Total	977	501	476
	Rural	926	468	458
	Urban	51	33	18
Deoghar	Total	586	337	249
	Rural	438	263	175
	Urban	148	74	74
Godda	Total	433	216	217
	Rural	425	211	214
	Urban	8	5	3
Sahibganj	Total	850	301	549
	Rural	783	280	503
	Urban	67	21	46
Pakaur *	Total	560	235	325
	Rural	525	214	311
	Urban	35	21	14

Contd.

Contd.

1	2	3	4	5
Dumka	Total	826	451	375
	Rural	720	383	337
	Urban	106	68	38
Dhanbad	Total	2,018	1,026	992
	Rural	1,001	535	466
	Urban	1,017	491	526
Bokaro *	Total	1,093	581	512
	Rural	658	349	309
	Urban	435	232	203
Ranchi	Total	1,195	628	567
	Rural	576	292	284
	Urban	619	336	283
Lohardaga	Total	118	47	71
	Rural	109	44	65
	Urban	9	3	6
Gumla	Total	426	213	213
	Rural	389	191	198
	Urban	37	22	15
Pashchimi Singhbhum	Total	957	484	473
	Rural	718	370	348
	Urban	239	114	125
Purbi Singhbhum	Total	2,932	1,631	1,301
	Rural	606	290	316
	Urban	2,326	1,341	985
ORISSA	Total	30,766	17,138	13,628
	Rural	20,785	10,993	9,792
	Urban	9,981	6,145	3,836
Bargarh *	Total	1,705	903	802
	Rural	1,615	856	759
	Urban	90	47	43
Jharsuguda *	Total	589	309	280
	Rural	215	121	94
	Urban	374	188	186

Contd.

Contd.

1	2	3	4	5
Sambalpur	Total	808	430	378
	Rural	515	284	231
	Urban	293	146	147
Debagarh *	Total	199	91	108
	Rural	132	62	70
	Urban	67	29	38
Sundargarh	Total	1,592	811	781
	Rural	585	287	298
	Urban	1,007	524	483
Kendujhar	Total	880	464	416
	Rural	766	408	358
	Urban	114	56	58
Mayurbhanj	Total	1,101	503	598
	Rural	894	413	481
	Urban	207	90	117
Baleshwar	Total	1,815	798	1,017
	Rural	1,468	642	826
	Urban	347	156	191
Bhadrak *	Total	1,112	608	504
	Rural	891	496	395
	Urban	221	112	109
Kendrapara *	Total	1,019	588	431
	Rural	949	554	395
	Urban	70	34	36
Jagatsinghapur *	Total	797	507	290
	Rural	752	478	274
	Urban	45	29	16
Cuttack	Total	2,534	1,498	1,036
	Rural	1,138	622	516
	Urban	1,396	876	520
Jajapur *	Total	1,445	741	704
	Rural	1,368	703	665
	Urban	77	38	39

Contd.

Contd.

1	2	3	4	5
Dhenkanal	Total	1,048	732	316
	Rural	810	507	303
	Urban	238	225	13
Anugul *	Total	571	315	256
	Rural	461	259	202
	Urban	110	56	54
Nayagarh *	Total	414	238	176
	Rural	395	231	164
	Urban	19	7	12
Khordha *	Total	3,949	2,813	1,136
	Rural	670	380	290
	Urban	3,279	2,433	846
Puri	Total	1,197	669	528
	Rural	674	346	328
	Urban	523	323	200
Ganjam	Total	1,773	921	852
	Rural	1,218	606	612
	Urban	555	315	240
Gajapati *	Total	237	134	103
	Rural	171	92	79
	Urban	66	42	24
Kandhamal	Total	254	127	127
	Rural	198	100	98
	Urban	56	27	29
Baudh *	Total	261	155	106
	Rural	255	154	101
	Urban	6	1	5
Sonapur *	Total	504	275	229
	Rural	438	245	193
	Urban	66	30	36
Balangir	Total	1,507	794	713
	Rural	1,292	683	609
	Urban	215	111	104

Contd.

Contd.

1	2	3	4	5
Nuapada *	Total	484	277	207
	Rural	448	257	191
	Urban	36	20	16
Kalahandi	Total	1,143	629	514
	Rural	1,038	561	477
	Urban	105	68	37
Rayagada *	Total	415	200	215
	Rural	310	138	172
	Urban	105	62	43
Nabarangapur *	Total	683	276	407
	Rural	542	245	297
	Urban	141	31	110
Koraput	Total	549	246	303
	Rural	422	190	232
	Urban	127	56	71
Malkangiri *	Total	181	86	95
	Rural	155	73	82
	Urban	26	13	13
CHHATTISGARH	Total	20,077	9,749	10,328
	Rural	13,963	6,897	7,066
	Urban	6,114	2,852	3,262
Koriya *	Total	464	222	242
	Rural	322	148	174
	Urban	142	74	68
Surguja	Total	1,189	591	598
	Rural	1,101	544	557
	Urban	88	47	41
Jashpur *	Total	305	143	162
	Rural	266	122	144
	Urban	39	21	18
Raigarh	Total	1,617	864	753
	Rural	1,271	710	561
	Urban	346	154	192

Contd.

Contd.

1	2	3	4	5
Korba *	Total	1,064	473	591
	Rural	681	301	380
	Urban	383	172	211
Janjgir - Champa*	Total	2,201	1,064	1,137
	Rural	1,508	772	736
	Urban	693	292	401
Bilaspur	Total	2,593	1,267	1,326
	Rural	1,774	828	946
	Urban	819	439	380
Kawardha *	Total	867	410	457
	Rural	636	313	323
	Urban	231	97	134
Rajnandgaon	Total	1,069	538	531
	Rural	655	354	301
	Urban	414	184	230
Durg	Total	2,497	1,222	1,275
	Rural	1,267	642	625
	Urban	1,230	580	650
Raipur	Total	3,435	1,653	1,782
	Rural	2,126	1,045	1,081
	Urban	1,309	608	701
Mahasamund *	Total	1,049	516	533
	Rural	824	419	405
	Urban	225	97	128
Dhamtari *	Total	716	314	402
	Rural	626	270	356
	Urban	90	44	46
Kanker *	Total	290	130	160
	Rural	273	126	147
	Urban	17	4	13
Bastar	Total	543	268	275
	Rural	471	239	232
	Urban	72	29	43

Contd.

Contd.

1	2	3	4	5
Dantewada*	Total	178	74	104
	Rural	162	64	98
	Urban	16	10	6
MADHYA PRADESH	Total	41,952	24,338	17,614
	Rural	28,673	16,638	12,035
	Urban	13,279	7,700	5,579
Sheopur *	Total	326	226	100
	Rural	274	186	88
	Urban	52	40	12
Morena	Total	937	676	261
	Rural	730	538	192
	Urban	207	138	69
Bhind	Total	658	488	170
	Rural	476	356	120
	Urban	182	132	50
Gwalior	Total	741	512	229
	Rural	276	192	84
	Urban	465	320	145
Datia	Total	375	250	125
	Rural	285	182	103
	Urban	90	68	22
Shivpuri	Total	710	390	320
	Rural	465	271	194
	Urban	245	119	126
Guna	Total	1,021	583	438
	Rural	725	416	309
	Urban	296	167	129
Tikamgarh	Total	550	322	228
	Rural	431	252	179
	Urban	119	70	49
Chhatarpur	Total	775	468	307
	Rural	615	369	246
	Urban	160	99	61

Contd.

Contd.

1	2	3	4	5
Panna	Total	588	353	235
	Rural	535	323	212
	Urban	53	30	23
Sagar	Total	1,137	729	408
	Rural	793	510	283
	Urban	344	219	125
Damoh	Total	523	347	176
	Rural	410	269	141
	Urban	113	78	35
Satna	Total	1,828	1,014	814
	Rural	1,288	732	556
	Urban	540	282	258
Rewa	Total	2,112	1,113	999
	Rural	1,761	927	834
	Urban	351	186	165
Umaria *	Total	365	204	161
	Rural	309	174	135
	Urban	56	30	26
Shahdol	Total	1,631	779	852
	Rural	1,311	621	690
	Urban	320	158	162
Sidhi	Total	2,583	1,200	1,383
	Rural	2,230	1,040	1,190
	Urban	353	160	193
Neemuch *	Total	366	227	139
	Rural	196	105	91
	Urban	170	122	48
Mandsaur	Total	751	361	390
	Rural	569	256	313
	Urban	182	105	77
Ratlam	Total	637	362	275
	Rural	309	150	159
	Urban	328	212	116

Contd.

Contd.

1	2	3	4	5
Ujjain	Total	1,618	965	653
	Rural	633	360	273
	Urban	985	605	380
Shajapur	Total	667	388	279
	Rural	463	267	196
	Urban	204	121	83
Dewas	Total	897	560	337
	Rural	650	430	220
	Urban	247	130	117
Jhabua	Total	655	339	316
	Rural	519	256	263
	Urban	136	83	53
Dhar	Total	1,198	728	470
	Rural	987	614	373
	Urban	211	114	97
Indore	Total	1,980	1,023	957
	Rural	632	324	308
	Urban	1,348	699	649
West Nimar	Total	1,364	856	508
	Rural	1,016	653	363
	Urban	348	203	145
Barwani *	Total	574	338	236
	Rural	408	233	175
	Urban	166	105	61
East Nimar	Total	1,442	827	615
	Rural	844	520	324
	Urban	598	307	291
Rajgarh	Total	786	469	317
	Rural	658	381	277
	Urban	128	88	40
Vidisha	Total	730	445	285
	Rural	519	329	190
	Urban	211	116	95

Contd.

Contd.

1	2	3	4	5
Bhopal	Total	1,058	655	403
	Rural	124	71	53
	Urban	934	584	350
Sehore	Total	813	496	317
	Rural	683	412	271
	Urban	130	84	46
Raisen	Total	580	401	179
	Rural	460	319	141
	Urban	120	82	38
Betul	Total	827	475	352
	Rural	649	381	268
	Urban	178	94	84
Harda	Total	485	293	192
	Rural	406	255	151
	Urban	79	38	41
Hoshangabad	Total	845	565	280
	Rural	537	366	171
	Urban	308	199	109
Katni *	Total	956	577	379
	Rural	787	483	304
	Urban	169	94	75
Jabalpur	Total	1,883	1,067	816
	Rural	609	364	245
	Urban	1,274	703	571
Narsimhapur	Total	605	375	230
	Rural	461	294	167
	Urban	144	81	63
Dindori *	Total	747	384	363
	Rural	734	380	354
	Urban	13	4	9
Mandla	Total	713	434	279
	Rural	554	333	221
	Urban	159	101	58

Contd.

Contd.

1	2	3	4	5
Chhindwara	Total	667	372	295
	Rural	360	188	172
	Urban	307	184	123
Seoni	Total	482	267	215
	Rural	419	236	183
	Urban	63	31	32
Balaghat	Total	766	435	331
	Rural	573	320	253
	Urban	193	115	78
GUJARAT	Total	19,743	12,016	7,727
	Rural	8,343	4,801	3,542
	Urban	11,400	7,215	4,185
Kachchh	Total	501	262	239
	Rural	186	120	66
	Urban	315	142	173
Banas Kantha	Total	1,620	950	670
	Rural	1,145	631	514
	Urban	475	319	156
Patan *	Total	313	191	122
	Rural	182	102	80
	Urban	131	89	42
Mahesana	Total	515	308	207
	Rural	258	150	108
	Urban	257	158	99
Sabar Kantha	Total	1,037	597	440
	Rural	808	445	363
	Urban	229	152	77
Gandhinagar	Total	490	312	178
	Rural	112	56	56
	Urban	378	256	122
Ahmadabad	Total	2,362	1,529	833
	Rural	270	143	127
	Urban	2,092	1,386	706

Contd.

Contd.

1	2	3	4	5
Surendranagar	Total	541	328	213
	Rural	290	172	118
	Urban	251	156	95
Rajkot	Total	1,286	801	485
	Rural	576	365	211
	Urban	710	436	274
Jamnagar	Total	988	693	295
	Rural	296	184	112
	Urban	692	509	183
Porbandar *	Total	428	235	193
	Rural	181	96	85
	Urban	247	139	108
Junagadh	Total	1,205	720	485
	Rural	756	459	297
	Urban	449	261	188
Amreli	Total	481	291	190
	Rural	275	156	119
	Urban	206	135	71
Bhavnagar	Total	1,104	706	398
	Rural	397	242	155
	Urban	707	464	243
Anand *	Total	599	395	204
	Rural	169	98	71
	Urban	430	297	133
Kheda	Total	873	531	342
	Rural	353	177	176
	Urban	520	354	166
Panch Mahals	Total	889	530	359
	Rural	626	369	257
	Urban	263	161	102
Dohad *	Totai	213	111	102
	Rural	151	77	74
	Urban	62	34	28

Contd.

Contd.

1	2	3	4	5
Vadodara	Total	1,284	782	502
	Rural	397	232	165
	Urban	887	550	337
Narmada *	Total	95	65	30
	Rural	54	38	16
	Urban	41	27	14
Bharuch	Total	468	274	194
	Rural	191	101	90
	Urban	277	173	104
Surat	Total	1,710	975	735
	Rural	325	196	129
	Urban	1,385	779	606
The Dangs	Total	38	20	18
	Rural	38	20	18
	Urban	-	-	-
Navsari *	Total	376	223	153
	Rural	157	90	67
	Urban	219	133	86
Valsad	Total	327	187	140
	Rural	150	82	68
	Urban	177	105	72
DAMAN & DIU	Total	15	6	9
	Rural	7	2	5
	Urban	8	4	4
Diu	Total	8	5	3
	Rural	4	1	3
	Urban	4	4	-
Daman	Total	7	1	6
	Rural	3	1	2
	Urban	4	-	4
DADRA & NAGAR HAVELI	Total	49	20	29
	Rural	38	14	24
	Urban	11	6	5

Contd.

Contd.

1	2	3	4	5
MAHARASHTRA	Total	58,321	28,447	29,874
	Rural	22,432	12,077	10,355
	Urban	35,889	16,370	19,519
Nandurbar *	Total	376	174	202
	Rural	196	90	106
	Urban	180	84	96
Dhule	Total	581	282	299
	Rural	312	150	162
	Urban	269	132	137
Jalgaon	Total	1,935	944	991
	Rural	1,153	557	596
	Urban	782	387	395
Buldana	Total	1,121	641	480
	Rural	751	411	340
	Urban	370	230	140
Akola	Total	1,124	607	517
	Rural	457	268	189
	Urban	667	339	328
Washim *	Total	499	275	224
	Rural	379	211	168
	Urban	120	64	56
Amravati	Total	1,712	901	811
	Rural	1,037	526	511
	Urban	675	375	300
Wardha	Total	657	351	306
	Rural	406	220	186
	Urban	251	131	120
Nagpur	Total	2,793	1,330	1,463
	Rural	685	379	306
	Urban	2,108	951	1,157
Bhandara	Total	457	255	202
	Rural	377	210	167
	Urban	80	45	35

Contd.

Contd.

1	2	3	4	5
Gondiya *	Total	606	305	301
	Rural	458	227	231
	Urban	148	78	70
Gadchiroli	Total	446	208	238
	Rural	396	180	216
	Urban	50	28	22
Chandrapur	Total	1,114	578	536
	Rural	678	329	349
	Urban	436	249	187
Yavatmal	Total	1,809	1,101	708
	Rural	1,428	901	527
	Urban	381	200	181
Nanded	Total	2,022	1,083	939
	Rural	970	525	445
	Urban	1,052	558	494
Hingoli *	Total	448	256	192
	Rural	330	206	124
	Urban	118	50	68
Parbhani	Total	771	469	302
	Rural	383	247	136
	Urban	388	222	166
Jalna	Total	924	524	400
	Rural	662	362	300
	Urban	262	162	100
Aurangabad	Total	1,456	819	637
	Rural	870	468	402
	Urban	586	351	235
Nashik	Total	2,178	1,220	958
	Rural	888	481	407
	Urban	1,290	739	551
Thane	Total	3,141	1,471	1,670
	Rural	576	303	273
	Urban	2,565	1,168	1,397

Contd.

Contd.

1	2	3	4	5
Mumbai (Suburban) *	Total	4,498	2,922	1,576
	Rural	-	-	-
	Urban	4,498	2,922	1,576
Mumbai	Total	9,628	3,182	6,446
	Rural	-	-	-
	Urban	9,628	3,182	6,446
Raigarh	Total	728	408	320
	Rural	339	183	156
	Urban	389	225	164
Pune	Total	4,514	1,585	2,929
	Rural	874	463	411
	Urban	3,640	1,122	2,518
Ahmadnagar	Total	2,181	1,222	959
	Rural	1,462	786	676
	Urban	719	436	283
Bid	Total	723	399	324
	Rural	542	294	248
	Urban	181	105	76
Latur	Total	1,565	814	751
	Rural	900	474	426
	Urban	665	340	325
Osmanabad	Total	1,084	596	488
	Rural	887	502	385
	Urban	197	94	103
Solapur	Total	2,547	1,390	1,157
	Rural	1,517	841	676
	Urban	1,030	549	481
Satara	Total	1,301	652	649
	Rural	899	450	449
	Urban	402	202	200
Ratnagiri	Total	518	276	242
	Rural	300	168	132
	Urban	218	108	110

Contd.

Contd.

1	2	3	4	5
Sindhudurg	Total	180	87	93
	Rural	151	67	84
	Urban	29	20	9
Kolhapur	Total	1,122	531	591
	Rural	510	240	270
	Urban	612	291	321
Sangli	Total	1,562	589	973
	Rural	659	358	301
	Urban	903	231	672
ANDHRA PRADESH	Total	57,150	30,073	27,077
	Rural	35,923	17,941	17,982
	Urban	21,227	12,132	9,095
Adilabad	Total	1,415	738	677
	Rural	1,008	524	484
	Urban	407	214	193
Nizamabad	Total	1,887	1,010	877
	Rural	1,604	843	761
	Urban	283	167	116
Karimnagar	Total	3,880	2,029	1,851
	Rural	2,333	1,257	1,076
	Urban	1,547	772	775
Medak	Total	1,954	1,054	900
	Rural	1,707	932	775
	Urban	247	122	125
Hyderabad	Total	3,414	2,077	1,337
	Rural	-	-	-
	Urban	3,414	2,077	1,337
Rangareddi	Total	2,517	1,241	1,276
	Rural	1,572	757	815
	Urban	945	484	461
Mahbubnagar	Total	3,031	1,503	1,528
	Rural	2,562	1,251	1,311
	Urban	469	252	217

Contd.

Contd.

1	2	3	4	5
Nalgonda	Total	2,680	1,361	1,319
	Rural	2,187	1,099	1,088
	Urban	493	262	231
Warangal	Total	1,803	849	954
	Rural	1,249	603	646
	Urban	554	246	308
Khammam	Total	1,563	761	802
	Rural	1,187	567	620
	Urban	376	194	182
Srikakulam	Total	2,146	1,056	1,090
	Rural	1,910	946	964
	Urban	236	110	126
Vizianagaram	Total	1,634	798	836
	Rural	1,268	600	668
	Urban	366	198	168
Visakhapatnam	Total	2,533	1,386	1,147
	Rural	875	419	456
	Urban	1,658	967	691
East Godavari	Total	3,196	1,889	1,307
	Rural	1,541	733	808
	Urban	1,655	1,156	499
West Godavari	Total	3,122	1,710	1,412
	Rural	1,549	739	810
	Urban	1,573	971	602
Krishna	Total	2,316	1,206	1,110
	Rural	1,374	651	723
	Urban	942	555	387
Guntur	Total	3,461	1,858	1,603
	Rural	2,074	1,066	1,008
	Urban	1,387	792	595
Prakasam	Total	2,192	1,137	1,055
	Rural	1,361	704	657
	Urban	831	433	398

Contd.

Contd.

1	2	3	4	5
Nellore	Total	2,432	1,294	1,138
	Rural	1,756	873	883
	Urban	676	421	255
Cuddapah	Total	1,797	896	901
	Rural	1,315	639	676
	Urban	482	257	225
Kurnool	Total	2,555	1,280	1,275
	Rural	1,889	927	962
	Urban	666	353	313
Anantapur	Total	2,991	1,489	1,502
	Rural	1,879	893	986
	Urban	1,112	596	516
Chittoor	Total	2,631	1,451	1,180
	Rural	1,723	918	805
	Urban	908	533	375
KARNATAKA	Total	26,206	12,726	13,480
	Rural	15,535	7,288	8,247
	Urban	10,671	5,438	5,233
Belgaum	Total	2,641	1,107	1,534
	Rural	1,793	741	1,052
	Urban	848	366	482
Bagalkot *	Total	1,447	415	1,032
	Rural	754	212	542
	Urban	693	203	490
Bijapur	Total	1,385	666	719
	Rural	904	426	478
	Urban	481	240	241
Gulbarga	Total	2,071	1,108	963
	Rural	1,225	647	578
	Urban	846	461	385
Bidar	Total	1,475	784	691
	Rural	1,056	561	495
	Urban	419	223	196

Contd.

Contd.

1	2	3	4	5
Raichur	Total	944	456	488
	Rural	508	216	292
	Urban	436	240	196
Koppal	Total	887	406	481
	Rural	673	312	361
	Urban	214	94	120
Gadag *	Total	477	223	254
	Rural	230	116	114
	Urban	247	107	140
Dharwad	Total	712	410	302
	Rural	236	130	106
	Urban	476	280	196
Uttara Kannada	Total	448	222	226
	Rural	273	129	144
	Urban	175	93	82
Haveri *	Total	799	414	385
	Rural	586	290	296
	Urban	213	124	89
Bellary	Total	1,679	704	975
	Rural	972	387	585
	Urban	707	317	390
Chitradurga	Total	707	327	380
	Rural	491	216	275
	Urban	216	111	105
Davanagere	Total	669	304	365
	Rural	350	152	198
	Urban	319	152	167
Shimoga	Total	700	329	371
	Rural	465	218	247
	Urban	235	111	124
Udupi *	Total	176	109	67
	Rural	119	72	47
	Urban	57	37	20

Contd.

Contd.

1	2	3	4	5
Chikmagalur	Total	397	186	211
	Rural	181	87	94
	Urban	216	99	117
Tumkur	Total	1,589	823	766
	Rural	1,031	525	506
	Urban	558	298	260
Kolar	Total	1,685	814	871
	Rural	1,311	623	688
	Urban	374	191	183
Bangalore	Total	2,128	1,192	936
	Rural	224	101	123
	Urban	1,904	1,091	813
Bangalore Rural	Total	701	356	345
	Rural	509	246	263
	Urban	192	110	82
Mandya	Total	746	431	315
	Rural	621	352	269
	Urban	125	79	46
Hassan	Total	415	225	190
	Rural	264	145	119
	Urban	151	80	71
Dakshina Kannada	Total	401	233	168
	Rural	143	75	68
	Urban	258	158	100
Kodagu	Total	81	43	38
	Rural	55	28	27
	Urban	26	15	11
Mysore	Total	563	281	282
	Rural	327	154	173
	Urban	236	127	109
Chamarajanagar *	Total	283	158	125
	Rural	234	127	107
	Urban	49	31	18

Contd.

Contd.

1	2	3	4	5
GOA	Total	515	295	220
	Rural	200	100	100
	Urban	315	195	120
North Goa	Total	243	142	101
	Rural	103	57	46
	Urban	140	85	55
South Goa	Total	272	153	119
	Rural	97	43	54
	Urban	175	110	65
LAKSHADWEEP	Total	4	2	2
	Rural	-	-	-
	Urban	4	2	2
KERALA	Total	9,476	5,315	4,161
	Rural	6,147	3,286	2,861
	Urban	3,329	2,029	1,300
Kasaragod	Total	271	145	126
	Rural	208	111	97
	Urban	63	34	29
Kannur	Total	659	364	295
	Rural	297	144	153
	Urban	362	220	142
Wayanad	Total	190	114	76
	Rural	177	108	69
	Urban	13	6	7
Kozhikode	Total	631	334	297
	Rural	430	204	226
	Urban	201	130	71
Malappuram	Total	906	510	396
	Rural	783	435	348
	Urban	123	75	48
Palakkad	Total	924	527	397
	Rural	655	356	299
	Urban	269	171	98

Contd.

Contd.

1	2	3	4	5
Thrissur	Total	973	573	400
	Rural	534	298	236
	Urban	439	275	164
Ernakulam	Total	929	540	389
	Rural	357	199	158
	Urban	572	341	231
Idukki	Total	305	191	114
	Rural	261	156	105
	Urban	44	35	9
Kottayam	Total	618	377	241
	Rural	437	254	183
	Urban	181	123	58
Alappuzha	Total	577	292	285
	Rural	349	161	188
	Urban	228	131	97
Pathanamthitta	Total	355	208	147
	Rural	291	164	127
	Urban	64	44	20
Kollam	Total	947	526	421
	Rural	669	364	305
	Urban	278	162	116
Thiruvananthapuram	Total	1,191	614	577
	Rural	699	332	367
	Urban	492	282	210
TAMIL NADU	Total	17,756	9,303	8,453
	Rural	6,994	3,534	3,460
	Urban	10,762	5,769	4,993
Thiruvallur	Total	1,078	449	629
	Rural	438	202	236
	Urban	640	247	393
Chennai	Total	1,566	696	870
	Rural	-	-	-
	Urban	1,566	696	870

Contd.

Contd.

1	2	3	4	5
Kancheepuram	Total	772	406	366
	Rural	333	180	153
	Urban	439	226	213
Vellore	Total	1,283	646	637
	Rural	681	340	341
	Urban	602	306	296
Dharmapuri	Total	612	310	302
	Rural	538	275	263
	Urban	74	35	39
Tiruvannamalai	Total	787	518	269
	Rural	273	132	141
	Urban	514	386	128
Viluppuram	Total	524	261	263
	Rural	411	209	202
	Urban	113	52	61
Salem	Total	782	418	364
	Rural	419	232	187
	Urban	363	186	177
Namakkal	Total	296	145	151
	Rural	174	83	91
	Urban	122	62	60
Erode	Total	747	419	328
	Rural	157	82	75
	Urban	590	337	253
The Nilgiris	Total	168	93	75
	Rural	33	16	17
	Urban	135	77	58
Coimbatore	Total	1,431	799	632
	Rural	339	155	184
	Urban	1,092	644	448
Dindigul	Total	397	191	206
	Rural	227	113	114
	Urban	170	78	92

Contd.

Contd.

1	2	3	4	5
Karur *	Total	412	251	161
	Rural	49	27	22
	Urban	363	224	139
Tiruchirappalli	Total	590	312	278
	Rural	147	75	72
	Urban	443	237	206
Perambalur *	Total	67	32	35
	Rural	64	30	34
	Urban	3	2	1
Ariyalur *	Total	37	15	22
	Rural	33	13	20
	Urban	4	2	2
Cuddalore	Total	400	205	195
	Rural	205	101	104
	Urban	195	104	91
Nagapattinam *	Total	671	347	324
	Rural	277	146	131
	Urban	394	201	193
Thiruvarur	Total	166	89	77
	Rural	85	40	45
	Urban	81	49	32
Thanjavur	Total	1,026	643	383
	Rural	378	217	161
	Urban	648	426	222
Pudukkottai	Total	435	243	192
	Rural	383	219	164
	Urban	52	24	28
Sivaganga	Total	272	128	144
	Rural	205	90	115
	Urban	67	38	29
Madurai	Total	894	466	428
	Rural	249	127	122
	Urban	645	339	306

Contd.

Contd.

1	2	3	4	5
Theni *	Total	212	108	104
	Rural	69	32	37
	Urban	143	76	67
Virudhunagar	Total	327	168	159
	Rural	163	84	79
	Urban	164	84	80
Ramanathapuram	Total	331	202	129
	Rural	150	75	75
	Urban	181	127	54
Thoothukkudi	Total	431	231	200
	Rural	171	90	81
	Urban	260	141	119
Tirunelveli	Total	540	279	261
	Rural	203	96	107
	Urban	337	183	154
Kanniyakumari	Total	502	233	269
	Rural	140	53	87
	Urban	362	180	182
PONDICHERRY	Total	371	226	145
	Rural	65	37	28
	Urban	306	189	117
Yanam	Total	26	17	9
	Rural	-	-	-
	Urban	26	17	9
Pondicherry	Total	253	154	99
	Rural	36	21	15
	Urban	217	133	84
Mahe	Total	10	7	3
	Rural	-	-	-
	Urban	10	7	3
Karaikal	Total	82	48	34
	Rural	29	16	13
	Urban	53	32	21

Contd.

Contd.

1	2	3	4	5
ANDAMAN &	Total	62	37	25
NICOBAR ISLANDS	Rural	42	25	17
	Urban	20	12	8
Andamans	Total	54	31	23
	Rural	34	19	15
	Urban	20	12	8
Nicobars	Total	8	6	2
	Rural	8	6	2
	Urban	-	-	-

Bibliography

Allport, R., "Transport Services for the Urban Poor" *conference paper* "Infrastructure for Development"; 31 May - 2 June 2000, London

Booth, D, Hanmer, L, Lovell, E., "Poverty and Transport - a report prepared for the World Bank in collaboration with DFID"; *chapter 4 "Transport and urban poverty"*; 06/2000

Brinkley, Elena, "Louise Brooks, Richard Arlen Cast in Beggars of Life." *Hollywood Daily Citizen*, United States, February 3, 1928.

Cal, P.C, "Impacts of Urban Transport on the Poor in Manila", *WB UTS Review*, Yoko-hama Conference, 12/2000

Collier, Lionel, "Beggars of Life." *Kinematograph Weekly*, September 13, 1928.

Deniz, B, Christine K, *Urban Poverty*, Draft 08/2000

Diaz, O, Godard, X. "Poverty and Urban Transport - French experience in developing cities; World Bank TWUTD; 09/2000

Elbadrawi, H, Ospina, D, Shen, L. D, Zhao, F., At-grade Busway Planning Guide; Florida International University; 12/1998

Gannon, C, Liu, Z., *Poverty and Transport*; TWU-30; 09/1997

Gannon, C, Liu, Z., "Transport: Infrastructure and Services: Outline", chapter 4.2 Policy *Tools Urban Transport, Draft*; 08/2000

Harrison, P. S., "Beggars of Life - with Wallace Beery, Richard Arlen and Louise Brooks." *Harrison's Reports*, September 29, 1928.

P., J. E. "Beggars of Life." *Billboard*, September 29, 1928.

Zimmerman, Katherine, "Beery Scores in Character Role in Beggars of Life." *New York Telegram*, September 24, 1928.

Index